PRAISING IN BLACK AND WHITE

Praising in

BLACK

a n d

WHITE

Unity and Diversity in Christian Worship

BRENDA EATMAN AGHAHOWA

United Church Press
Cleveland, Ohio

United Church Press, Cleveland, Ohio 44115
© 1996 by Brenda Eatman Aghahowa

Pages 206–207 constitute an extension of this
copyright page.

Printed in the United States of America on acid-free paper
01   00   99   98   97   96   5   4   3   2   1

Library of Congress Cataloging-in-Publication Data
Aghahowa, Brenda Eatman, 1957–
     Praising in black and white : unity and diversity in Christian
worship / Brenda Eatman Aghahowa.
         p.   cm.
     Based on the author's thesis (doctoral)—University of Chicago,
1991, originally presented under the title: Charismata and formalism.
     Includes bibliographical references and index.
     ISBN 0-8298-1134-6 (alk. paper)
     1. Public worship—Comparative studies.   2. United Church of
Christ—Liturgy.   3. Assemblies of God—Liturgy.   4. Afro-American
Pentecostal churches—Illinois—Chicago—Case studies.
     5. Liberalism (Religion)—Protestant churches—Case studies.
     6. Liberalism (Religion)—Illinois—Chicago—Case studies.
     7. Chicago (Ill.)—Church history—20th century.   8. Afro-Americans—
Illinois—Chicago—Religion.   I. Title.
BV198.A35   1996
264'.00973—dc20
                                                          96-34339
                                                              CIP

—

To the memory of my parents,
Willie Clarence and Julious Mae Eatman,
without whose lifelong sacrifices none of my past, present,
or future accomplishments would be possible

—

CONTENTS

ACKNOWLEDGMENTS

It is impossible to complete a work of this scope without support of all kinds—academic, emotional, spiritual, practical and financial—from very many people. Volumes would be required to thank each and every person who contributed in some way to the content of this work and/or to my well being as I struggled to finish it. While it is not possible to thank all, it is fitting and proper to mention the most crucial supporters.

This work began as a doctoral dissertation. Thus, I extend warm gratitude to the University of Chicago Divinity School faculty members who served so ably on my dissertation reading committee. With patience, care and erudition, Dr. Martin E. Marty (adviser) and the two readers, Dr. Anne Carr and Dr. Philip Devenish, offered thoughtful critique of this work chapter by chapter, year after year.

The Rev. Dr. James H. Hargett has been the most significant mentor in my pilgrimage as "learned minister." He and the Rev. Mr. Edward Peecher were gracious and courageous enough to allow their congregations to be studied and surveyed for this project. Indeed, these two pastors permitted serious academic scrutiny of their own philosophies and practices of worship, risking both praise and blame. Without their cooperation, and that of their congregations, this work would not have been possible. To them and their members, who have been very good sports, I owe a great debt.

I gained rich insights into African American worship from an ecumenical group of scholars, including the Rev. Dr. Homer U. Ashby Jr. (Presbyterian), the Rev. Dr. Hycel B. Taylor (Baptist), and the late Dr. Nathan Jones (Catholic). Chaplaincy training in clinical pastoral education (CPE) enhanced my understanding of the relationship between worship, pastoral care, and the psychotherapeutic disciplines. In this regard, I must acknowledge gratefully the Rev. Dr. George P. Polk of Baltimore; and the Rev. Dr. Robert A. Young Jr. and the Rev. Dr. Luther Mauney, both of the Program of Patient Counseling at Virginia Commonwealth University's Medical College of Virginia, Richmond.

No book ever sees the light of day without the serious dedication and flexibility of a superb typist. Gwendolyn Barnes is to be commended for her expert final preparation of this manuscript—both in its dissertation-defense form and in its final form for publication by the United Church Press.

Speaking of the publisher, much gratitude to Kim Sadler and her staff for sharing in the vision of this book and investing in its publication.

"Eternal" indebtedness to God the Savior, for vibrant spirituality; to God the Holy Spirit, for inspiring me with the thoughts and ideas contained in this work; and to God the Creator, for using so many along the way to nurture me in the faith and bring me to this point of achievement. Among these, I thank especially: the Rev. Dr. E. Theophilus Caviness, lead pastor of the Greater Abyssinia Baptist Church in my native Cleveland, Ohio; Church of God in Christ Bishop Carlis L. Moody, Evanston, Illinois; Presbyterian pastor the Rev. Ms. Cheryl Hooker Shoals, Belmont, North Carolina; the Rev. Ms. Jerri Bender Harrison, a Chicago-area pastor in the African Methodist Episcopal (AME) denomination; and the Rev. Dr. Robert M. Franklin Jr., a Church of God in Christ minister who is director of the Program of Black Church Studies at Emory University's Candler School of Theology, Atlanta.

Love and laughter shared with my maternal grandmother, Janie Mae Brown, and my sister, Janice Ann Eatman, both Clevelanders, have undergirded me at all times. Others who have "held up my arms," as it were, throughout this long, arduous process by way of prayer and other forms of encouragement and support include the following: Debra J. Bonds, Minneapolis, Minn.; Cheryl L. Martin; General "Bill" Morrison and Quentine Gabriel, both of Cleveland, Ohio; Dr. Dennis Kimbro, author of *Think and Grow Rich: A Black Choice,* Atlanta, Ga.; Barbara Simmons Taylor, Edwin and Violet McKinney, Arnold and Ora Lewis, Sammie and Binetta Lane, Dorothy Roulette, the Rev. Ms. Julie Ruth Harley, Dorothy G. Tarr, Esther Hill, Cherry Jones, the Alvin Washington family, Phyllis Williams, Ronald High, the Rudy/Saucier family, the Rev. Ms. Leslie R. Dowdell, the Rev. Dr. Yvonne Delk (my "mother in the ministry"), the Rev. Ms. Mary Parish, the Rev. Ms. Khani Bell Hawkins, the Rev. Ms. Zenobia Brooks, Pastor Richard D. Henton, Shirley Patton, Willie Lee Hart, Bob Black, and Audrey Williams and my other local sorors of Delta Sigma Theta Sorority, Inc., all of the Chicago area. You are all treasures!

Lastly, my deepest love, passion, and devotion must be expressed to my husband, the Rev. Dr. Stephen I. Aghahowa. His affection and good humor, alongside the continual giggly smiles of our two small daughters, Stephanie and Brenda Jr. ("B.J."), never fail to energize me, providing the determination, strength, and joy to persevere and to be my best.

FOREWORD

Some people call them "culture wars." These are conflicts over values, morals, expressions. Sometimes they are provoked by ideologies: left versus right; pro-life versus pro-choice; "family values" versus "liberalism"; old religion versus New Age are typical. More often they are rooted in basic human differentiations in a time when people look to groups to provide their identity. Then factors such as these come into play: race, ethnicity, gender, age, religion, and class. Or: black versus white; Hispanic versus Anglo; straight versus gay or male versus female; retirees versus under-thirties; Muslim versus Christian; rich versus poor.

These differentiations and conflicts between groups representing them cause fissures down the middle of church bodies. For years, debates over ordination of gays or over homosexual lifestyles have threatened to divide denomination after denomination. The conflicts these represent demand separate treatment in different books from this one, though some of them are implied here. What the list in the first paragraph does not include is classification based on *taste*. Yet aesthetic expression, in surrounding world and gathered church alike, divides believers as much as anything else. This book does address that issue, if from fresh angles of vision.

Taste. It pervades talk in what we used to call the secular world. Some malls have chosen to purge their halls of boisterous teenagers by playing classical music on the system. Thus Bach and Boccherini, played insistently and "tuned up" over the loudspeakers, will drive the young ones to the parking lot and the hamburger-dealing hangouts, just as amplified rap will lead seniors into exodus and exile from CD emporia. Some of the battles in the culture wars have to do with taste in the arts; witness the ways "cultural elites" line up against "family values" forces in battles over the National Endowment for the Arts or the National Endowment for the Humanities. On a smaller battlefield but for inducing no less intense battles, produce a new hymnbook and watch Christians fight over inclusive language or the dropping of militant-sounding hymns.

So party lines begin to develop. On one hand are the devotees of market-researched megamall music, whose praise songs echo the muffling beat of onk-chugga-onk-chugga-onk that rides with elevator patrons or afflicts captive audiences on airplanes awaiting clearance on runways. Aesthetic cultural warriors who oppose this will grumble: "If the only way to get to heaven, Martha, is by worshiping with *that* in our ears, we just aren't going!" Or: "Praise songs. They are all about one word, God—sung in two syllables—lasting three hours." And on the other side are the high-church liturgiologists, traditionalists who insist on preserving their versions of retrieved ancient Christian worship. They get perceived as dogmatic: "What's the difference between a liturgiologist and a terrorist?" Answer: "You can negotiate with a terrorist."

Ecumenical movements can talk all they want about the apostolic succession of bishops, the real presence of Christ in the Lord's Supper, Baptist soul liberty, or Catholic Christology. They may come to all the agreements they wish and sign all the concordats they desire: if they do not pay attention to what people see and hear and sense when they come to the sanctuary; if they do not take seriously the love Christians have for familiar forms and the distaste they express for the challenging, they will not do justice to the situation and cannot speak meaningfully to tensions in culture and congregation.

Onto that battlefield scene steps Brenda Eatman Aghahowa, not as cultural warrior but as potential truce-maker who has taken and described two of many possible "sides" in worship expression, and has endeavored here to work toward peace or at least mutual understanding and mutual appreciation. She is not saying of one form of worship—call it ecstatic, or expressive—"you *have* to like this." She is saying to those who find it naturally alien or uncongenial: "Please understand this, and how it makes the presence of God vivid and the love of humans palpable." She even moves on to say how such worship may contain elements that can enhance other styles. Such borrowing is not part of the feared "dumbing down" of worship, which is what its critics imply is a consequence of participating in its style and spreading it.

As for one of those other styles, which she characterizes as formal or mainstream, the issue is not fear of "dumbing down" but of "toning down." She is saying to the exuberantly impatient that they do not have to find themselves regularly or finally at home in what will appear to them to be staidness or ennui-inducing. She is saying: There are more ways than one to worship God. This set of people has found themselves at home in worship patterns that reflect their more ordered culture styles. They are not "less religious" for their choice; they are "being Christian" in a different way. You may never make the switch to their style, but the church will be better off if you can see their form as legitimate, can understand how they worship (liturgy = the people's service), and might even learn from and discreetly borrow from some of what they aspire to do.

This would be a very unsatisfying book if Dr. Eatman Aghahowa were plugging a style halfway between everything else. One of the reasons ecumenical worship tends not to take off is this: worshipers of one tradition have a sense that when an ecumenical hymnbook, liturgy, or guide to worship gets published, it will choose only the safe, middle-of-the-road expressions. Thus, musically, there would be no really soulful gospel music or really gospel-filled soul music: just toned down, compromised, and compromisingly "acceptable" reminiscences of rich traditions. On the other side, there would be no Catholic chant that evokes the Middle Ages; no divine elemental roar of the organ for Lutherans; no pure Anglican hymns or Presbyterian plainsong. Just committee-chosen "easy listening" patterns that offend none and thus also rouse no one. So the people reject the experiments at compromise and head back for home to styles congenial to them.

So it is with other elements of worship. Pentecostals would not get to speak in tongues; they would just stiffly raise their arms and waggle their fingers. Anglicans or the Orthodox would not be allowed the "smells and bells" of high-church or Eastern liturgy. They would get sermons telling them that people *used* to use incense and reach for the transcendent. And the worshiper in either setting would get not the best but, if not the worst, the most mediocre elements of the tradition that envelops the regular attenders.

Dr. Eatman Aghahowa is not promoting such weak and waffling alternatives. She has chosen a much more difficult task. She has chosen the route of critical affirmation: she *participates* in both modes and invites us to; she *appreciates* the two patterns she chooses to keep on inheriting and making her own; she *understands* two styles; she sets both in *cultural context,* as she says we all must. One of the strongest features of the book is evident in her ability to give a faithful accounting of what goes on in places and forms of worship usually unfrequented by any but devotees. Another strong feature is the quotations from the (admittedly semiscientific) social science research she has done, overhearing people give their views. I urge those with passions for precision not to dismiss those wonderfully imprecise and thus faithful interpretations and opinions.

Working with Dr. Eatman Aghahowa during the earlier phases of her research and writing, I would often jar and chide her: "Brenda, when you describe Pentecostal worship, you really are describing home; the place where your heart lives; where real worship goes on." Yes, of course. Then she would report on African American churches that express themselves in modes that militants dismiss as Euro- or white confinements. "Friend, when you describe more formal worship, you really are showing that you are drawn to the effort to give expression to a culture in which you are also at home, and are really affirming that true worship goes on in patterns that many people with whom you grew up would reject, aren't you?" Yes, of course.

Yes, of course. Yes, of course. I think in her duality of affirmations and critiques, she was giving a worship analogue to what W. E. B. DuBois had spoken of as a "doubleness" felt by every African American. But she implicitly shows that in some way or other each of us lives with some sort of doubleness. For some it is as we glide between what gets called "sacred" and "profane" dimensions of culture; between "religious" and "secular." For others this doubleness is part of our ability to affirm one style of conduct in some aspects of life and another in other aspects. Those who have it made, who have found the "one way" and the "absolute" and the "only divinely prescribed" form of worship or anything else Christian, will have real trouble with this book. Most of us who are on the Way, receiving elements of Truth, and enjoying aspects of the Life, however, are not likely to be free to live with only one mode of expression. We are trapped in doubleness, in multiplicity. By going deep into singular expressions, the author helps us make our way as she, to our delight, keeps making hers.

Martin E. Marty
The University of Chicago

AUTHOR'S NOTE: THE ISSUE OF INCLUSIVE LANGUAGE

Author and editors have been studious about the use of inclusive language throughout this book, to avoid the exclusive imagery in terms like "father" or "he" (in reference to God) and "Lord" (when referring to God or Jesus). The latter term is viewed in certain liberal mainline circles as having overtones of political subordination inappropriate to the spiritual relationship of follower to God.

These issues are nonexistent, even anathema and considered heretical, in churches like the one referred to here as "Fire Baptized," and sometimes even at churches like "Grace," where trained clergy believe inclusive language is a significant issue worthy of attention, but the church folk in the pew do not necessarily agree. It has been my lifelong experience in black churches of various theological bents that the spiritual and sociopolitical focus tends to be on issues of race, with little or no attention given to issues of sexism. Thus, many of these Christians, if they even knew there was such a thing as inclusive language, would wonder what all the fuss is about.

Occasional inclusion in this book of quotes from the King James Version, often replete with male imagery, has been done for one main reason: The KJV seems to be *the* cherished version of the Bible for many Pentecostal and conservative Christians. To be sure, this is the case for members at Fire Baptized. Further, it is my own personal feeling that trying to alter certain biblical passages (like the one from Psalm 150 in chapter 1) in order to make them inclusive destroys their essential flavor and makes their reading rather awkward.

In the spirit of love, humility, unity, and ecumenical cooperation promoted by this work, in the spirit of appreciating these Christians as they are, and not necessarily as some think they *should* be and believe, or would *wish* them to be and believe, I have intentionally opted to leave quotes from people in the pew as is. Let's hear these worshipers' exact words so that we can get a feel for their theological beliefs. Let them say what they want to say, in the ways in which they are most comfortable saying it. Love requires that we respect them where they are and not impose on them alien requirements regarding their use of language.

~ 1 ~
PRAISING: VARIATIONS ON A THEME

"Now there are varieties of gifts, but the same Spirit."
—*1 Corinthians 12:4, RSV*

It is Sunday in Chicago, and the variety of Christian and other worship experiences to be enjoyed in a metropolis this size is impressive. There is diversity in terms of the hour of worship; worshipers' nationalities, races, and ethnicities; and the style, form, content, and theological orientation of the worship itself.

One may choose, for instance, to experience all the splendor and grandeur of Catholic Mass at Holy Name Cathedral downtown or opt for the quiet piety of services at smaller mainline Protestant churches tucked away on equally quiet residential streets on the city's northwest side. Certainly, one may elect to travel to Chicago's largely black South Side to experience all the color, fervor, and excitement of worship as it has been shaped by the descendants of slaves. Whether one seeks ecstasy, majesty, or some other quality of worship, choices abound.

Perhaps the categories implied are too neat, both in terms of the city's geography and in terms of worship content. For there are white Pentecostal churches all over the city, as there are also sedate black mainline churches around town. Further, with respect to worship content, a single worship service at any given church—particularly in many black churches—often represents an interesting mixture of splendor, quiet, and fervent spirit.

Christian worship, in Chicago and around the world, can be compared to classical music, which has a thematic melody followed by variations on that theme. The variations on the theme of Christian worship—offering public, corporate homage and praise to God in the name of Jesus Christ—are infinite. And each spiritual "strain" is beautiful to the spiritual senses in its own way.

Unfortunately, spiritually tonal discord often occurs among Christians who fail to appreciate worship strains different from their own preferred style of worship. Those who prefer the classical allure of Bach and those who like to clap and sway to the pulsating contemporary gospel rhythms of the Mississippi Mass Choir frequently turn their noses up at one another in spiritually arrogant fashion. Both genres of music offer a theologically sound, Christian message and simply offer variations on a theme of musical praise.

The study at hand, which began as a doctoral dissertation, provides an in-depth examination of the contrasting worship styles of two Chicago congregations--one Pentecostal, one liberal mainline—and asks the question: What can worshipers of each of the two churches appreciate about the worship form of the other? What can they, in humility, learn from one another?

With the idea of variations on a theme as its foundation, this work will seek to serve as a vehicle for ecumenical understanding and Christian unity. Certainly, enhancement of these can heighten the appeal of Christianity for unchurched persons, who often are put off by Christians' seeming lack of tolerance for differences among themselves, whether these relate to worship, theology, or other concerns.

The springboard for discussion will be a detailed analysis of worship at two case study churches, which happen to be African American—one affiliated with the United Church of Christ and one within the Assemblies of God denomination. Nevertheless, the challenges these Christians face in shaping meaningful worship are of common concern throughout Christendom. Thus, the work is intended as a helpful resource or handbook for planners, instructors, and students of worship, and for all who worship—regardless of their Christian denomination.

"Charismatic": Don't All Christians Have the Gift of "Charis" or Grace?

From the infinite diversity of Christian worship forms, we will consider two broad categories, which for the sake of simplification, I label "charismatic" and "formal." By *charismatic* I mean styles of worship that are very lively or ecstatic, in which spontaneity of response to the immediate move of God's Spirit is prominent and the Pentecostal spiritual gifts are in operation. I designate as *formal* those worship forms that are rather quiet, meditative, stately, or majestic, in which a printed order of worship is strictly adhered to and from which spontaneous demonstrations in response to the Spirit's move are largely absent.

Given the controversy and negative connotations that often accompany the term charismatic, I am tempted to throw it out and coin something new, something neutral or generic. (I like, for instance, the adjective *effervescent* to describe Pentecostal and other lively forms of worship.) To throw out the term, however, would be to contradict one of the primary aims of this work, which is to help create appreciation for Pentecostal or charismatic worship—worship in which charismata, or the Pentecostal grace gifts, are in operation.

Robert H. Culpepper's discussion on this issue, in *Evaluating the Charismatic Movement,* is instructive:

> There are some outside the charismatic movement who strongly object to the adjective "charismatic" as a description of the movement. Pointing out that the word "charismatic" is derived from the Greek noun charis, grace, they emphasize that all of God's gifts are gifts of [God's] grace. . . . There is a sense in which the validity of this criticism must be admitted. All Christians have the gift (charisma) of eternal life (Rom. 6:23), and the Holy Spirit has been given to all who belong to Christ (Acts 2:38; Rom. 8:9). Thus, in the broad sense all Christians are charismatic, Still, it is true that the gifts of the Holy Spirit, particularly the more spectacular ones mentioned in 1 Corinthians 12:7–11, received little attention in Christendom outside of main-line Pentecostal circles until Neo-Pentecostalism or the charismatic movement appeared. Therefore, in a narrower sense, the use of the adjective "charismatic" as a description of this particular movement may be accepted.[1]

Also helpful in Culpepper's work is his focus on British charismatic author Michael Harper's illumination of the five Greek words used in

1 Corinthians 12 to designate spiritual gifts:

1. *Pneumatika* (12:1). This literally means "spirituals," or spiritual endowments, as distinguished from natural gifts.
2. *Charismata* (charis). This connotes that spiritual gifts have nothing to do with human merit.
3. *Diakoniai* "services" (12:5). This term indicates that spiritual gifts are avenues of service for helping others.
4. *Energemata* "powers" (12:6). This term characterizes spiritual gifts as momentary bursts of spiritual power or energy rather than permanent endowments.
5. *Phanerosis*, "manifestation" (12:7). This means that unlike fruits of the Spirit—which are invisible graces—the gifts can be seen, heard, or felt.

Culpepper points out that throughout this passage Paul emphasizes that all varieties of gifts have but one divine source, and that God's purpose in manifesting them is the common good.[2]

It is high time for Pentecostals to stop feeling the need to be apologetic and/or defensive about what are biblically sound spiritual gifts and forms of worship. Thus, I have opted to use the spiritual term *charismatic*, rather than something more "acceptable" to opponents of this type of worship.

Because charismatic worship is foreign to many in the Christian body, it is often viewed as frightening and/or as an unacceptable and inauthentic form of worship. Charismata often are ridiculed because many people fail to understand and appreciate their manifestation. Effort must be made to demystify these special gifts, not to deny their existence or their biblical authenticity.

The Question of "Authentic" Christian Worship

In *Praising in Black and White* I seek to examine a variety of stark contrasts that are liturgical, theological, and sociological in nature. The two black churches highlighted here are affiliated with two predominantly white denominations. One of the churches is liberal mainline, the other Pentecostal. One church offers worship that is highly Afrocentric in style and flavor; worship at the other church is very Eurocentric in tone and feeling.

Attention to issues of personal spirituality dominates worship at the one church, while discussions of the church's role in politics and the shaping of public policy dominate sermonizing and ethos at the other.

One could go on and on about the "black and white" issues to be uncovered and treated here. The idea, though, is not to promote a gray, uniform blending of the two styles of worship. Rather, I hope to affirm the stark differences as biblically and theologically *authentic* in order to enhance unity and ecumenical cooperation in the Christian body.

Having experienced for many years close ties to both liberal mainline and Pentecostal worshipers, I have observed a great deal of narrowness of perspective and outright bigotry on both sides of the fence with respect to worship. Many members of both types of churches often feel that their faith group has the only authentically Christian way of worshiping, and they act as if their denomination or local church has cornered the market on spiritually satisfying, meaningful worship.

As an African American clergyperson who is a member of a black church in a mostly white liberal mainline denomination, my spiritual roots are in predominantly black denominations. Through the years, the following too-common worship scenarios have provided much laughter as well as frustration and deep theological reflection.

At times I have invited black Pentecostal friends to experience worship at my black liberal mainline church. After the hour-long service is ended, their response is inevitably something like, "Well, let me go get some *real* church now!" Or they may respond with questions like, "Do you really *like* this? Can you possibly get anything of spiritual value or uplift from this? You don't really consider that dull, dry, bland, *formal* service *real* worship, do you?"

Conversely, as a member of both black Pentecostal and Baptist churches in years past, I occasionally had the opportunity to invite (mostly) white liberal mainline Protestants to share in worship. The mainline worshipers, at times throughout the service, would ask various questions that required "translation" or explanation of elements distinctive to black and/or Pentecostal worship. These included emotional shouting, rhythmic swaying and clapping of choir members in time to the music, dancing for joy in the aisles, falling (as though in a faint) under the power of the Holy Spirit, and speaking in tongues.

After an intense two- or three-hour service, it would be clear that the uninitiated visitor was thinking silently, "These people have lost it! They are crazy!" Verbally, however, the polite responses were inevitably something on the order of, "My, what a l-o-o-o-n-n-n-g service! Is the service always this long? Your church members really get into it, don't they? But, come now, you folks don't really consider all that emotionalism, that swinging-from-the-rafters-type *charismatic* service, *real* worship? Worship should be reverent and dignified, shouldn't it?"

The questions that both Pentecostal and Mainline worshipers have asked me over and over again--sometimes directly, sometimes subtly and unconsciously—is this: "Is that other form of worship "real" (genuine, biblically valid or *authentic*) Christian worship?" They often answer their own question in the negative, either directly to me at the moment or subtly by not returning for a second helping of the other (foreign) style of worship.

Their attitude is that both styles could not possibly constitute "real," authentic Christian worship. After all, they seem to say, Christian worship is *only* that which is charismatic and highly spirited or *only* that which is formal, quiet, and more meditative.

Clearly, there are misconceptions, misinformation, misunderstandings, stereotypes, and the need for spiritual growth on both sides. It is true that formal worship, at its worst, can be little more than dead ritualism. Likewise, charismatic-type worship, at its worst, can be merely a display of emotionalism. Some Christians in both types of churches lack spiritual depth. But while distortions can develop in either form, both forms are extremely rich at their best and truest. The failure of many people to recognize this simple fact often has caused me to shake my head in disgust, tear out my hair, and cry "Time out!"—both figuratively and literally.

Over the years I have sought to serve as an ambassador of sorts (and referee in some instances), to promote understanding and appreciation through dialogue and informal "field trips" like those described earlier. The central questions of this book have arisen out of frustration over the narrowness of perspective and spiritual myopia in both camps where worship is concerned. This book has also grown out of my own appreciation and understanding of the strengths and limitations of these two contrasting forms of worship. It attempts to illustrate what proponents of each form can appreciate about the other and how they can enhance their own form of worship by learning from the other.

The Matter of Appreciation and Unity: Why Study a Contrasting Form of Worship?

These issues are not raised here merely for the purpose of academic exercise. There are at least three reasons—two spiritual, one practical—for Christian worshipers to attempt seriously to appreciate the diversity of worship within the body of Christ. These three reasons relate to the second great commandment of Jesus, the biblical call for unity (vs. schism) in the body, and the matter of church growth.

The second great commandment of Jesus—that <u>Christians ought to love their neighbors as themselves</u> (Matt. 22:39)—<u>suggests that one take one's neighbor seriously, esteeming him or her as highly as oneself</u>. It is hard to love as oneself a person one views as liturgically, spiritually, intellectually, or otherwise inferior. In reference to appreciating worship styles different from one's own, loving one's neighbor as oneself requires spiritual maturity, tolerance, and humility. These qualities are evidenced in worshipers who may prefer a particular form of worship but are aware of its shortcomings as well as its strengths, and who can see God at work in differing styles as well.

The matter of appreciating diversity within the body of Christ is also critical to unity and ecumenical cooperation. The apostle Paul's discussion of unity in the church, found in 1 Corinthians 12, is instructive. There, he describes the body of Christ as having many members with different functions. "There are varieties of gifts, but the same Spirit." (1 Cor. 12:4). To paraphrase the insight, we might state that although there are many forms of worship, the same Spirit causes worshipers to be nourished by them all.

In this well-beloved chapter, Paul suggests that each member of Christ's body needs every other member in order for the whole to function properly. "The eye cannot say to the hand, 'I have no need of you,' nor again the head to the feet, 'I have no need of you'. . . . But God has so composed the body . . . that there may be no discord in the body, but that the members may have the same care for one another." (1 Cor. 12:21, 24, 25, RSV). The analogy fits, whether applied to a local element of the body of Christ (a congregation) or to the body of Christ universal.

The call is to "unity in diversity"—to unity in purpose, despite Christians' diverse spiritual gifts, styles of worship, and other considerations. The idea found in John 17:11 (RSV) "that they may [all] be one" (i.e., be unified) is also found here and throughout the New Testament.

Further, the gifts and other considerations mean nothing without love, Paul goes on to suggest in 1 Corinthians 13 (the famous 'love chapter'): "If I speak in the tongues of men and angels, but have not love, I am a noisy gong or a clanging cymbal" (1 Cor. 13:1ff, RSV). Again, it is impossible to love one's neighbor as oneself if one does not understand or appreciate the neighbor. It is impossible to have a truly collegial, fruitful relationship between persons who basically disrespect one another and/or view one another as second-class citizens.

Clearly, schism and lack of love exist in the Christian body. Nowhere is divisiveness more pronounced than in matters of worship. But until contrasting groups of worshipers can honestly say to one another, "While I prefer my own style of worship, I appreciate the richness and integrity of yours," unity and cooperation in the body will continue to elude the Christian family. The result will be that many unchurched persons will elude it as well, preferring not to be a part of a divided, squabbling, ungracious religious family.

All the well-intentioned talk in certain circles of the body of Christ about the need for ecumenical cooperation around issues of justice and peace can be nullified by the lack of tolerance and understanding between proponents of either formal or charismatic worship. Talk of ecumenism is meaningless until each camp puts away disparaging epithets (like "Bible thumpers" and "ungodly secular humanists") and recognizes the basic spiritual integrity and the undergirding theological orientation of the other form of worship.

The strengthening and increased unity of the entire body of Christ, along with enhancement of one's preferred worship style, result from believers beginning to appreciate Christian worship forms other than their own. Such results are the key aim of this work.

The third reason that Christians should pay serious attention to contrasting worship forms is practical, and has to do with church growth. When I was struggling to decide on a title for this work, I suggested to the publisher *The Ecstasy and the Majesty: An Exploration of Issues in Worship for Pentecostal and Liberal Mainline Churches in America,* attempting a play on the expression "the agony and the ecstasy." At points, though, I was inclined to call it *The Agonizing Ecstasy and the Agony of the Ecstasy.* This working title refers to the problematic euphoria that accompanies the fast numerical growth of many conservative and Pentecostal churches at this juncture in history versus the depression resulting from this trend for those in the statistically declining liberal mainline churches, which often lose members to the growing ones.

Many sources document the numerical decline of liberal mainline denominations, in contrast to the numerically thriving conservative and charismatic-type churches. An excellent work is *American Mainline Religion: Its Changing Shape and Future,*[3] by Wade Clark Roof and William McKinney, which draws heavily on statistics from the National Council of Churches' *Yearbook of American and Canadian Churches.*

My own assessment of the decline is that liberal mainline religion's meaningful, but often sterile, worship does not "meet people where they live," so to speak. It does not satisfy their deepest spiritual and emotional hungers and needs. A lack of spiritual vitality in worship and the overall ambiance of many such congregations means low attendance in worship (typical attendance is only 33 percent of recorded membership) and failure to attract new members, especially young adults and youth, who are the future of any congregation.

Maybe even more compelling than official statistics are real-life examples of these trends. Two church properties sit side by side on the north side of 154th Street in a quiet residential area about two miles from my home in the Chicago suburb of South Holland. Around 11:15 on any given Sunday morning, the traffic jam in and around the parking lot of the New Christian Valley Full Gospel Baptist Church, pastored by Bishop H. Daniel Wilson, suggests that something very exciting is happening in worship each week. This black church features a lively, ecstatic worship style. The worshipers from one of two earlier services spill out of the church excitedly, making room for those anxious to get in for the 11:30 service.

Next door, the now defunct Thornridge United Church of Christ, sat shuttered and silent on a lovely campus, a mausoleum by comparison. The church remained in this condition for one year, before reopening as Covenant UCC, a black new church start, the first such by the UCC in this area since the early 1960s. Chicago's south suburbs are rapidly changing in racial composition. Thus churches like Thornridge, which refuse to change with their neighborhood by enhancing their worship style to attract new (as well as existing) residents from the area's racially and theologically diverse population, will dwindle and die. Meanwhile, other churches with livelier worship that meets prospective members' spiritual, emotional, and cultural needs will thrive. For many liberal mainline churches, then, appreciating the strengths of contrasting worship forms may be important for the sake of sheer survival.

Charismatic churches have experienced impressive numerical growth over the last twenty or thirty years, often at the expense of the liberal mainline churches. However, these churches are robbed of even more growth by failings that include a lack of intellectual thoughtfulness and a failure to relate the Bible to social justice issues in much of their worship. Highly educated persons and political activists veer toward the liberal mainline denominations in order to relate their faith in concrete ways to such pressing social concerns as homelessness, unemployment, nuclear war, the ecology, institutional racism, and the like.

The spiritual mandates to love neighbor as self and to work toward unity in the body of Christ, along with practical concerns about church growth, compel worshipers of both charismatic and liberal mainline churches to look seriously at other forms of worship. Studying contrasting worship styles may enable congregants to improve their own worship and heighten attendance, church growth, and retention of members.

Who's in the Mainline?

Perhaps a brief word of clarification on the author's use of the term mainline is in order. Roof and McKinney offer help here, describing a fragmented mainline, consisting of liberal, moderate, and conservative communions— some numerically large, some statistically small—all helping to shape the mores and values of the vast majority of Americans. Thus, Presbyterians, Southern Baptists, Pentecostals, Catholics, and most other Christian denominations would be considered part of the mainline, even though the groups differ in size, vitality and "claim upon the American way."[4]

When I use the term *mainline,* then, I will modify it with one of the adjectives *liberal, moderate,* or *conservative.* This book is concerned primarily with the so-called liberal mainline churches. Roof and McKinney state that three churches make up the heart of the historic Protestant mainline—the

Episcopalian, the Presbyterian, and what is now called the United Church of Christ. They classify these "colonial big three" as liberal mainline.[5]

Most interesting is their discussion of the considerable cultural influence of these groups in contrast to their lack of spiritual vitality and numerical strength:

> Liberal Protestantism's cultural influence is greater than its lack of
> religious vitality suggests. Known for its close ties historically with the
> northern and eastern establishment, it still is a power and presence of
> some significance though less so than in the first part of the twentieth
> century. Persons within this tradition are disproportionately represent-
> ed among the nation's civic and corporate elite. . . . Politically the power
> of liberal Protestants continues to be fairly strong despite the gradual
> erosion of WASP influence throughout this century: all three religious
> groups have far more members in the U.S. Senate and House of Rep-
> resentatives than would be expected based on their aggregate sizes.[6]

This information strongly supports the assertion I make frequently in this work that one of the strengths of liberal mainline worship and worship life is that they take seriously the relationship of the gospel to social action. To a great degree, individuals' quality of life can be improved spiritually and emotionally by prayer. But it can be improved practically only through public policy and legislation that insure a solid education, jobs that pay a living wage, decent and affordable housing, etc. While liberal Protestantism will have to attend to matters of personal spirituality in order to increase numerically, conservative (particularly Pentecostal) Protestantism will have to attend to matters of social justice to grow theologically and in faithfulness to the full meaning of the gospel.

Strengths and Limitations of Worship Defined

Implicit in the suggestion that both worshiping communities can enhance their worship by paying attention to the strengths of each other's (and their own) mode of worship, is the thought that each worship form also has limitations or shortcomings. As this book progresses, my definitions of worship strengths and limitations will serve as the basis for critique of worship in the two study churches. Thus, I offer definitions for consideration early on.

In my estimation, a *worship strength* is that which:

○ Increases the believer's love of God and neighbor, in keeping with the two great commandments of Jesus given in Matthew 22:37–40: My neighbor is not just the person who lives next door or the one with whom I am comfortable; it is anyone in God's creation, regardless of race, class, ethnicity, or geographical location.

○ Gives vitality to worship, a consistent liveliness and freshness that create in worshipers both an eagerness to attend worship from week to week, and the energy and joy to get through the six days that follow.

○ Promotes holism in congregants' religious expression; it allows the worshipers to be themselves, to be the spiritual, emotional, physical, social and intellectual beings they are.

○ Gives the worshiper both a sense of the *immanence* (closeness) of God and of God's majesty and *transcendence* (greatness, splendor, removedness).

○ Helps the believer to apply biblical truths or principles to everyday life and to see (or at least reflect on) God acting around him or her in daily existence, thus enabling worship to continue on a personal level between public worship services.

○ Increases the worshiper's desire and ability to exercise the various spiritual disciplines (prayer, fasting, keeping a spiritual journal, meditation, home Bible study), and thus enhances his or her personal spirituality.

○ Provides religious meaning for action in spheres of life outside the church, such as the social, political, and economic arenas.

○ Promotes full seeing and hearing of sacred actions, utterances, and songs intended for the entire congregation.

Conversely, a *worship limitation* or shortcoming is that which:

○ Decreases love for (and attention to) God and neighbor.

○ Gives worship a stale, routinized aura or leads worshipers to think, "If I don't attend worship, I won't miss much." Thus, it lessens attendance.

○ Overemphasizes certain elements of human nature at the expense of the others (intellectualism over spiritual development, emotionalism over thoughtfulness, etc.).

○ Overemphasizes immanence almost to the utter exclusion of creating a majestic sense of God, or vice versa.

o Hinders the worshiper's ability to apply biblical truths or principles to everyday life.

o Fails to excite the worshiper about spiritual disciplines or to provide appropriate tools for developing vital personal spirituality.

o Fails to provide religious meaning for social action in other spheres of life outside the church.

o Hinders full seeing and hearing of sacred actions, utterances, and songs intended for the entire congregation.

As research and personal experience indicate, certain limitations in both liberal mainline and Pentecostal worship forms have serious consequences for these churches. Acknowledging and correcting such limitations possibly could help to reverse the much-bemoaned membership decline in liberal mainline churches and help the growing Pentecostal churches to cure their sociopolitical myopia. Given the centrality of ritual life in most churches, it seems highly plausible that both these troubles stem at least in part from shortcomings in worship.

Theological Grounding for Charismatic and Formal Worship Styles

"God is not hard of hearing." So goes the song of liberal mainliners who complain about the loud volume of the praise offered in charismatic, ecstatic, and other enthusiastic forms of worship. Pentecostal worshipers usually respond, "And He's not dead or nervous either. Anything dead ought to be buried." [Use of "Lord" and "He" for God throughout this discussion is intentional, since attention to the issue of inclusive language is often either nonexistent or anathema in Pentecostal circles.]

Both sets of worshipers are correct. For without question, there are theological, biblical merit and precedent for both formal (quiet, meditative) worship, as well as charismatic (loud, enthusiastic) worship. While both forms help worshipers to appreciate God's immanence and transcendence to a certain extent (as theologically they should, since God is both close to and removed from humanity), each form tends to emphasize more heavily one or the other of these attributes of God, giving each its essential flavor or character.

Biblical support abounds for the enthusiastic, highly fervent, effervescent character of worship one finds in charismatic and Pentecostal churches. In such worship, the immanence or closeness of God is emphasized. Over and above the general liveliness of other ecstatic worship, the various charismata (tongues, interpretation of tongues, divine healing, prophecy, and the like) are also in evidence.

Psalm 150 immediately comes to mind: "Praise the Lord! . . . Praise him with trumpet sound; praise him with lute and harp! Praise him with timbrel and *dance*; praise him with strings and pipe! Praise him with sounding cymbals; praise him with *loud* clashing cymbals! Let everything that breathes praise the Lord!" (Ps. 150:3–6, RSV; emphasis mine).

Throughout the psalms we are encouraged to give loud, ebullient praise to God with voice, dance, and all manner of instruments. This essentially is what one finds in Pentecostal worship—loud, exuberant praise. Voices and arms are lifted to God in adoration and surrender, and musical praise is offered on the organ, piano, synthesizer, guitar, saxophone, tambourine, drums, and other instruments.

Vocal and musical praise often give way to spontaneous dancing. Not only does the psalmist command us to dance in worship, but one may recall David dancing furiously before the ark of the covenant when it was returned to Jerusalem and Moses' sister Miriam leading the women in dance after the crossing of the Red Sea (Exod. 15:20).

Thus, 2 Samuel 6:14, 15 (RSV) states: "And David danced before the Lord with all his might. . . . So David and all the house of Israel brought up the ark of the Lord with shouting, and with the sound of the horn." This is not bland, quiet worship. This is a spiritual happening, and it is the essence of much Pentecostal, indeed African American, worship.

One finds basis in the Old Testament, too, for ardent prayer; the pouring out of one's soul to God. Impassioned, unscripted prayer, by both the general laity and worship leaders, is another mark of charismatic worship. Throughout the psalms especially, one experiences the pouring out of the soul in prayers of repentance, of rejoicing, of agony over affliction and oppression of enemies, and so on.

In the New Testament, one finds in 1 Corinthians 12–14 descriptions of enthusiastic worship at Corinth. This worship involves operation of the gifts of the Spirit (tongues, interpretation of tongues, prophecy, healing, etc.). Paul also explains how these gifts are to be used in worship. Jesus encourages believers to worship "in spirit (with vitality?) and in truth" (John 4:24).

In Revelation, John provides images of what worship is like in heaven and, as many Pentecostals believe, what it will be like after the rapture of the church:

> Then I looked, and I heard around the throne and the living creatures
> and the elders the voice of many angels, numbering myriads of myri-
> ads and thousands of thousands, saying with a loud voice, "Worthy
> is the Lamb who was slain, to receive power and wealth and wisdom
> and might and honor and glory and blessing!" And I heard every
> creature in heaven and on earth and under the earth and in the sea,
> and all therein, saying, "To him who sits upon the throne and to the
> Lamb be blessing and honor and glory and might forever and ever!"
> And the four living creatures said, "Amen!" and the elders fell down
> and worshiped. (Rev. 5:11–14, RSV)

The images John presents are of worshipers giving animated, enthusiastic praise before the throne of God night and day. Indeed, all of creation (in heaven, on earth, under the earth, and in the sea) is pictured as joyously praising God. The Revelation passage calls to mind imagery from Isaiah: "the mountains and the hills before you shall break forth into singing, and all the trees of the field shall clap their hands" (55:12b, RSV).

Also from John come harsh words for the "lukewarm churches." God told John to write to the church at Laodicea:

> I know your works: you are neither cold nor hot. Would that you
> were cold or hot! So, because you are lukewarm, and neither cold
> nor hot, I will spew you out of my mouth. For you say, I am rich, I
> have prospered, and I need nothing; not knowing that you are
> wretched, pitiable, poor, blind, and naked. Therefore I counsel you to
> buy from me gold refined by fire, that you may be rich, and white
> garments to clothe you and to keep the shame of your nakedness
> from being seen, and salve to anoint your eyes, that you may see.
> Those whom I love, I reprove and chasten; so be zealous and repent.
> (Rev. 3:15–19, RSV)

Thus, the lukewarm churches are told to get in gear and be zealous, to be excited about their faith, and to repent of their lukewarmness. In the Old Testament as well we find this rebuke—largely a moral complaint—directed at those given to solemn assemblies that are little more than dead ritualism. God says through the prophet Amos:

> I hate, I despise your feasts, and I take no delight in your solemn assemblies. Even though you offer me your burnt offerings and cereal offerings, I will not accept them, and the peace offerings of your fatted beasts I will not look upon. Take away from me the noise of your songs; to the melody of your harps I will not listen. But let justice roll down like waters, and righteousness like an everflowing stream. (Amos 5:21—24, RSV)

The first chapter of Isaiah is equally strong on the dead ritualism of those who fail to do the true will of God. God said through Isaiah:

> Bring no more vain offerings; incense is an abomination to me. New moon and sabbath and the calling of assemblies—I cannot endure iniquity and solemn assembly. Your new moons and your appointed feasts my soul hates; they have become a burden to me. I am weary of bearing them. When you spread forth your hands, I will hide my eyes from you; even though you make many prayers, I will not listen; your hands are full of blood. Wash yourselves; make yourselves clean; remove the evil of your doings from before my eyes; cease to do evil, learn to do good; seek justice, correct oppression; defend the fatherless, plead for the widow. Come now, let us reason together, says the Lord: though your sins are like scarlet, they shall be as white as snow; though they be red like crimson, they shall become like wool. (Isa. 1:13–18, RSV)

A wealth of commands, admonitions, and information throughout the scriptures provide biblical, theological grounding for enthusiastic worship, coupled with godly living, righteousness, and activism.

Certainly, there also is call in Scripture for the quieter, grander, more formal type of worship. Descriptions of Solomon's temple in 1 Kings 7, for instance, depict a very majestic, ornate structure; a magnificent edifice with furnishings of gold and brass, and carvings of cherubim, lions, and palm trees all around. The worship service at which the temple was dedicated in 1 Kings 8 appears to be a mixture of solemnity, mystery, prayer, repentance, and joyful praise.

When one thinks of the Israelite high priest entering the Holy of Holies to offer sacrifices for the sins of the people once a year and of the veil separating the Holy of Holies from the general sanctuary of the tabernacle, one envisions a worship that is grand, quiet, almost dark and mysterious in nature, and certainly solemn. In Hebrews 9:1–7, the writer powerfully sets the stage for, creates the mood of, the annual Great Day of Atonement prescribed in Leviticus 23:27.

The mystery, removedness, and transcendence of God, of which one often gets a sense in much formal worship, strongly comes through in the account of the law being handed down at Mount Sinai:

> On the morning of the third day there were thunders and lightnings, and a thick cloud upon the mountain, and a very loud trumpet blast, so that all the people who were in the camp trembled. Then Moses brought the people out of the camp to meet God; and they took their stand at the foot of the mountain. And Mount Sinai was wrapped in smoke, because the Lord descended upon it in fire; and the smoke of it went up like the smoke of a kiln, and the whole mountain quaked greatly. And as the sound of the trumpet grew louder and louder, Moses spoke, and God answered him in thunder. And the Lord came down upon Mount Sinai, to the top of the mountain, and the Lord called Moses to the top of the mountain, and Moses went up. (Exod. 19:16–20, RSV)

The Old Testament includes other accounts of God's presence being manifest in worship by a cloud of smoke and by fire. These include the account of Isaiah in the temple (Isa. 6:1–4), the account of fire coming down from heaven and consuming an offering on the altar (2 Chron. 7:1), and accounts like the following, describing what occurred when the ark of the covenant was brought to Solomon's temple:

> And it was the duty of the trumpeters and singers to make themselves
> heard in unison in praise and thanksgiving to the Lord, and when the
> song was raised, with trumpets and cymbals and other musical
> instruments, in praise to the Lord, "For he is good, for his steadfast
> love endures for ever," the house, the house of the Lord, was *filled*
> *with a cloud,* so that the priests could not stand to minister because
> of the cloud; for the glory of the Lord filled the house of God.
> (2 Chron. 5:13, 14, RSV; emphasis mine)

We have here, perhaps, the precedent for much of the "bells and smells" variety of worship to be encountered in some denominations that offer a highly liturgical, formal service.

The psalms speak of exuberant praise, but they also speak often of waiting quietly in fear before God. "A God feared in the council of the holy ones, great and awesome above all . . ." (Ps. 89:7, RSV). Here we see the idea of fearful reverence of God. Psalm 130:5 (RSV) states, "I wait for the Lord, my soul waits, and in his word I hope." The idea of waiting quietly for and before God in prayer, hope, and study of the Word shines through here.

Isaiah 40:31 (RSV) also speaks of the strength that comes from waiting quietly for and before God in prayer: "But they that wait for the Lord shall renew their strength, they shall mount up with wings like eagles, they shall run and not be weary, they shall walk and not faint." One sees again and again in the Old Testament the idea of waiting quietly, patiently, and hopefully before God.

New Testament support of quiet thoughtfulness in worship is heard indirectly in Paul's liturgical complaints regarding certain abuses in charismatic worship in some churches at Corinth. Specifically, 1 Corinthians 14 is devoted to the spiritual gift of speaking in tongues and how to use it for the edification of those present in worship. In some Corinthian charismatic churches, believers spoke in tongues when there was no one present to interpret their spiritual messages to the congregation. In other instances, more than one person would attempt to prophesy at once. "For God is not a God of confusion but of peace" (1 Cor. 14:33a). Here, Paul calls not for an end to speaking in tongues or other charismatic gifts, but for orderliness in their exercise during enthusiastic worship services (i.e., one person prophesying at a time). He also calls generally for practices that heighten understanding (i.e., speaking in tongues for the congregation only when an interpreter is present to edify the body). The challenge in these churches was clearly to learn to balance liturgical discipline and spiritual enthusiasm.

Scholars such as James D. G. Dunn, in *Unity and Diversity in the New Testament,*[7] argue that there was great diversity of worship styles among Christians of the New Testament church. Some were more given to solemn assemblies, preserving a great deal of Jewish ritual and aura in their worship, while others were more given to charismata, to enthusiastic worship.

Dunn describes communities of Jewish Christians, Hellenistic Jewish Christians (or those significantly influenced by Greek culture), and charismatic Christians, like those at Corinth. Each community had its own form of worship. Other scholars, like J. Wendell Mapson Jr. and Ferdinand Hahn, describe the same diversity:

> In a sense, it is misleading to speak of the New Testament church; rather, it is more accurate to speak of the churches of the New Testament. The New Testament reveals not one form of worship but several. Distinctions in worship forms existed among the early Aramaic-speaking community, the Hellenistic Jewish community, the early Gentile community, and the sub-apostolic period. This multiplicity of forms suggests that not only between churches but also within each church existed a freedom and spontaneity, devoid of the formality and rigidity that would later characterize Christian worship.[8]

Hahn observes that "There is no trace of any obligatory liturgical order [in the New Testament]. We must instead think in terms of great freedom and variety in the structuring of worship."[9]

This diversity of forms is clear from Paul's ministerial and evangelistic efforts. One does not get the sense that, as he visited the various worshiping communities, he took a worship manual or standardized liturgy that he then imposed on all the churches. Rather, Paul seemed to affirm the diversity he found, while speaking out on various excesses, intolerances, abuses of liberty, and practices that tended to heighten division rather than increase harmony in congregations.

So, too, today's Christians who wish to follow biblical norms, must learn to affirm and appreciate the basic integrity of other "authentic" Christian worship forms, while also critiquing in love practices or perspectives that make for "inauthentic" worship. Inauthentic worship is that which exhibits many of the limitations described earlier and, thus, fails to glorify God, edify worshipers, and inspire men and women to vital spirituality and to tasks of Christian social action.

Preview of Chapters: A Look Ahead

Thus far, we have set forth the principle aim of the work (promoting the appreciation of worship forms different from one's own, for the dual purpose of enhancing one's own worship and increasing ecumenical unity and cooperation). We have also provided theological grounding for the two worship styles under consideration and offered some thoughts regarding what constitutes a worship strength or limitation. Having laid this initial groundwork, we will build on it in coming chapters as we explore a variety of issues in worship facing liberal mainline and Pentecostal churches.

The exploration begins with theoretical discussion of the general concepts of worship and black worship in chapter 2. Among other definitions of worship, we will examine the notions of *Gottesdienst* and *leitourgia* (the Greek word from which the term liturgy is derived), with special attention given to their dual meanings as both human beings' service to God and God's service to human beings.

In order for those unfamiliar with black worship to understand much of the detailed description and analysis of worship in the two churches studied in chapters 3 and 4, it will be necessary to pay serious attention to black worship as a category unto itself. While black worship is not monolithic (some forms of it being Afrocentric and some decidedly Eurocentric in flavor), the chapter calls for recognition of certain distinctive features of African American worship that are enduring, regardless of denomination or geographic location. The African roots of this worship are highlighted as is discourse on the related issue of *liturgical imperialism*.

Chapter 3 showcases the elegant, majestic worship of Grace United

Church of Christ. Planning, gender inclusiveness, and attention to the relationship of the gospel to social issues are the hallmarks of worship at this "silk stocking," upscale black church. Its professional chancel choir, accompanied by brass and/or string ensembles for special worship services, expertly renders classical sacred pieces and Negro spirituals. Its strengths, however, are its weaknesses. Worship leaders have in effect "planned out"the spontaneity of the Spirit. Too much attention is given to global matters and not enough to issues of personal spirituality. Choral and hymn music are culturally alien. In-depth analysis of the worship uncovers a variety of identity crises—liturgical, spiritual, and socioeconomic—as this aging congregation struggles internally over worship matters and its future survival.

The undeniably ecstatic worship of Fire Baptized Assembly of God Church is the focus of chapter 4. Worship features operation of the Holy Spirit charismata, a high degree of spontaneity, holistic participation by worshipers, Bible-centered preaching that enables worshipers to apply biblical principles to everyday situations, emphasis on spiritual disciplines, much personal attention to worshipers, and an evangelistic thrust. Its limitations include the failure of the worship to provide religious meaning for activism in political, social, and other societal arenas. This is startling, given the history of African Americans as a religiously activist people. While black in flavor and style, the worship is not black in content in this regard. The service is also male-dominated and reveals insensitivity to the pastoral-care needs of this youthful, hurting congregation.

After enduring four chapters of what the "experts" have to say about worship, lay readers will have the opportunity to hear others just like themselves air their views on what they would change about their worship. I encourage you, as a reader, to try to find yourself somewhere in this chapter. It is highly likely that you will resonate with at least some of the comments made by church members of Grace and/or Fire Baptized about what makes worship special and what makes it dead ritualism or less than effective.

Surveys collected within the two congregations will be analyzed qualitatively. In these surveys I asked respondents to comment about worship strengths and limitations and to define in their own words the meaning of eight basic Christian concepts: God, Christ, Holy Spirit, sin, salvation, body of Christ, the world, and the Bible. I asked them about these concepts in order to gain some idea of how much basic theological information worshipers are receiving and retaining from worship and other sources. This is the information that is vital for one-on-one evangelism—sharing the good news of Christ with unchurched persons who might be prospective members of their churches.

The final chapter of the book will provide an epilogue of sorts, an update or follow-up on worship changes made at the two study churches since the original research was completed. This chapter also will provide more in-depth treatment of certain issues raised in uncovering the strengths and limitations of worship in both churches. These include: evangelism and church growth; the gospel and sociopolitical activism; the "women's question."

Study questions cap the discussion at the end of each chapter. Designed to make the reader both stretch in current thinking about worship and wrestle with important issues that affect worship, these questions can be used for either individual or group study. They can serve as a guide or a conversational starting point for persons serving on worship or pastoral search committees, professors of worship or ministry, theological students, judicatory or denominational officials, and certainly, pastors and church lay members--anyone wanting to lead or participate in dialogue about what worship can and should be. Chapter 6 ends with a sample "Worship Rating Form" rather than study questions. It is hoped that this will be a useful tool as well for dialogue and worship evaluation.

Study Questions

1. Cite some scriptures in both the Old and New Testaments that might serve as the basis for:
   a. ecstatic worship featuring fervent spirit, dance, and/or a variety of instruments.
   b. formal worship that is quiet, majestic, and meditative.
2. What are some important spiritual and practical reasons for learning to appreciate worship forms different from one's own?
3. What are some strengths, some qualities and elements of worship, that make it both meaningful and enjoyable for you? What are some qualities or elements of worship that limit its spiritual effectiveness and enjoyability? Answer the questions both out of your appreciation for your preferred worship style and out of appreciation for a contrasting worship style.

~ 2 ~
DEFINITIONS OF PRAISING AND A LOOK AT BLACK WORSHIP

I was glad when they said unto me, "Let us go into the house of the Lord!"
—Psalm 122:1, KJV

Despite the diversity of ways we flesh out worship in actual ritual performance from denomination to denomination, from church to church, and from culture to culture, there is some unity in the form of definitions and common purposes. In chapter 5, worshipers will share what *they* think worship should be and do. For the moment, however, we turn to theoretical discussion by scholars to gain expert insight into the art of praise.

The two congregations under consideration in this book are both predominantly black in predominantly white denominational structures. One offers worship that is Afrocentric in flavor, the other has a more traditional Eurocentric liturgical style.

Without serious attention to black worship as a category unto itself, much of the analysis in chapters 3 and 4 will not make sense to those unfamiliar with black worship. Thus, alongside the rather generic discussion of worship here, we offer insights from black intellectuals on "praising in black" and how this differs from Eurocentric worship. We also offer a rationale for highlighting differences between the two styles in the midst of discussions of unity.

Toward a Definition of Worship

In discussing the various ways in which Christian thinkers speak about worship, James White, professor of Christian worship at Perkins School of Theology, Southern Methodist University, shows affinity for Lutheran theologian Peter Brunner's term, *Gottesdienst*.[1] For White, the word "carries a fine ambiguity, reflecting both God's service to humans and humans' service to God. Brunner capitalizes on this ambiguity and speaks of the 'duality' of worship," says White.[2]

Discussion of the term by John Reumann further illuminates this duality:

> The German "Gottesdienst" means "service to God." but the tricky
> question is whether to take the genitive, "Gottes-," "God's service,"
> as an objective or subjective genitive. The former would make God
> the object of the action in serving; Gottesdienst in this sense would
> be "serving God" and implies much of what "worship" does—
> honor, veneration, acts of homage, e.g. in cult. The subjective geni-
> tive, however, takes the "Gottes-" part of the compound as the
> subject of the action of serving, and so the sense is "God's serving
> us." Worship, on that reading, means when God ministers to [us]
> and brings the Good News and . . . grace into [our] lives.[3]

The latter definition of the term means, "God doing something for us which we cannot do for ourselves," Reumann continues. He suggests that German scholar Ferdinand Hahn understands the term in just that sense:

> The basis of worship is God's saving action; word and sacraments
> are God's service to the community. Coupled with it is, however, also
> a reciprocal aspect, the response side from [human beings], namely
> service by the community before God. But as Professor Hahn reads
> the New Testament—and again this is characteristic of Evangelical
> thought, in light of Romans 12—the church's service before God
> takes place in the world and especially takes the form of service to
> the [sister or] brother.[4]

Thus, it seems that the term, from Hahn's point of view, provides two dualities: (1) God's service to human beings and (2) human beings' service to God. The latter is seen not only as public religious ritual, but as social action as well.

This theme of worship as both religious ritual and social action in the world is also developed in Frank Senn's discussion of the Greek term *leitourgia*, from which the word *liturgy* is derived:

> *Leitourgia* derives from *leiton*, "pertaining to the people," and *ergon*, meaning "work" or "service." The term is used variously in the New Testament to refer to the priestly service of Zechariah in the Temple (Luke 1:23), the sacrificial ministry of Christ (Heb. 8:6), the worship of the church (Acts 13:2), and the collecting of money for the poor and suffering saints (2 Cor. 9:12). In these New Testament uses of *leitourgia* the public and social dimensions of cult are exemplified. In its specific Christian use, liturgy is not only public worship but also social action.[5]

A look at the secular roots of our English word *worship* provides another definition or understanding of the word, an understanding that is perhaps implicit in the first two terms (*Gottesdienst* and *leitourgia*). White traces its origin to the Old English word *weorthscipe*, which signifies attributing worth, value, or respect to someone. He points out that it "was and still is used to address various lord mayors in England, and the Anglican wedding service since 1549 has contained that wonderful pledge: 'with my body I thee worship.' . . . The basic insight we gain is that worship means attributing value and esteem or ascribing worth to another being."[6]

Thus, worship is the duality of God's service to human beings and human beings' service to God, as the work of the people (both in terms of ritual and social action) and as adoration and reverential fear of God. This in no way exhausts the ways of thinking about worship.

White reminds us, for instance, of Paul W. Hoon's discussion (in *The Integrity of Worship*) of worship as "revelation" and "response," and of Evelyn Underhill's suggestion that, "worship, in all its grades and kinds, is the response of the creature to the eternal."[7] Further, White suggests that a survey of the enduring forms of Christian worship—of the seven classical liturgical families (St. Basil, Gallic, Byzantine, Roman rite, Western Syrian, Eastern Syrian, and Alexandrian) and of the seven Protestant liturgical families (Lutheran, Reformed, Anglican, Free Church, Quaker, Methodist, and Pentecostal)—would provide additional food for thought and "help others clarify for themselves what they mean when speaking of 'Christian worship.'"[8]

Why Distinguish "Black" Worship from Other Forms?

It will not be possible to understand the description of worship in the two black congregations without first seeking some understanding of the distinguishing characteristics common to much black worship, and of its African origins. Some may ask, "Why talk about *black* worship at all? Why raise barriers? We're all Christians, and we all worship. Worship is (or should be) generic." It might be instructive for any of that mindset to consider the remarks of black Catholic scholar Cyprian Lamar Rowe, regarding declarations like "We're all human," or, in this case, "We're all Christians who worship":

> Whenever we hear someone say, "We are all human," as if it therefore is quite clear that we are all the same, we must be very careful. Humanity provides a potential. Culture actualizes the potential. I suggest that *there can be no really true and helpful discussion of the sameness of human beings until there is an understanding of our cultural differences.* . . . Obvious truths can conceal very cunning, very destructive lies. So the statement, "We're all human," can be used to camouflage or sweep under the carpet real differences of culture, of identity, of gifts. It can become a lie. There is a psychic as well as an historical *truth* in Matthew's conviction that if Jesus is the one who is to come, he must come out of the progeny of Abraham. To forget who we are and where we come from is to invite death to ourselves and destruction to our people.[9]

Rowe asserts that for Blacks and whites (or any other contrasting racial ethnic groups) to engage in dialogue about worship (or any other topic, for that matter), superficially glossing over significant cultural differences, is to foster a false cooperation—to create a lie. Indeed, the beauty of true dialogue is that each party has something unique and special to contribute to the conversation, and is allowed to do so. Citing Psalm 137, "How could we sing a song of the Lord in a foreign land? If I forget you, Jerusalem, may my right hand be forgotten?," Rowe points out that the psalmist is saying, "I must not forget, because the Lord gives us our culture as a primary witness." Rowe concludes:

> *If I throw this aside in the interest of some vague commonness,* I am working against what God has clearly indicated I should do. . . . If I do not share myself and all that I am, then I share nothing. Some people appear to think that all the discussion about and attempts to experience ourselves as Blacks is a negative reaction. They do not understand. They see it as fragmenting us, tearing us apart. They ask, "Why do you not talk about similarities, rather than our differences?" But *until there is an absolute respect for our differences and a cherishing of a variety in culture and in gifts, there can be no talk about similarities that is of genuine and true value.*[10]

In the interest of increased cooperation, then—not only between liberal mainline and Pentecostal Christians, but also between Christians of varying racial and ethnic backgrounds (either within the same faith group or in contrasting faith groups)—Rowe would argue that true cooperation requires us to cease regarding diversity as a hindrance to unity. Rather, we must begin to appreciate differences and to regard them as a mark of God's infinite creativity.

Liturgical Imperialism

Rowe suggests that for African Americans to affirm their own distinctiveness in no way constitutes a denial of others. Perhaps, on the contrary, for others to deny the uniqueness of black worship (and to deny the *validity* of the existence of such uniqueness) constitutes a kind of *liturgical imperialism* that suggests, "They (African Americans) should worship like us."

Finally, commenting on such imperialism, Rowe describes a Ghanaian novel, *The Torrent,* which he recommends to anyone who desires a better understanding of the predicament of Blacks in a mostly white society. The novel describes a British-run secondary school in Ghana that endeavors to "turn bushboys from their 'savage' condition into 'civilized' people." In so doing, the students are taught to reject much of their own culture in favor of European norms, including the stricture that "one should worship God quietly and with physical restraint, not with emotional rejoicing and body movement." Rowe observes that:

> This kind of *psychic and cultural imperialism* can be stark and bold or it can be a very subtle process. In either case, it has devastating effects on the persons whose culture is not respected and understood. Such a person loses the ability to know where truth is and even to enter into the process of arriving at truth. The whole epistemological procedure which has been part of that person's inheritance is fouled up. What Afro-Americans are asserting, with their growing freedom to face these problems, is that they want to revive a manner of arriving at and perceiving truth that is congenial to their deep cultural traditions. What is involved in this is *not a denial* of what others do, but an *affirmation* of what the Lord has wrought in us, a different people and a people who are chosen, in the same way other peoples are chosen.[11]

Generally, then, *liturgical imperialism* has to do with the imposition of Euro-American worship preferences on Christians of African or other descent. It is related to the notion of cultural Christianity, which links Euro-American culture and Christianity, as if the two were one, and views Euro-American worship styles as normative and superior.

This issue is very close to home for me, as my minister-husband is a Nigerian by birth who grew up under the influence of missionaries of an American fundamentalist denomination in the 1940s and 1950s. His love-hate relationship with that particular group eventually prompted him to choose the National Baptist Convention of the USA, an African American denomination, for his ordination, rather than his original faith group. His ambivalence toward the denomination in which he was first spiritually nurtured stems from a great deal of rage over losing some of his own rich traditions, only to come to the United States for seminary and discover that African Americans are reclaiming a lot of what he has lost!

Some of the missionaries responsible for his very fine academic and religious education, as a youth and beyond, required those who took on Christianity to put aside many of their own worship styles and rich cultural traditions. They did this in the mistaken belief that these were connected in some instances with the worship of tribal idols. For example, Stephen was required to take on a "Christian" name at baptism. Apparently, his own very meaningful birth name, Iyalekhuosa (pronounced ee-yah-lay-HOE-sah, which means, "God's pardon"), was not good enough.

Western suits and dresses often replace the more colorful, beautifully woven traditional garb at worship. Certainly, the style of worship, while spirited anyway, is still more formal and subdued than it would be without the influence of the missionaries.

Liturgical imperialism can be imposed by European Americans on African Americans and others, or even by others on themselves (e.g., by African Americans on other African Americans, by Hispanic Americans on other Hispanic Americans, by Korean Americans on other Korean Americans, etc.). For this to occur (for Blacks, for example, to victimize other Blacks by liturgical imperialism), usually indicates the presence of an identity crisis in the congregation. That is, some congregants wish to include more elements of African American heritage in the worship while others reject these traditions, perhaps previously having run away from black denominations specifically to avoid them.

Insights from African American theologian Henry L. Mitchell address these matters of identity crisis and the value of maintaining one's own cultural practices in worship.[12] Mitchell describes the experiences of a group of black ministers who spent a summer in West Africa participating in the Martin Luther King Jr. Program in Black Church Studies (which he directed in Rochester, New York). The purpose of the trip was to enable these minister-scholars "to see, from a scholarly perspective, the usefulness and validity of Black-culture practices." Mitchell goes on to explain that this experience was necessary because "very often, in our thinking, our traditional practices of Black folk religion seemed to be an interim kind of thing: done for the time being, because that was what moved people and

program." Viewing African patterns in black American worship as an interim kind of state until black church members become more educated,
Mitchell explains, is unacceptable. Because these traditions have integrity
and represent Blacks historically and psychically at deep levels, they are not
to be done away with. Nor are they to be merely tolerated until the masses
of folk come "up" to the level of the trained black clergy. Rather they are to
be celebrated, preserved, refined, and shared with the world. Mitchell states
later in his article that African culture, as manifested in worship and in
other aspects of black American life, "refuses to be obliterated" and "cannot be readily erased."[13]

Basically, what we are addressing here and encouraging readers to think
about, is the need to distinguish—in worship and other areas of spiritual
life—that which is universally Christian from that which is culture-specific. If
we can begin to rid ourselves of various types of cultural-spiritual imperialism and try to view things through the broad lens of Christ's saving, inclusive
love, then our perspectives on such issues as worship, women in positions of
ecclesiastical authority, and the church's involvement in social action will
tend more toward tolerance and unity than toward divisiveness, spiritual
arrogance, and exclusion.

Black American Worship: Its African Roots

Mitchell also provides help in discerning some characteristics of African
culture that are carried over into the worship and everyday life of African
Americans. Among other issues, he talks about the black African worldview, the notion of extended family, and the person in West African culture.

The worldview of African traditional religion does not allow for a sepa-
ration of sacred culture from secular culture. "African culture is decidedly
not dualistic. It has a holistic world view, which is only the tip of an iceberg
of contrast between Western or Euro-American culture and African culture," Mitchell comments.[14]

African scholars, including John S. Pobee, formerly of the University of
Ghana, discuss the importance of ancestors to the living and how reverence
for ancestors, who are a part of the spirit world, points to a meshing of
sacred and secular cultures. Pobee notes, for instance, the Ghanaian Akan

tribal customs of putting down the first morsel of food for the ancestors and of pouring some drink on the ground for ancestors before eating or taking a drink.

> Behind all such acts, at both the individual and communal levels, stands the rationale that a person is surrounded by numerous hosts of spirit-beings, some good, some evil, which can and do influence the course of human life for good or for ill. Consequently, their good will is actively and constantly sought, thereby acknowledging the dependence of the living on the spirit world. In this connection, *Akan society hardly draws any distinction between the sacred and the secular.* This is not the same thing as saying that African religion is sacralist, i.e., so preoccupied with the sacred as to prejudice the material well-being of the community and to impede [human] control over [the] environment. Rather the sacred, described by Rudolph Otto as *mysterium tremendum et fascinosum* and representing integrity and order beyond [human] control and challenging [humankind] to the pursuit of development and perfection, on the one hand, and the secular, representing integrity and order such as are within the comprehensive control of [humanity], on the other hand, are not alternatives; rather, they are two complementary ways of looking on reality.[15]

Mitchell contends that the African worldview is based on the extended family. "People in African cultural traditions know no other way to relate to each other. . . . Every woman is mother, aunt, grandmother, sister or daughter, and there is no title for a person whose respect and status is in any way to be disassociated from one's own family."[16]

His comments are born out and amplified by Africans themselves, who speak often of the importance of community with respect to the African worldview. Says Mercy Amba Oduyoye, lecturer at the University of Ibadan, Nigeria:

> Africans recognize life as *life-in-community.* We can truly know ourselves if we remain true to our community, past and present. The concept of individual success or failure is secondary. The ethnic group, the village, the locality, are crucial in one's estimation of

oneself. Our nature as beings-in-relation is a two-way relation: with God and with our fellow human-beings. Expand the communal ideology of clans and ethnic groups to nations and you have a societal system in which none is left in want of basic needs.[17]

United Methodist elder Gwinyai H. Muzorewa, of Zimbabwe, treats the same theme:

> So we find that African humanity is primarily defined by a sense of belonging, serving one's own folk, and kinship. For the African, it is not enough to be a human being; unless one shares a *sense of community,* one can easily turn out to be an enemy. African theology may derive the criteria for belonging to a community of believers from this traditional concept of humanity in community. Such a definition of the community of believers takes collective survival very seriously. Thus two major concerns of African theology, solidarity and humanization, find clear expression in the context of the community.[18]

Yet the African concept of community is not stifling to the individual or to the development of individual gifts. As J. Deotis Roberts suggests in describing the work of Aylward Shorter on the content of African traditional religions, the "life-in-community" concept has to do with the nature of community, *freedom of the individual within community,* as well as responsibility of the individual for the community.[19]

Mitchell agrees, stating that, with respect to the *person,* African culture seems "more declarative of the uniqueness of each human being and of the fact that that uniqueness ought to be held in utter awe and reverence." This stands in sharp contrast to the culture of mainstream America:

> White people read music and are criticized when they do not follow what is on the paper. A Black person who is trying to be middle class and wants to be like White folks says, "She don't know how to play what's on the paper. She play anything she feel like playing." Well, that is exactly what African art invites, because African art is done with the understanding that *everybody is artist.* Everybody fulfills himself/herself as he/she feels like being fulfilled, in whatever it is one

happens to be doing. . . . *It is understood* that everybody fashions his
[or her] own offering of praise to God in his [or her] own way. . . .
One is supposed to know the theme well enough to use it in the fashion that befits one's spirit. You will hear folk in the congregation say,
"Sing your song, child!" And when they say it, they themselves are,
in a vicarious way, fulfilled. It is understood that it is "*your* song"
and that Beethoven, or whoever, just sort of gave you the initial
theme on which you thereafter improvised.[20]

As Roberts notes, "one cannot claim absolute continuity between
African traditional religion and black religious experience. . . . Too much
time and too many circumstances divide Africans from Afro-Americans."[21]
Yet, he suggests, it is clear that many Africanisms did in fact survive slavery
and continue to this day:

The divergence between E. Franklin Frazier and Melville Herskovits
as to the extent to which Africanisms have survived slavery among
blacks in the United States has been much discussed. The slave
system broke down the linguistic and cultural patterns of the
Africans. Yet the influence of African music, rhythm, and dance
is unmistakable in black culture. It is quite obvious that slaves did
not come to America without any religious traditions. In a word,
since Africa is a historic reality for blacks, the African background
to the understanding of black religious experience will always be
important. Any enlightenment we can bring through studies made
by Africans themselves is needed.[22]

Drawing on Roberts's remarks here as well as similar insights from other
scholars and a lifetime of personal experience in the black church, it seems
safe to make the following assertion: As a result of African cultural heritage—combined with the culturally homogenizing effects of the American
slavery experience, Jim Crowism, and continuing discrimination—there are
some enduring characteristics of black worship, and these are evident without regard to denomination or American geographical location. As we continue our discussion of the general characteristics of black worship and then
go on to describe worship in the two black congregations, we will readily

see the continuity of the holistic African worldview, the notions of extended family and community, and the view of the person as Mitchell and the others have described them.

Enduring Characteristics of Black Worship

James Cone, in "Sanctification, Liberation, and Black Worship,"[23] offers great help in speaking about characteristics of black worship. He outlines six principal components of black worship: preaching, singing, shouting, conversion, prayer, and testimony.[24]

For Cone, the black preacher is primarily a prophet and the sermon "a prophetic oration wherein the preacher 'tells it like it is' according to the divine Spirit who speaks through the preacher."[25] Cone says the sermon in the black church is not intended to be "an intellectual discourse on things divine or human."

> That would make the preached Word a human word and thus dependent upon the intellectual capacity of the preacher. In order to separate the preached Word from ordinary human discourse and thereby connect it with prophecy, the black church *emphasizes the role of the Spirit in preaching.* No one is an authentic preacher in the black tradition until called by the Spirit. No person, according to this tradition, should decide to enter the ministry on his or her own volition. Preaching is not a human choice; it is a divine choice.[26]

Cone further emphasizes the role of the Spirit in the sermon event by describing black preaching as essentially "telling the story," and as "proclaiming with appropriate *rhythm* and passion the connection between the Bible and the history of black people." Spirit-filled, Spirit-inspired presentation of the Word is then coupled with informal "call and response"[27] between preacher and hearers. "Amen," "Praise the Lord," "Hallelujah," and other affirmations voiced spontaneously by the people as they hear the sermon help the preacher know that he or she is on the right track, and that what he or she says "rings true to the Spirit's presence in their midst."[28]

For Cone, *song* in the black worship experience opens the people's hearts for God's Spirit and intensifies the power of the Spirit's presence. Says Cone, "It is possible to 'have church,' as the people would say, without outstanding preaching, but not without good singing. Good singing is indispensable for black worship, for it can fill the vacuum of a poor sermon.[29] "Good singing" from the black church vantage point is impassioned, intense, emotional, and spiritually powerful. This is because the soloists and choir members are full of *conviction* about whatever sermon they deliver in song—be it about God's grace, God's provision, God's salvation, whatever.

In the black church, it is not enough for singing to be technically correct. The priority, to echo Mitchell's comments on improvisation, is to know the main melody well enough to offer musical praise in your own way; thus, the common introduction of soloists, "Sister Sally will come to us *in her own way*, singing, 'I Must Tell Jesus,'" or whatever selection. Further, the singer is to offer musical praise in such a way as to bring home biblical truths in a compelling fashion for the hearers.

As the Spirit meets the Spirit, as Spirit-inspired soloist touches the hearts of Spirit-moved hearers, often, "all holy hell breaks loose," in the words of Northwestern University professor Leon Forrest.[30] What results is the "shout" that, Cone says, refers not to sound but to bodily movement in response to the Spirit's presence in the worship.

> The Spirit is God's way of being with the people, enabling them to
> shout for joy when the people have no empirical evidence in their
> lives to warrant happiness. The Spirit sometimes makes you run and
> clap your hands; at other times, you want just to sit still and perhaps
> pat your feet, wave your hands, and hum the melody of a song:
> "Ain't no harm to praise the Lord."[31]

To this list of responses to the Spirit's movement in the worship service, one might add crying, dancing, and (particularly in Pentecostal churches, but not limited to these) speaking in tongues and other charismata.

Forrest, in a *Chicago* magazine article on worship in several Chicago black Baptist churches, provides a colorful description of "the shout" or of "getting happy" in response to Spirit-filled singing. Observing worship at Christian Tabernacle on the South Side, Forrest writes:

The choir here is professional and solemn in the beginning, and then all holy hell breaks loose. On this Sunday, tenor Melvin Smothers leads in a voice of power and fire heading toward furor. The song is "He Walks with Me," and when Smothers disengages himself from the body of the choir—"Got a new walk . . . got a new talk" and begins to speak in a witness-bearing, singsong voice, I'm reminded that theater emerged from religion. It is the force of the music—the obsessive and repetitive rhythm—tied to lyrics suggesting a reordering out of chaos that leads one from a state of self-possession to the momentary state of blessed assurance, when you "take hold of your life through Jesus Christ." The singer—as caught-up spiritual performer—is in control and then loses control over his spirit. When he appears on the verge of losing control, he is actually opening himself up to be taken over by the Holy Spirit. And that is why Melvin Smothers and the others can "get happy." Just now two young men become so enraptured that they can't break the spell. Nurses move quickly to the rescue, but the lads are starting into a holy jumping, stomping dance to Jesus, and they are [speaking] in tongues.[32]

Cone has much to say about the phenomenon of "shouting" and how difficult it is for the uninitiated to grasp its meaning:

For white intellectuals, including theologians, black folks' shouting is perhaps the most bizarre event in their worship services. White intellectuals often identify shouting in the black church with similar events in white churches, trying to give a *common* sociological and psychological reason for the phenomenon. Such an approach is not only grossly misleading from my theological perspective but also from the premises and procedures that white scholars claim guided their examination. How is it possible to speak of a *common* sociological and psychological reason for religious ecstasy among blacks and whites when they have radically different social and political environments, thereby creating differing psychological and religious orientations? It is absurd on sociological, psychological, and theological grounds to contend that the Ku Klux Klansman and the black person who escaped him are shouting for the same or similar reasons in their respective church services. Because whites and blacks have different historical and theological contexts out of which their worship services arise, they do not shout for the same reasons. The authentic dimension of black people's shouting is found in the joy the people experience when God's spirit visits their worship and stamps a new identity upon their personhood in contrast to their oppressed status in white society. This and this alone is what the shouting is about.[33]

Cone speaks of shouting in terms of dying and rising again, as a conversion experience. Although conversion is a one-time event associated with baptism in one sense, he says, in another sense "one is continually converted anew to the power of the Spirit and this is usually connected with shouting."[34]

It is possible to take issue with Cone's linking of shouting and conversion simply because there is abuse of shouting in some black churches. African Americans know what the phenomenon looks like. Thus, some shout whether or not they've been converted by baptism or whether or not they've been "converted" in the second sense Cone speaks of—that is, spiritually renewed by God's Spirit in worship. This is because spiritual enthusiasm is highly valued and prized in black churches.

When some speak of "conversion," in typical evangelical-Pentecostal terms, the individual who is converted has received Christ as personal Savior, resulting in having a transformed heart and living a transformed life on a daily basis through the empowerment of the Holy Spirit. Some have had this experience of conversion; some have not but shout anyway. They shout artificially, and the seeming spirituality exhibited in worship somehow does not carry over into personal behavior and relationships after worship is over.

The spiritual "glow" derived from shouting in authentic black worship lasts longer than the duration of the shout itself, and longer than the length of the worship service, for those who are truly converted (converted in either of the two senses Cone suggests or in the evangelical-Pentecostal sense). For the truly converted, the glow of authentic black worship often lasts until it is time to spiritually "recharge" at the next scheduled worship service.

But Cone is correct in identifying conversion as a significant emphasis in black worship. Nearly all black services include an "altar call" near the end of worship. The call is for the unchurched, who are invited to come forward to join the church ("The doors of the church are open") and/or to receive

Christ as personal Savior. As Cone points out, the altar is also for the churched who care to renew their commitment to the faith. It might be added that the altar is also the place where the churched and unchurched symbolically can leave their burdens. "Take your burdens to the Lord and leave them there," as the song goes.

In terms of renewing one's commitment to the faith, Cone notes that such renewal is often expressed in testimony:

> To testify is to stand before the congregation and bear witness to
> one's determination to keep on the "gospel shoes." "I don't know
> about you," a sister might say, "but I intend to make it to the end of
> my journey. I started this journey twenty-five years ago, and I can't
> turn back now. I know the way is difficult and the road is rocky. I've
> been in the valley, and I have a few more mountains to climb. But I
> want you to know this morning that I ain't going to let a little trou-
> ble get in the way of me seeing my Jesus."[35]

The last element of black worship Cone highlights is prayer. African Americans believe they have a direct line to God in prayer; that, as is often sung in the black church, "Jesus is on the main line." Prayer is as impassioned as singing and preaching. "Black prayer should be heard and not read, because the rhythm of the language is as crucial to its meaning as is the content of the petition," Cone remarks.[36] In other words, style and content are inextricably linked.

> The *style* of black worship is constituent of its *content,* and both
> elements point to the theme of liberation. *Unlike whites who often
> drive a wedge between content and style in worship (as in their
> secular-sacred distinction), blacks believe that a sermon's content is
> inseparable from the way in which it is proclaimed.* Blacks are deeply
> concerned about how things are said in prayer and testimony and
> their effect upon those who hear it. The way I say "I love the Lord,
> he heard my cry" cannot be separated from my intended meaning as
> derived from my existential and historical setting. For example, if
> I am one who has just escaped from slavery and my affirmation is
> motivated by that event, I will express my faith-claim with the
> *passion* and *ecstasy* of one who was once lost and now found.

> There will be *no detachment* in my proclamation of freedom. Only
> those who do not know bondage existentially can speak of liberation
> "objectively." *Only those who have not been in the "valley of death"*
> *can sing the songs of Zion as if they are uninvolved.*[37]

In summation of Cone's points, the "presence of the divine Spirit . . .
accounts for the *intensity* in which black people engage in worship. There is
no understanding of black worship apart from the rhythm of song and
sermon, the passion of prayer and testimony, the ecstasy of the shout and
conversion as the people project their humanity in the togetherness of the
Spirit."[38]

Cone's discussion of black worship centers around things like ecstasy,
passion, intensity, and liberation (as in freedom of body movement, freedom
of verbal affirmation and response, freedom to improvise musically, freedom
to respond to the Spirit's movement in the service in any number of ways).
Some of the same ideas are echoed and augmented by at least one other
African American scholar, the late Dr. Nathan Jones, formerly a Catholic
consultant of black church education and pastoral ministry in Chicago.

In his book *Sharing the Old, Old Story*,[39] Jones develops a schema of the
religious expectations of African Americans using phrases and terms that
describe nine different aspects of black religious experience. He touches on
issues like the charismatic nature of black worship (recall Cone on passion
in preaching, prayers and singing, which stems from conversion by the Spirit), its immediacy (which can be likened to Cone's intensity), and its general
affective nature (related to Cone's comments on detachment in much Euro-
American worship). Jones's discussion of the nine descriptive phrases, and
their relationship to Cone's concepts, are summarized in the sections that
follow.

1. "I Have Come to Feel God's Presence Near"

Black worship and religious experience emphasize the *subjective* and
intuitive (feeling), rather than objective, abstract, or rational thinking, Jones
says.[40] Jones does not suggest that black worship is strictly subjective or
emotional, that it is mindless. On the contrary, a great deal of thought is
necessary to link black struggles for equality and justice in a mostly white
society to the gospel message.

Yet, the most renowned and powerful black preachers (like the Rev. Dr. Martin Luther King Jr., the Rev. Mr. Jesse Jackson, the Rev. Dr. James Forbes, and others) consistently package sophisticated theological and political concerns in a charismatic, colorful fashion so that their audiences not only *learn* something important intellectually that relates to their faith but also *feel* God's Spirit active in their midst. Dry, abstract discourses linking the gospel and liberation issues do not go over well with most black religious audiences, no matter how brilliant in content.

It is probably fair, then, to say that African Americans are often an *affective* people in worship, which is Jones's point. But to push the point too far and assume that African Americans don't think at all in worship would be an inexcusable denial of their history as a religiously activist people. It need not be recounted in detail here, but it is commonly known that African Americans historically have organized and mobilized for social action in the black church since other options in the wider society have not always been open to them. The current rash of black church fires around the United States set by racial bigots is a powerful testimony of the sociopolitical significance of these institutions. These churches pose a real threat to those who still erroneously believe that blacks are inferior and are to be kept "in their place" in the societal order.

Historically, the black church has been the only organization African Americans could truly call their own. They have derived (and continue to derive) not only the intellectual, cognitive information, but the spiritual vision, energy, and creativity needed to launch and carry out crucial political and social movements *from* their affective worship and vibrant spirituality. Further, as Clarence Rivers poignantly states, the Western/Euro-American worship tendency toward puritanism (i.e., detachment and suspicion of involving emotion and enjoyment) "has no exclusive claim to religiousness, nor has discursiveness an exclusive claim to intellectuality. *Emotion is also a way of knowing and relating to the world.*"[41]

2. *"Make It Plain, [Rev]!"*

The learning in black religious experience is largely *inductive*, rather than *deductive*, with emphasis on the concrete. In spelling out the implications of this for catechesis in black churches, Jones observes a "serious concern for lively presentations, story-telling, drama, and arts in catechesis in black churches with a special attention given to the relationship of message to life."[42]

3. *"Reach Out and Touch Your Neighbor"*

Frequent visitors to black worship will know of its relational character. Worshipers might be instructed to ask the names of those sitting next to them, to shake hands with people around them, or to turn to their neighbors and say, "God bless you" or "I don't know what *you* came to do, but *I* came to praise the Lord." Or they might be instructed to leave their seats for a brief period of time and go around the sanctuary to hug and greet as many people as they can. Often, for the benediction, worshipers may be asked to join hands, even across aisles, for the final doxology. All will sway together rhythmically in time to the music as they sing a gospel version of "Praise God from Whom All Blessings Flow." The clasped hands are lifted to the ceiling as the final Amen of a threefold "Amen" concludes the doxology.

Jones further observes that black religious experience *relates* to theology, and vice versa. "Theology as well as catechesis uninformed by daily life is virtually meaningless."[43] Thus, the implications for catechesis and worship are "emphasis on *participatory learning* where everybody has a role. Relationships in the learning community are taken seriously, enriching the quality of the session. We are all lifelong learners in the school of faith. *Testifying* gives persons confidence in community, removes barriers between self, God, and others, while it *edifies* the hearers."[44]

Black worship is *participative,* Jones says, as indicated, for example, by the informal "call and response" between minister and worshipers. But also, through testifying (another term encountered in Cone's work), people relate to one another and relate the faith to life, thus edifying (or spiritually building up) all present.

In many black churches, it is clear from the testimonies and other elements of worship that the *members have a heavy emotional investment in one another.* They are not simply smiling politely and superficially on Sunday and having no relationship during the rest of the week. They are involved in one another's lives—sharing struggles and convictions in testimony, and carrying one another's burdens in prayer. Black worship is relational.

4. *"Let Go and Let God"*

Black religious experience is *circular,* rather than linear in approach to communication. Jones notes an "openness to spontaneity and God's movement, especially in celebration and prayer." He observes "less emphasis on printed materials and greater emphasis on creating a prayerful mood, calling forth the learner's deepest needs, and bringing these to prayer. *No one is hurried. The order of the worship service or liturgy is not the overriding concern.*"[45]

Evidence for the spontaneous and unhurried worship Jones observes is to be found in the practice of some black Pentecostal churches that dispense with any printed order of worship at all. But even in most black churches, where a printed order of worship is used, the unspoken understanding of the congregation is that the printed order is *not* set in concrete and is subject to change. This freedom exists in the spirit of "letting go and letting God."

Depending on how the Spirit moves, the choir *might* sing the selections listed in the program, or it might not. At the pastor's or choir leader's direction, choir members might sing something else that seems more appropriate for the needs of the congregation on that particular day.

The pastor *might* preach from the notes or manuscript prepared for that day, or s/he might be led a different direction entirely by the Spirit. Commonly, a black pastor might say to a congregation something like, "Church, I was planning to preach from Isaiah 6:8 today, but the Lord is directing me to deal with 2 Peter 3:10 instead. So just bear with me." The informal affirmations always come immediately, heartily, and in great quantity: "Help yourself, Rev!" "Well, that's all right!" "Amen!" "Fix it up real good now!" "Take your time!"

And the pastor *will* take his or her time, as will the choir, and other participants in the service, resulting in worship length anywhere from two hours each Sunday at some churches to three hours (or more) at others. For the most part, members do not complain about the length of their worship service or suggest that it should be scaled down to, say, an hour. Every portion of the service "ministers" or provides spiritual uplift and edification. Whether it is the prayer time (when everyone is encouraged to go forward to the altar), the praise time (or the time of "shouting" and rejoicing), testifying, congregational singing, the sermon, the call to Christian discipleship, or even the offertory period—no element or moment in the service is considered dull, a waste of time, unimportant, or uninspiring.

Often, too, highly joyful worship is a very positive alternative to what is waiting at home. It is a pleasure for many African Americans intentionally to leave behind the stresses and strains of home life. These pressures are either intensified and/or caused at least in part by larger societal problems and factors related to the continued second-class citizenship of Blacks in America.

African Americans continue to face discrimination in the job market and in the search for housing. They encounter far higher rates of race-related police brutality in their communities than in others. They confront these and other problems *in addition* to the spiraling inflation and other concerns that *all* Americans face. This added stress takes its toll on African Americans' health and personal relationships, as evidenced by higher rates among Blacks of divorce and single parenthood; of cancer, hypertension, infant mortality, and the like.

So the church is a welcome refuge. For a few hours on Sunday (and perhaps on selected evenings during the week), there is shelter from the storm. There joy, relief, solace, affirmation, and escape can be found in a warm, intimate, ecstatic worship environment, which ultimately points the black Christian back to the world and equips him or her for living, social action, and evangelism in the world.

Certainly, socioeconomic factors also partly determine how much time people spend at church and why. Of nearly 2.5 million black families in the United States, about 31 percent (almost one-third) live below the poverty level (according to 1993 U.S. Census Bureau statistics). This compares with 12.3 percent for the general population.[46]

Given these economic realities, there often is little money for expensive diversions. Thus the church serves as a social meeting place as well. Sometimes there are also theological prohibitions against many of the available social entertainments in the wider society, particularly in the more conservative denominations.

But, again, even the African Americans who enjoy a certain measure of educational, professional, and financial success endure a profound sense of alienation and precariousness of position in a mostly white society. Since

African Americans have *not* "arrived" in terms of equality and full acceptance in the larger society, feeling "at home" in worship with others who
share one's culture, struggles, and experiences is a high point of the week
for many.

The black church, therefore, serves an important social as well as spiri-
tual/religious role. For large numbers of African Americans (particularly
those in the Pentecostal-Holiness tradition who worship several times a
week), it would be safe to guess that worship is practically "the only game
in town" in terms of social outlets. Furthermore, the best black worship is
always highly enjoyable and never boring. It provides a "good time in the
Lord" because of its spontaneity and other joyous elements.

5. "We Want Some of the Action"

Black religious experience is communal rather than hierarchical, Jones
stresses, elaborating on his third point about the relational nature of black
worship and religious experience. The implication for catechesis is that it is
planned in such a way as to maximize participation by the total community. "No 'Lone Ranger' shows here," he says.[47] Again, the informal "call and
response" between minister and congregation during the sermon makes for
a colorful dialogue in community rather than a lecture or one-way communication. The sermon is thus a communal event.

Similarly, choral selections are also communal events that "maximize participation by the total community." Choral selections, like sermons, are
punctuated throughout with the informal affirmations of worshipers:
"Amen!," "Sing your song, girl!," "Yes!," "Thank you, Jesus!," "Well!
Well!," and the like. In this way, choral music is shaped by the total community and, as such, is the property of the total community. A musical selection
is not simply performance by the choir. It is a communal happening.

6. "Everybody Talkin' 'bout Heaven Ain't Goin' There"

Black religious experience is praxis-oriented. Religious instruction and
preaching lead a congregation into action for justice. "Action/reflection is
the Church's model. Christian education must be informed and transformed

by action. Action must not be hasty but rather shaped by careful reflection in community," Jones says.[48]

Jones seems to reiterate an earlier point—that charismatic worship/religious experience and thoughtfulness with respect to the larger social questions often go hand in hand. To present the choice of *either* thought-provoking, sedate worship or charismatic, mindless worship, as some do, is to present false alternatives. Charisma and thought-provoking, action-oriented content often go together in black churches, and indeed they must.

It is critical that the two (lively worship that is personally nurturing and thought-provoking worship that leads to social action) go together, not only in black churches but in all churches. Some might suggest, for instance, that the liberal mainline churches' dramatic decline in membership over the last thirty years or so (in contrast to a corresponding dramatic increase in membership in the conservative, Pentecostal, and evangelical churches) has much to do with the sterile, intellectual worship of these churches—worship that is unappealing to the youth they fail to attract and hold.

7. *"God's Not Finished with Us Yet"*

Black worship/religious experience is process-oriented rather than static. Says Jones, "No form of catechesis is absolute. Christian life by its very nature is movement, change, pilgrimage—for such is God's action among [the] people."[49]

8. *"God's Grace Will Run Ahead of You"*

Black worship is charismatic, "drawing forth the gifts of the Holy Spirit present in the community of believers." Jones remarks in this regard, "Community gathers around the charisma of a minister of the Word, the catechist. However, it is imperative that the minister have personally experienced the overwhelming power of God's mystery and that he/she is free and willing to share this relationship with others."[50] Jones emphasizes here (as does Cone) both the *charisma* of the African American preacher and the necessity of this person having a *personal experience of conversion,* an experience about which he or she is willing to testify to others.

9. *"My Soul's So Happy I Can't Sit Down"*

Jones wants to emphasize the immediacy of God's presence in the life of the believer. He refers to this as "realized eschatology," a concept Cone emphasizes as well in the following passage:

> The black church congregation is an eschatological community that lives as if the end of time is already at hand. The difference between the earliest Christian community as an eschatological congregation and the black church community is this: The post-Easter community expected a complete cosmic transformation in Jesus' immediate return because the end was at hand; the eschatological significance of the black community is found in the people's believing that the Spirit of Jesus is coming to visit them in the worship service each time two or three are gathered in [God's] name, and to bestow upon them a new vision of their future humanity. This eschatological revolution is not so much a cosmic change as it is a change in the people's identity, wherein they are no longer named by the world but named by the Spirit of Jesus.[51]

What comes through from both Jones's and Cone's comments on the eschatological nature of black worship is the emphasis on the *immanence* or immediate closeness of God in worship, as opposed to *transcendence* or removedness of a God who is high and lifted up—up and above this earthly realm and earthly affairs.

Jones talks about experiencing the immediacy of God's presence in black worship in terms of "feeling the presence of the Spirit moving across the altar of your heart in real ways and not vicariously."[52] God's presence is given expression in outward manifestations of "shouting" (recall Cone). Once again, shouting is not just verbal exclamation but also body movement: running the aisles, foot tapping, dancing, clapping, and hand waving.

In a 1985 series of lectures on black worship at Chicago's McCormick Theological Seminary, Jones also spoke of "silent shouting" or "glowing." He noted that the faces of the quieter "saints," who are not as demonstrative in praise during black worship, seem to exhibit a supernatural glow of joy and contentment in response to the Spirit's immediate presence in worship.

To be sure, this is not all that can be said either on worship as a general category or on black worship in particular. Obviously, the distinctive features of black worship that Cone, Jones, and others lift up reflect black worship at its best—when it is most successful. All black churches do not attain the worship heights described here, nor does any one black church perfectly exhibit the best combination of these features all the time. But it is hoped that against this backdrop of information readers can judge for themselves the success of black worship in the two study churches as the next chapters unfold.

Study Questions

1. Explain the dual meanings of the terms *Gottesdienst* and *leitourgia*. What are the implications for lay participation in worship and the church's involvement in social action?
2. Why is it important to distinguish black worship from other worship? What are its enduring features?
3. What does liturgical imperialism mean? Can you think of examples of this, either in your denomination currently or in world church history?

- 3 -
PRAISING AS MAJESTIC, SPIRITUAL HOMAGE

In the year King Uzziah died I saw God sitting upon a throne, high and lifted up; and God's train filled the temple. And above God stood the seraphim; each had six wings: with two he covered his face, and with two he covered his feet, and with two he flew. And one called to another and said, "Holy, holy, holy is the Lord of hosts; the whole earth is full of his glory."
—Isaiah 6:1–3, RSV

This chapter and the next will examine closely the Sunday worship of two contrasting churches, detailing both the strengths and limitations of worship that I observed some years ago during my doctoral research. Later in the book, we will observe how the worship of these two churches has changed since. For now, however, we "freeze" in time, as it were, the worship as I encountered it then. This examination will be useful to those affiliated with churches whose worship still looks like these two did at that time, and to anyone who cares to grow from the "timeless" perspectives offered here.

The elegant, formal, majestic worship of a United Church of Christ congregation is the focus here. We will examine liturgical structure as well as factors including: similarity or dissimilarity to prescribed denominational liturgy; what is communicated in worship by architecture, vestments, ministerial style and the like; the resulting tone of worship; and strengths and limitations of worship and related issues.

"Grace" United Church of Christ: General Description of Congregation

"Grace" United Church of Christ (not its real name) is a middle- and upper-middle-class black congregation on Chicago's South Side. The name "Grace" has been selected because of the overall spiritual ambiance of the church and the pastor's thrust in ministry and preaching.

That emphasis or thrust is not evangelism, spiritual gifts, the fruit of the Holy Spirit, the judgment of God, rules and regulations that constitute "holy living," or other orientations typical of more conservative churches. Rather, what comes through quite strongly is an emphasis on God's grace in providing salvation through Jesus Christ.

The ministry at Grace has other foci as well. For example, the pastor likes to wrestle with the gospel's relevance to major social issues, such as racism, sexism, the danger of nuclear holocaust, and other questions of justice and peace. Yet, overarching these particular concerns is the understanding of God's grace in saving humanity and in moving humankind toward establishing God's realm in some measure here on earth. I will elaborate on these emphases later.

Grace boasts some 750 core members and has 1,100 on its rolls. Members are largely black decision makers in town, including various elected officials, lawyers, judges, doctors, educators, financiers, psychologists, entrepreneurs, and other professionals. The congregation is aging, with two-thirds of its members being sixty-five years of age or older. It struggles to attract and keep younger members. The exact ratio of women to men is not known, but—as is the case in many black, and other, churches—there seem to be more women than men. Perhaps the proportion of women to men at Grace is 65 percent to 35 percent.

The church is situated in a lower-middle-class community on Chicago's southeast side. At the time of the church's transition from a white to a black congregation in 1953, the neighborhood was considered one of the primary areas for the city's African Americans to settle in because of the legal abolition of certain discriminatory real estate practices. The area is now economically depressed, however. In some respects, then, Grace is a commuting congregation. Many members, though certainly not all, come in from more-prosperous city and suburban communities to worship each Sunday.

Order of Service

Generally, the church strives for an elegant, well-planned worship service, about an hour and fifteen minutes long. The worship service lasts fifteen to thirty minutes longer on the first Sunday of each month, when communion is served.

It is important to note that the United Church of Christ resulted from the 1957 merger of the Congregational Christian Churches and the old German Evangelical and Reformed Church. Grace was on the Congregational side of the merger.

Its order of worship, then, varies little from one of several prescribed orders of worship found at the back of the *Pilgrim Hymnal*[1] of the Congregational Christian Churches. Both orders, the current and the denominational model, are provided in Exhibit 1. There seems to be only a minor rearrangement of the elements suggested in the prescribed order, plus the addition of a second Scripture lesson, announcements, recognition of visitors, and replacement of one of the hymns with a second choral selection.

Architecture

In *Christian Worship and Its Cultural Setting*, Frank Senn suggests that *everything* in worship communicates; no symbol is empty.[2] What is the significance of church architecture? James F. White believes it helps to both shape and misshape worship:

> At the same time architecture is accommodating worship, it is also
> in a subtle and inconspicuous way shaping that same worship. In the
> first place, the building helps define the meaning of worship for those
> gathered inside it. Try to preach against triumphalism in a baroque
> church! Try to teach the priesthood of all believers from a deep
> gothic chancel never occupied by any but ordained ministers! Second,
> the building dictates the possibilities open to us in our forms and
> styles of worship. We may want good congregational song, but do
> the acoustics swallow up each sound so that all seem mute? Or do

Exhibit 1

A suggested Order of Worship from the *Pilgrim Hymnal* of the Former Congregational Churches	Current Order of Worship for "Grace" UCC
○ Prelude	○ Prelude
○ Call to Worship	○ Call to Worship
○ Invocation	○ Processional Hymn
○ Lord's Prayer	○ Invocation
○ Hymn	○ Lord's Prayer
○ Responsive Reading	○ Response (Service Music "Oh Christ, Thou Lamb of God")
○ *Gloria Patri*	
○ Scripture Reading	○ Hebrew (Old Testament) Scripture Reading
○ Anthem	
○ Pastoral Prayer	○ Christian (New Testament) Scripture Reading
○ Offering and Dedication	
○ Hymn	○ *Gloria Patri*
○ Sermon	○ Anthem
○ Prayer	○ Of Parish Interest (Announcements)
○ Hymn	
○ Benediction	○ Offertory and Doxology
○ Postlude	○ Recognition of Visitors
	○ Call to Prayer (Choral Response)
	○ Pastoral Prayer (Choral Response)
	○ Spiritual or Gospel Choral Selection
	○ Sermon
	○ Closing Hymn
	○ Benediction
	○ Postlude

we have to give up any hope of movement by the congregation
because everyone is *neatly filed away in pews*? We soon realize that
architecture presents both opportunities and limiting factors; some
possibilities are opened and others closed. We could worship only
with difficulty without buildings; often we worship with difficulty
because of them.[3]

Architectural plans and blueprints for the Grace building, constructed in
1914, long have been lost. Thus, no sophisticated description of the edifice
is available. The four-story, brown brick structure has been adequately
described by Pastor A. as, "grotesque of exterior and grand of interior."
Yet, it can be fairly said that judged on the basis of White's four criteria of
good church architecture—utility, simplicity, flexibility, and intimacy[4]— the
Grace sanctuary gets only fair marks.

The sanctuary is generally quite handsome. It is oblong in shape, and the
basic floor plan is that of many Protestant churches—the well known
"meeting hall with a stage."[5]

Pale green walls (painted white by the end of my thesis research) are
graced by eight rather subdued, stained glass windows with pale green backgrounds. There are four windows on each side of the sanctuary. One huge
stained glass window, also with pale green background, takes up most of the
back wall. The window depicts Jesus teaching women and children—an
appropriate backdrop for the baptisms that take place at the baptismal font,
located just in front of the window at the main entrance to the sanctuary.

Hanging at even intervals over the aisles throughout the sanctuary are
rather ornate lighting fixtures. Some track lighting recently has been added
to spotlight the choir at the front.

Up front, a dark mahogany pulpit is situated at center on a raised, car-
peted platform. This contrasts with the pulpit desk location at the four
white UCC churches I visited for comparison's sake during my doctoral
research. The white churches—two of Congregational background and two
of Evangelical and Reformed heritage—all had the altar at the center, with
a small lectern for lay readers at one end of the chancel or pulpit area and a
more elaborate, sometimes higher, pulpit desk at the other.

As Frank Senn has noted, the central pulpit may suggest—consciously or
unconsciously—that the Word precedes the sacraments in importance. The

message may be the exact opposite at the four white UCC churches—with worshipers feeling that the sacraments precede the Word in importance.

Behind the Grace pulpit desk are three high-backed armchairs with red cushions, used by clergy and other worship leaders. The center chair has a higher back than the other two. A rich-looking liturgical parament hangs in front of the desk. Its color, like the color of the parament on the altar table below it, varies with the church season.

The altar table rests on the sanctuary floor just beneath the pulpit desk and bears a cross with the Greek symbol "IHS," meaning Jesus Christ. Standing floor candles are also seen in the altar area. On some Sundays, the total number of candles is fourteen—seven on each side representing the seven days of Creation and the seven last words of Jesus, Grace's pastor explains. On other Sundays there are ten candles, representing the ten commandments.

Twelve red-cushioned armchairs, six on either side of the altar table, face the congregation. They are reserved for Grace's diaconate (deacon) board members, who sit alternately male-female during the service. Pastor A. says this practice has been held over from one of his predecessors who had a Baptist background. This predecessor brought with him the black Baptist tradition of seating deacons down front. The diaconate board has a maximum of thirty members, fifteen women and fifteen men. While twelve members sit facing the congregation, the remaining members who attend any given Sunday sit in the first few pews of the center section.

Behind the clergy chairs on the pulpit, a mahogany partition separates the clergy area from another raised section above it for choir members. Worshipers in the first few rows of pews cannot see the choir members when the choir is seated. Centered on the wall above the choir members' heads is a large mahogany cross. Exhibit 2 presents an illustration of the worship space at Grace UCC.

In all, the sanctuary has a look of elegance. The arched center ceiling is high, but not so high as to destroy a feeling of intimacy. Further, the acoustics for hymn singing and other music are good. For simplicity and intimacy, the sanctuary fares well. Utility and flexibility are another matter.

The sanctuary is located on the second floor, a major drawback for an elderly congregation. The church has no elevator, and an electric chair-lift is inoperable. Many do not like to use it when it is working. Thus, it is not

Exhibit 2. Worship Space for Grace UCC

Exit

Exit

Pews for choir members

} Choir loft (elevated above chancel)

Organ

Chairs for worship leaders → ○   ○

} Raised pulpit (chancel) area

Pulpit desk

Piano

○ ○ ○ ○ ○   ○   Altar table   ○   ○ ○ ○ ○ ○

Chairs for deacons   Standing candles   Chairs for deacons

South section of pews   Center section of pews   North section of pews

Stained glass windows

Stained glass windows

Informational table   Baptismal font

Ushers pew

South Entrance   North Entrance

Stained glass window

easy for older folk to get up to the sanctuary for worship and, afterwards, back down to the ground floor, which contains a large social hall. In addition, the church has a considerable volume of funerals, as one might expect of an older congregation, and the pallbearers (often elderly) have great difficulty getting caskets up and down the stairs.

Pastor A. says that, on the average Sunday, the attendance in many mainline churches is generally only about one-third of official membership. In the case of Grace, which seems to fit this rule of thumb, would attendance be helped by an elevator or chair-lift? How many elderly or disabled members skip worship because of these physical limitations?

Second, the rows and rows of immovable pews do limit flexibility and hamper movement such as liturgical dance, because everyone is "neatly filed away" in them, to use White's image. Generally, there is very little movement by worshipers during the service. Perhaps this is not a major concern for members of a largely elderly congregation, who often have little inclination or agility to move around a great deal.

Worshipers sit and stand when they are supposed to, as for hymns and special service music, like the *Gloria Patri*. But mostly they are seated. Ushers always take up the offering by passing collection trays down the pews. Deacons distribute the communion wafers and grape juice. There is no kneeling at the altar for prayers of solace, repentance, or healing. The overall effect of architecture on worship, then, is that the elegant Grace sanctuary, coupled with other items to be discussed shortly, can make for a rather stiff or stilted service.

Worship Ritual

The service begins officially at 10:15 with a fifteen-minute meditation period. At that time, two acolytes, usually children, enter the sanctuary from doors on either side of the chancel area and light the standing floor candles.

A lay reader, usually a member of the diaconate board, then reads from the pulpit desk, "The Lord is in His holy temple. Let all the earth keep silence before Him." Immediately following this brief reading, a choir member sings the same message, after which the period of silent meditation begins. The church minister of music then plays preludial music until 10:30.

A few minutes before 10:30, the pastor, followed on some Sundays by the church's student ministry intern and/or lay liturgists, enters the sanctuary from a side door at the right of the chancel area and climbs the steps to the pulpit. Just behind the senior minister and other worship leaders are members of the diaconate board. Again, alternating male and female, they sit facing the congregation, six deacons on either side of the altar table, in chairs on the sanctuary floor in front of the raised pulpit area.

At exactly 10:30, worship ritual begins. The watchwords are *order, planning, dignity, majesty, grandeur, and awe.* The pastor, a fifty-six-year-old alumnus of Oxford, Yale, and Colgate-Rochester Divinity School, among other institutions, rises to begin the service. This tall, light complexioned African American man, with double chin and salt-and-pepper hair, wears half-bifocals and a black liturgical robe with stole of appropriate color for the church season. On communion Sundays, he wears a white robe. As he eloquently gives the Call to Worship—usually one of several brief adorations listed in the front of the *United Church of Christ Hymnal*[6]—he looks every bit the part of "learned clergy."

The Chancel Choir of some fifteen members, which sings most Sundays, gives a brief choral response to the Call to Worship from the back of the sanctuary. With grand gesture, the pastor then motions for the congregation to stand for the singing of the processional hymn. The congregation sings while the robed choir members process down the left aisle of the church to the front of the sanctuary, then through a side door and up to the choir loft on a level above the pulpit.

What follows is an extremely orderly and meaningful affair. Ushers, smartly and uniformly dressed, march down the twin aisles of the sanctuary at designated points in the service to seat latecomers, pass out bulletins, and the like. Parishioners stand and sit on cue for hymns, the *Gloria Patri,* and the Doxology, "Praise God from Whom All Blessings Flow."

Choir members, who are musically well trained and include some professional singers, expertly perform classical sacred pieces and spirituals. Occasionally, they perform gospel songs. Usually, however, the Celestial Choir or young adult choir performs the gospels on the third Sunday of each month.

It is clear to any worshiper on most Sundays that a great deal of planning has gone on prior to worship. The chosen scripture readings and the sermon theme are usually coordinated with the choral and hymn selections for the day. For instance, on a Sunday when the pastor preached "The Good Shepherd," based on the text in John where Jesus so describes himself, the day's anthem related to the idea of shepherding, as did the hymns and pastoral prayer.

The church has no worship committee. Rather, the pastor plans the worship alone and selects hymns. Of course, he is assisted in the execution of worship by the diaconate board members, liturgists, and the choir. The minister of music is responsible for selecting special service music—choral responses and such—and choral pieces. The pastor submits sermon titles and scripture selections to the minister of music several weeks—and in some cases months—in advance to allow adequate time for the selection and preparation of music to complement sermon themes.

It is hard to match the splendor of worship at Grace during key seasons of the Christian year, splendor created in large part by special music. For example, the Chancel Choir, guest soloists, and a small orchestral ensemble render pieces from Handel's "Messiah" during the Advent/Christmas season. A brass choir of trumpets majestically announces the risen Christ on Easter morning. The effect is a feeling of awe, perhaps, as the worshiper is given a sense of the majesty, removedness, and transcendence of God.

Worship Strengths

Planning, Music

The strengths and attractions of Grace worship are many. Obviously, the planning of music, scripture readings, preaching, and prayers to revolve around a single theme and/or to relate to the season of the church year makes for a very meaningful worship experience. Certainly, brevity is appreciated by this very busy group of professionals and by older members who have limited energy.

The variety of music is another draw. While some African American choirs perform only gospels, Grace choirs provide classical sacred pieces, spirituals from the American slavery era, and some gospels. This fits with the observation of liturgiologist Frank Senn, who asserts, "The overall range of the music used in black worship represents a versatility of which few white congregations could boast."[7]

Gender Inclusiveness

Gender inclusiveness is another strength of this worship. Pastor A. and certain worship practices continually affirm women worshipers, both explicitly and implicitly, as first-class citizens in God's family and in God's ministry. They are affirmed explicitly by the pastor's consistent use of inclusive language in sermons, scripture readings, and hymns. They are affirmed implicitly at deep levels of the subconscious by the profound symbolism of the male/female/male/female seating of diaconate board members in the altar area, and the frequent presence in the pulpit of women liturgists and/or the student minister, who is a woman.

Grace's pastor does more than simply give lip service to the idea of women being equal partners in ministry. He consistently gives them substantive roles to play. This is no small achievement in a black church—or in any church, for that matter. Attention to issues of sexism is perhaps even more critical in black churches than in white churches, because African American women bear the double "cross" of discrimination, being both black and female.

It is commonly held that women constitute nearly two-thirds of the membership of most black churches. They do most of the fundraising, organizing, and teaching of Sunday school. Yet, somehow it is felt that their gifts end there. It is evident, however, that even as God called and equipped Deborah of the Old Testament for her position as judge (the highest position of her day for either a man or woman) and equipped the New Testament's Phoebe and the apostle Junias, or Julia, for the positions of ecclesiastical authority they held, God continues to call and prepare women to lead churches and denominations in our time. Thus, Grace's pastor gets high marks for the inclusive tone of worship services at Grace and for his generally inclusive style of shared ministry with women.

Grace's services are also inclusive religiously. Through scholarly reading and dialogue with persons of the Jewish faith, Pastor A. is aware that some Jews feel Christians exhibit anti-Semitism in the designations "Old" and "New" Testament, as if the Old Testament—the sole basis for Jewish faith—is incomplete and superseded by the New Testament. From the Christian perspective, perhaps this is true. Yet, Pastor A. has begun referring to the Old Testament Scripture as the "Hebrew Scripture," out of deference to Jewish brothers and sisters, and the New Testament Scripture as the "Christian Scripture."

Whether or not one agrees with Pastor A.'s designations or the reason for them, worshipers and others might give him credit for attempts to lower and alleviate as many barriers as possible between various segments of God's creation. Under Pastor A.'s leadership, Grace members have visited a synagogue for worship and members of that synagogue have visited Grace for worship. To be sure, there is no lack of creativity in Pastor A.'s ministry at Grace.

Preaching: The Gospel and Social Concerns

Another strength of Grace worship is the solid attention given in sermons to relating the gospel to various issues of justice and peace. Especially appreciated is Pastor A.'s wrestling with such topics as:

o   The issue of apartheid in South Africa.
o   The possibility of nuclear annihilation and our role in peacemaking.
o   America's blasé, almost arrogant attitude about its technological progress and capabilities in the aftermath of the *Challenger* explosion. (What a shock that our space technicians failed to such a major degree in this instance.)
o   Civil rights issues, such as persistent institutional racism, both in the church and other sectors of society.

While one may or may not sympathize with the pastor's stances, his wrestlings with tension in Scripture—his struggling, for instance, with the meaning of the two different creation accounts in Genesis—are thought-provoking. The sermons abound with information and insights related to black history and events of recent political history of particular interest to African Americans.

Grace worshipers were asked one Sunday, for instance, to consider the deep biblical symbolism of black American civil rights leaders embracing South Africa's Anglican Archbishop Desmond Tutu at a Washington rally during his U.S. tour. Pastor A. likened the embrace to the biblical Joseph embracing his brothers who had earlier sold him into slavery. According to Pastor A., scholars suggest that the slave trade in Africa could not have survived and thrived unless Africans themselves helped by selling their own brothers and sisters. Thus, in one sense, African Americans embracing Tutu, an African, represented the same act of forgiveness that Joseph extended to his brothers. "As for you, you meant evil against me, but God meant it for good, to bring it about that many people should be kept alive, as they are today," Joseph told his brothers in Genesis 50:20 (RSV). African Americans can say something like that to Africans: "Your selling us to slave traders for gain was evil, but God ultimately used these circumstances for good, so that centuries later, we are now able to assist you in your struggle for liberation and for a higher quality of life." Many at Grace had not previously encountered this perspective or this bit of black history.

Clearly, the sermons are provocative, eloquent, and creative to a high degree. They touch on important issues that are rarely, if ever, dealt with in many Pentecostal and Evangelical churches.

Worship Limitations

Cultural Capitulation, Gospel "Muzak"

It is evident that Grace worship has considerable strengths at its best. Yet, these strengths are coupled with some very serious flaws. Indeed, in many instances, its strengths are its shortcomings.

Perhaps its major failing is that it resembles black worship only to a limited extent. The indication from scholars, and from a lifetime of personal experience as well, is that black worship as a genre generally is vibrant, colorful, and highly participatory. Worship at Grace, while meaningful in content, is often stiff and lifeless in tone. This is not merely the writer's observation; many Grace members themselves voice this same judgment. Their opinions of their worship will be explored more fully in chapter 5.

African American visitors, and some whites as well, often comment on how "white" Grace worship seems. Naturally, the reference is to the subdued, sedate, traditional variety of worship to be encountered at many white liberal mainline churches and not to white Pentecostal worship, which is typically very lively.

The effect of Grace's architecture on its worship was mentioned earlier. However, the worship's stiltedness is not entirely the fault of the architecture. In equally elegant sanctuaries in other black congregations, the tone and feel of worship are highly effervescent.

Ideally, the music should help take some of the chill off the worship. Yet, the church seems to strive too hard to be Euro-American musically and liturgically, and not hard enough to be true to the African roots of its parishioners. Both the hymnody and choral music are often culturally alien to this congregation.

The Chancel Choir, which sings three of four Sunday mornings each month, is a musically trained group led by a classically trained African American minister of music of Episcopalian background. Only persons who can read music and are familiar with the classics and spirituals are accepted after auditioning. This has been the case historically at Grace. The repertoire is heavily dependent on European classical sacred pieces and Negro spirituals. Only occasionally is there a contemporary gospel selection. Organ preludes and postludes invariably are European classical pieces. This means that the music is what some might call, "highbrow."

The pieces are usually beautifully done, and there are a few dynamic soloists. Execution of music by Grace choirs usually seems technically correct—one does not hear a lot of mistakes. It is clear that the choir members work hard in rehearsals on blending, the use of dynamics (i.e., degrees of softness and loudness), and other performance considerations.

Yet, the evaluation of this observer, of many Pentecostals, and of many Grace members themselves, of Grace's choral music would be that there usually is no "anointing" of the Holy Spirit, no Holy Spirit "punch," so to speak. In other words, the music sounds good, but—outwardly at least—many choir members do not seem to sing with any real conviction or excitement, with any sense that they really know what they are singing about. Many choir members seem focused on the notes they sing, but spiritually and emotionally detached from the message they offer.

It seems fair to say that, for those who are familiar with black gospel music, the gospels rendered at Grace often do not sound like gospels. They sound more like sanitized or "Muzak" versions of black religious music. In the words of one Grace parishioner, "choir members could be less operatic."

The spiritual vitality, improvisation, and fire, the sheer grit and gutsiness one associates with black church music and black church soloists as they offer musical praise generally do not characterize the music at Grace. Nor is the congregation's response to the music typical either. Amens, when heard at all, are "hushed," to use Pastor A.'s language, rather than hearty. Often, the response is the same as that of many white liberal mainline worshipers to music in their worship services, which is no affirmation voiced at all during the service.

As I visited various congregations for purposes of research, I came upon an outstanding bell choir at a white UCC church in a western Chicago suburb. One of the pieces played the morning I visited was an Easter hymn, "In Joseph's Lovely Garden," arranged by Betty Garee. It was a breathtaking selection, with a sparkling, tinkling finish. Yet, at its conclusion, and throughout the rendition as well, worshipers sat deadpan, expressing in no way, either to God or the musicians, any outward appreciation whatsoever for this splendid offering of musical praise. Those familiar with liberal mainline white worship may not find this surprising, but anyone who has had even limited exposure to worship of the masses of African Americans would be surprised at that lack of response in a black church.

Grayson Brown talks of some of the dangers and mistakes to be avoided in selecting music for black worship. He says we should not attempt to

> "make gospel music serious" by digging out the most complicated things the Fisk Jubilee Singers ever did and decide that those and those alone will be "good" Black music. Nor can we get anywhere by using anything (however good it is in itself) with the attitude that we are thereby "doing something for those people." If we can't do something for ourselves, if we can't enter into it, if we can't experience the thing we are doing, we should forget it.[8]

Is Grace guilty of making these mistakes? Perhaps so. While brilliant in themselves, many of the classical pieces are often lost on at least some of the congregation's members.

I shall never forget the comment of one older gentleman at Grace after a Sunday worship service during the Advent season in which special soloists and instrumentalists had been brought in to do pieces from Handel's "Messiah." Asked how he enjoyed the choral pieces, he responded "The music was good, but it wasn't spiritual." What he was clearly saying was that the pieces were musically outstanding but did not touch him. Most might agree that "Messiah" is biblically sound, meaningful, and moving as well, depending on who is performing it. Yet, somehow, this musical idiom did not touch this man in the deepest recesses of his heart. It was not what his spirit craved or needed that day. Maybe a rousing rendition of, "Go Tell It on the Mountain," might have "hit the spot" spiritually. Survey work and conversations with various Grace members suggest that many other parishioners would give the same evaluation as this man, not only of the music on that particular Sunday, but of much of the music generally at Grace.

Brown's point is well taken. No matter how "good" something is, if worshipers cannot enter into it, are not touched by it, worship planners should, in Brown's words, forget it. To be certain, the desire to broaden a congregation's horizons, musically and in other ways, in worship is admirable. Every human being has an intellect as well as a spirit, and intellect should be expanded and challenged in worship.

Yet, the human being is more than intellect. The human is spirit and emotion as well, and the best worship is *holistic,* ministering to the whole person. Grace members confirm that although Grace's music and homilies often satisfy their needs for knowledge and learning, their souls often go crying for personal nurture and uplift. Thus, while including classical music enhances the richness of worship in many ways, African Americans can worship without it most Sundays. In fact, most of them do. The issue of liturgical imperialism, raised earlier, enters here.

Given their general writings related to this issue, Brown, Cone, Henry Mitchell, and others—including many Grace members—would assert that it is time for black musicians and planners of worship to stop letting others set standards for them in terms of what makes for meaningful music ministry to black folk. African Americans must seek out their own musical resources— anthems by black composers, spirituals, meter hymns, favorite hymns of the black religious tradition, golden era gospel, and contemporary gospels— and select from that rich depository the very best. Resources from other traditions can be a supplement, rather than a staple, of black worship music diets.

African American music scholar J. Wendell Mapson Jr. suggests that the educational value of developing a music format that includes this variety of black music would be in "sharpening the appreciation and understanding of the variety of black music historically utilized in the black religious experience."[9] African Americans must preserve their own worship music idioms, for certainly no one else will. A people without a sense of its musical history (as well as its other history) is a people without a future. If African Americans focus on the musical idioms of other groups while ignoring their own, these forms will die. Such an occurrence would be an insult to God, who created Blacks with the musical color, flavor, and inclinations they have for God's glory. For Blacks to be themselves and to love who they are glorifies God.

In discussing the lack of genuine emotion and spiritual quality of music at Grace on most Sundays and the fact that the gospels do not sound like gospels, it should be noted that many Grace choir members would like the music to have a livelier, more compelling quality. It is not that they are incapable of rendering gospels to actually sound like black gospels. When these same choir members have performed in special Sunday afternoon concerts and the like with guest musicians, it is clear that the chancel group has the ability and the talent to render moving, "anointed" (i.e., supernaturally inspired and inspiring) gospel music.

Some members have told me that they feel Pastor A. stifles the emotional life of the church. Specifically, he squelches spontaneity in worship. My personal interview with Pastor A. would seem to bear out their assertions in this regard. I asked him specifically about the music and why it lacked the effervescence of music in most black churches. He said essentially that African Americans, because of the harshness of slavery, Jim Crowism, and other experiences in their history, have developed a very emotional style of worship in order just to survive. But that is not needed any more. He seemed to say, "Blacks have outgrown that." No longer should African Americans "emote [their] way through" religion, he says. Rather, they should "think [their] way through."

For Pastor A., worship has to do with thought and action. Worshipers are to reflect on the relationship of the gospel to the socioeconomic circumstances of African Americans, its relationship to the larger social questions, and then act on that. Emotion is to be controlled and not indulged in worship, he says. This perspective seems narrow and is perhaps an example of black self-embarrassment. Self-hatred seems too strong a term here.

All the seeming affirmations of blackness within the worship service—the use of Negro spirituals, sermons relating the gospel to the socioeconomic and political plight of African Americans, and the like—seem contradicted by this attitude of suppressing emotion in worship. Clarence Rivers's remarks on this issue, cited earlier, bear repeating: The Western/Euro-American worship tendency toward puritanism, toward detachment and suspicion of emotion and enjoyment "has no exclusive claim to religiousness, nor has discursiveness an exclusive claim to intellectuality. Emotion is also a way of knowing and relating to the world."[10]

For amplification of Rivers's ideas, Pastor A. and others might consult books like the National Office of Black Catholics' *This Far By Faith: American Black Worship and Its African Roots*, and filmstrips like "New Roads to Faith: Black Perspectives on Education," which link African religious traditions to current African American styles of worship. The similarities between much black American worship and much black African worship that has not been tampered with by white missionaries are astounding.

The tendencies to use the whole body to praise God, to use a variety of instruments, toward lively, effervescent worship in general, are all seen in authentic African worship. The survival of these qualities in the worship of many African Americans today is undeniable. Any planner of black worship who claims to takes seriously black culture and black heritage and yet stifles and discourages expression of genuine emotion in worship has failed to examine fully the nature of African worship, its survivals in African American worship, why those survivals make sense, and why they make for authentic, meaningful black worship.

Liturgical Imperialism

There is no doubt that Pastor A. does discourage expression of emotion in worship. For instance, he often distinguishes between a "hushed" Amen and a "loud, out-of-order" Amen. He told the congregation one Sunday during worship (apparently in response to criticism of the blandness of the worship), "Some think we ought to have an unthinking worship here at [Grace], where we bring in the band, and all shout up and down the aisles.

But the American Missionary Association tried to get us out of that. Emotions are to be controlled in worship, and reflection should take place."

The American Missionary Association (AMA) was the ecumenical organization, with many Congregationalist members, which helped establish schools, colleges, and churches in the South for the newly freed slaves after the Civil War. An earlier point must be reiterated: To suggest that no serious thinking goes on in effervescent black worship is to deny the history of African Americans as an activist people who often galvanize and mobilize in the black church. Pastor A.'s casting of the choices, then, as *either* having a thoughtful, sedate worship or having an emotional, unthinking worship flies in the face of the religious history of African Americans.

Once again, the idea of liturgical imperialism has surfaced in the reference to the American Missionary Association. We must ask: Did the AMA impose upon the African Americans it helped to educate, and for whom it established churches, a way of doing liturgy—and perhaps of doing other things as well—that was alien to them? Did these well-meaning whites, in effect, denigrate the very persons they wished to assist, rather than encouraging them to work at meaningful *integration* of Christian concepts and African culture? By virtue of the kindness of the AMA whites, did some African Americans in the Congregational tradition then overidentify with the whites, thereby dismissing their own authentic worship styles out of a sense of gratitude and indebtedness? If so, when does the debt to AMA end and black freedom to shape liturgy in a way congruent with the identity of African Americans as a people begin?

These are serious questions demanding serious reflection and action. They really suggest an *identity crisis* for the congregation, with respect to its worship at the very least. The future of Grace as a church, a church with many elderly members, may depend on what it does with its worship, especially its worship music.

Grace, which had two services each Sunday in days gone by, has lost a great number of members over the years and seems to have difficulty attracting and holding young adults and youth. It seems that Grace's worship does not have enough energy, vibrancy, or African flavor for the tastes and needs of many young adult African Americans—indeed, of many older Blacks either.

While Grace does have a few three- and four-generation families, some

Grace parents openly bemoan the fact that their young adult and teenage children worship at Grace's sister church, Trinity United Church of Christ, or at other churches. Trinity, pastored by the Rev. Dr. Jeremiah A. Wright Jr., is a 6,500-member black congregation with three very lively, almost Baptist/Pentecostal, worship services each Sunday. Its worship works very hard at being true to African American culture and its African roots. Trinity is the largest and fastest-growing church in the entire United Church of Christ denomination.

The features of black worship that Cone and Jones described—including informal call and response between minister and congregation, extemporaneous, heartfelt prayers (as opposed to the formal written prayers one hears at Grace), and the use of exciting contemporary gospel music as well as spirituals—are evident in Trinity's worship. Trinity members I have spoken with say they have overcome the large size of the congregation and find something meaningful, spiritually nourishing, and helpful, there.

Grace may have the most meaningful worship content of any church in the universe. And the worship there *is* meaningful, both for me and for many Grace members. However, if the content is not packaged in a way that people can receive it, the church can expect to die out along with its elderly members.

One can understand Pastor A.'s concern, and that of J. Wendell Mapson Jr. as well, regarding the manipulation of artificial, rather than genuine, emotion in worship. Some black churches do use contemporary gospel music and music that is not spiritually nourishing to "hype" emotion. Some substitute exciting music for sound biblical teaching and preaching. The result is rampant emotionalism in worship rather than the expression of genuine emotion. Hence Pastor A.'s caution in including too much contemporary gospel music in worship.

Mapson says that a lot of contemporary black gospel is packaged and labeled for mass distribution by record companies and is not spiritually edifying. It is written by musicians who lack spiritual depth and are just producing music for the sake of producing music.[11] Perhaps there is some truth to that. But there is also a considerable body of contemporary black gospel music available that is biblically and theologically sound that also happens to be exciting music. Such music, if done properly, will enhance the spiritual and emotional quality and appeal of the worship service. It will draw worshipers closer to God, allow them—both young and old—to affirm their culture and, at the same time, draw more young people to the church.

The Grace minister of music was asked why the choir does not perform more contemporary gospels. He confessed that he did not know many, since he comes from a rather "stuffed-shirt Episcopal" (A.M.E.—African Methodist Episcopal) background. This is not to suggest that worship in all A.M.E. churches is stuffy; it is not. But this is the way in which he described his own former churches.

He added that he would have to play gospels set down on sheet music exactly as they were written. Apparently, he does not play by ear and inspiration as do many African American church musicians, who often have no formal music training. He suggested that Grace may need to bring in another resource person just to do gospels.

Denomination versus Congregation

Pastor A. also said in his interview for this project that African Americans must take seriously the prescribed order of service that comes down "from on high," so to speak, from the UCC national office, now located in Cleveland. Black ministers who just "want to do their own thing" in worship, without paying attention to the prescribed worship from headquarters, really are not serious about being in the United Church of Christ, he said.

It is clear, however, that to take seriously the United Church of Christ is to take seriously the *autonomy of the local churches*. Local congregations are fierce about autonomy in this particular denomination. Indeed, it is doubtful that the 1957 merger would have occurred if those from the Congregational side had not been assured of it. Consider Article IV of Section 15 of the UCC Constitution and Bylaws:

> The *autonomy of the local church* is inherent and modifiable only by its own action. Nothing in this Constitution and Bylaws of the United Church of Christ shall destroy or limit the right of each local church to *continue to operate in the way customary to it*; nor shall be construed as giving to the General Synod, or to any Conference or Association now, or at any future time, the *power to abridge or impair* the autonomy of any local church in the management of its

own affairs, affairs which include, but are not limited to, the right
to retain or adopt its own methods of organization, *worship* and
education; to retain or secure its own charter and name; to adopt its
own constitution and bylaws; to formulate its own covenants and
confessions of faith; to admit members in its own way and to provide
for their discipline and dismissal; to call or dismiss its pastor or pastors by such procedure as it shall determine; to acquire, own, manage
and dispose of property and funds; to control its own benevolences;
and to withdraw by its own decision from the United Church of
Christ at any time without forfeiture of ownership or control of any
real or personal property owned by it.[12]

The tenacious insistence that each local congregation be able to do whatever it wishes in terms of worship and all other church matters is obvious
here.

Since I concluded my original research, both a new worship manual and
hymnal have been published by the UCC Office for Church Life and Leadership. What Section 15's Article IV suggests is that, as the new manual
arrives, for instance, at local UCC churches, planners of worship have at
least three options: they can follow the suggestions in it to the letter; they
can modify the suggestions; or they can dispense with the manual entirely
and structure worship "in the manner customary" to their local churches—
that is, continue to use the previous manual or other resources.

According to Section 15, then, and in keeping with the covenantal polity
of the UCC system in general, the manual is merely a guide. Freedom is
granted to structure worship in anyway meaningful to a particular congregation. African American UCC ministers are not strictly tied to the manual,
nor are any other UCC ministers. Visits to various black and white UCC
churches reveal that no one is strictly tied to prescribed UCC liturgy. There
is considerable diversity in worship styles within the denomination.

Once during a course on UCC history and polity at Chicago Theological
Seminary, instructor and CTS president, the Rev. Dr. Kenneth B. Smith
asked class members how many were in churches that actually use the UCC
hymnal. Less than half of the students responded affirmatively. Some UCC
churches still use the *Pilgrim Hymnal* (from the Congregational churches);
some still use the Evangelical and Reformed hymnal.[13] At least one black

church, Trinity, uses the *National Baptist Hymnal* as its mainstay of congregational song.[14] Many churches supplement the UCC hymnal with others. Grace might do the same—that is, supplement the UCC hymnal with musical resources more attuned to black religious heritage.

There is a body of religious music that seems to be commonly shared by African Americans across denominational and geographic lines, perhaps because most Blacks have their roots in slavery in the southern United States. Whether one visits an A.M.E., Baptist, Pentecostal, or other black church, one is likely to hear favorite hymns like "My Hope Is Built on Nothing Less," "Blessed Assurance," "There Is a Fountain," and "Great Is Thy Faithfulness." These, along with many other songs that have somehow become standards in black hymnody, are absent from the UCC hymnal.

This is not to suggest that black Christians are the only persons who sing these particular hymns. It does suggest, however, that certain hymns seem particularly meaningful to African Americans, regardless of the denomination or geographic location. Thus, black worship that does not include some of these as staples is impoverished, in the sense that a feeling of "at-home-ness" in worship is diminished. This is particularly applicable to a church like Grace where, again, most of the members are "transplants" from other denominations and did not grow up spiritually in the Congregationalist or Evangelical and Reformed tradition.

Indigenization and Holistic Worship

The issue here is *indigenization,* defined by James White as "the adapting of universal rites to the cultures and customs of various peoples in different parts of the world or in different groups within the same society."[15] White indicates this is a valid trend among denominations:

> Our times try to undo the medieval clericalization that compressed all liturgical books into clerical documents and the sixteenth-century standardization that made all books identical whether for clergy or laity. A variety of ministries in a variety of cultures demands a much more pluralistic approach to liturgical books. We may eventually see parallel service books put out by a single denomination, with several in effect at the same time. The notion that the advent of a new service

book makes its predecessor obsolete should by now be an obsolete
idea. We may see genuine liturgical pluralism with several alternative
routes of equal authority within the same denomination. The choice
of books would be tailored to fit the worship to the people and situation involved rather than vice versa."16

Serious efforts at indigenization in terms of hymnody and other elements
would make worship at Grace much more vibrant, emotionally satisfying to
worshipers, and pleasing to God.

André Godin quotes psychologist Abraham Maslow as saying (in
Religions, Values, and Peak-Experiences):

> Any religion, whether liberal or orthodox, theist or not, must be
> not only intellectually credible and morally worthy of respect but
> also emotionally satisfying. And I mean to include here emotions
> of the transcendent type corresponding to the need for respect, for
> giving, for humility, for worship, for sacrifice. . . . [Without this]
> all we now get is a *vague, cold philosophy of life, colorless, dull,
> unexciting, unemotional*, which fails to do what traditional religions
> accomplished in their great days . . . including wild, joyful, eruptive,
> emotionally satisfying experiences.17

Maslow's thought seems to argue against any view of worship that says the
only way to show reverence for God is to sit silently, motionlessly, and emo-
tionlessly dry-eyed in the pew.

It is ironic that it is perfectly acceptable to be the emotional, physical,
social beings that we are at every public event *except* worship. At sporting
events, tears roll down the faces of some as the national anthem is played.
Fans jump and cheer wildly for victorious athletes. (Who yelled louder than I
did at Northwestern University's Welsh-Ryan Arena during a rally for the
Wildcats football team upon its return from the 1996 Rose Bowl—
the team's first trip to that bowl in more than forty years?) Game show con-
testants literally jump up and down and vigorously hug and thump the backs
of overjoyed relatives who join them on stage after solving a crucial puzzle,
winning a match, or scoring a sufficient number of points to secure a jackpot.

Call to mind televised scenes from the July Fourth commemoration of the

Statue of Liberty's centennial. Miss Liberty, a mere concrete monument, received more exuberant praise and cheering in one weekend than Jesus Christ, Savior of the world, receives in a lifetime at many churches—a sad indictment. On visiting New York City's Battery Park that summer, I was told I would have to wait an hour simply to purchase a ticket to see the statue and yet another hour for the ferry to take me there. As I watched the mobs of enthused tourists ahead of me waiting patiently, it seemed to me that the statue had nearly become a national shrine. It seems that our priorities of what is *really* worth cheering and getting emotional about are all mixed up.

Some may say that worship is not like these events, nor should it be. Some may scoff at the idea that worship should be as exciting as secular public events, like football games or the Statue of Liberty celebration. But making worship emotionally satisfying and exciting is critical to attendance—particularly at liberal mainline churches like Grace, where attendance is usually only one-third of recorded membership.

Grace members have come to expect, for instance, that on the Sundays during football season when the Chicago Bears have a home game, many of the church's men will be absent. Further, these men are not at all embarrassed for their wives to go to church and report that their husbands, rather than accompanying them to worship, have left for Soldier Field several hours early in order to fight the traffic, park, and get seated well before the game begins at one o'clock. On Super Bowl Sunday—which is usually held in another city and conflicts most years with Grace's annual business meeting, held after worship on the last Sunday in January—male members continually remind the pastor of "the game," which will be televised long after worship has ended and several hours after the meeting. (Most members don't stay for these quarterly business meetings after worship anyway.) Nevertheless, the pastor is directly and indirectly cautioned to keep his sermon and the entire service as brief as possible.

This is the state of affairs at Grace and other churches like it. More enthusiasm and time are invested in other activities occurring on Sunday than in worship itself. At any church, clearly worship is competing with other attractions. Often worship loses the competition because these other attractions better meet certain human needs.

Sporting events, for example, require *holistic* involvement of spectators: emotional cheering and applause, which foster a sense of belonging (as a fan among many fans of a particular team); physical standing and jumping to one's feet; and cognitive scorekeeping and analysis of game plays. Mind, body, and spirit are all involved. Further, the results are often unpredictable. No one knows what will happen from one moment to the next. The result is an exciting, suspense-filled, fun event, which nourishes the human spirit in some important and healthy ways.

Responsible planners of worship cannot afford to shrug off or offhandedly dismiss these issues. Rather, they must grapple with them and begin to ask difficult questions: What intangibles does worship lack that make it less attractive than other competing Sunday options? What causes persons to place their loyalty with other events when there is a tempting choice?

The beauty of traditional African and African American worship is that it is *holistic*, as well as dynamic, in many of the same ways as exciting secular public events. Call to mind discussion in chapter 2 on the African worldview and on the absence of a division between the sacred and the secular in African culture. In holistic, dynamic worship, the whole self is engaged in the praise of God, and the movement of God's Spirit in the worship often makes the results unpredictable, rather than routinized, from Sunday to Sunday.

For these reasons, traditional African American worship is therapeutic— meaning it "ministers" to the human spirit in a way that other forms of worship are not and do not. It is a sad day for African Americans, and for God, when Blacks trade in holistic worship for something that is not holistic and, thus, less satisfying to many.

Preaching: Personal versus Global Concerns

Pastor A. is a lively preacher. Generally, he uses no manuscript for sermon delivery, and his extemporaneous sermonizing is typically fiery and impassioned. This stands in contrast to the emotional restraint he expects from the congregation. Nevertheless, his preaching is problematic for the congregation.

Nine of ten sermons seem to relate to issues of civil rights, sexism, and the like. Again, this is one of the strengths of Grace worship—that one receives food for thought on how the gospel relates to the larger social questions. Yet no one wants or needs to wrestle almost exclusively with these issues. In the words of one Grace member, "I like to hear about civil rights, but not every Sunday." Worship participants come to church with all kinds of needs and brokenness in their individual personal lives, and they need comfort as well as challenge to noble action.

They come as walking wounded, on the verge of divorce, depression or despair. They come facing major surgery. They come unforgiven, perhaps doubting that God's forgiveness is available to them. They come grieving over the loss or incarceration of loved ones. They suffer from broken relationships in their families, from frustration over discrimination and other issues in the workplace, and from anxiety over unemployment and/or financial stress.

In short, many are hurting and they need something practical in the sermons that will help them face and get through the coming week with joy, peace, and confidence that God cares for and will deliver them. If all they hear is the socially prophetic Word—words urging them to bring about social transformation and to right injustices in the larger society—they will not come back, or they will go away empty of personal solace and joy. It is hard to run out and save the world if your own personal world is falling down around you.

Unchurched and churched worshipers alike need to hear words of hope and consolation, conveyed in colorful biblical preaching and teaching that helps them with the practical situations of their everyday lives. They need to receive these messages alongside socially prophetic exhortations. If worshipers are not first healed spiritually and emotionally to a large degree, they will be unable to take on the social tasks that liberal mainline ministers often present them. Tasks that seem overwhelming in and of themselves may appear unbearable when coupled with an individual's personal crises and burdens.

It is my experience that in much liberal mainline preaching, the biblical text gets lost in social commentary, citations of various theologians, and humanistic and philosophical discussions. This is often true of Pastor A.'s sermons. While Grace members affirm and admire Pastor A.'s fine education and wide reading, many have indicated that they would appreciate fewer citations from Niebuhr, Barth, Bonhoeffer, and other theologians, and more from biblical figures. They seem to suggest that Pastor A. should stay closer to the biblical text and make it come alive, perhaps with story-telling—one of the great traditions of African American preachers.

The Grace congregation is not a seminary audience, and it is clear that references to these various theologians and their ideas often are lost on these worshipers. This is not because they are unintelligent or unable to comprehend what is being said. But some of what is presented is deeply complex conceptual material for persons not steeped in the study of theology. The preaching has to be less discursive and more human, containing characters, situations, and ideas to which people can relate.

Attention to individual personal spirituality is almost totally absent. Some within the United Church of Christ look on the prospect of increasing attention to issues of spiritual renewal as retrenchment from the denomination's historic commitment to social action. Quite the contrary: Vital spirituality must be the *foundation* of social action. Otherwise, Christians soon run out of human energy to persevere in social struggle. Furthermore, Christian social action runs the risk of becoming social action that could be pursued by any secular agency.

The choice of focusing on *either* social action *or* spirituality makes these two false alternatives, just as the choices of effervescent worship or thinking worship are false alternatives. In both cases, the two must go together.

With more emphasis on such topics as the gifts/fruit of the Holy Spirit in the believer's life and on spiritual disciplines (e.g., Bible reading, prayer, fasting, and keeping a diary of life experiences as they relate to the pilgrimage of faith), the spiritual appeal of Grace worship would be enhanced and the spiritual lives of the members would improve also.

If skillfully done, preaching that is more biblical (i.e., more focused on the richness of the text), as well as more inspirational and practical, will create in Grace's members a love for God's Word and a desire to study the Bible in personal devotion. There is apparently very little interest in the Bible at Grace.

For the most part, church members do not bring their Bibles to worship to follow along as scriptural passages are read and referred to. Nor does Pastor A. urge them to do so. Too frequently, the lay persons who serve as lectors during worship cannot quickly find a passage they are to read from the Bible on the pulpit desk. Sometimes they clearly show uncertainty as to whether the book in question is in the Old or New Testament. Then they stumble badly in the reading of the passage, betraying a serious lack of familiarity with the holy writ.

In light of Sunday school attendance, the lack of familiarity with Scripture seems understandable. Total attendance in Christian education classes on the average Sunday is about fifty persons—twenty adults and thirty children, out of 1,100 on the church rolls. Contrast this with Sunday school attendance at Pentecostal churches.

One Sunday, for research purposes, I visited a middle- to upper-middle-class white Assemblies of God congregation in a southwestern Chicago suburb. Of 1,700 members, 925 were reported to be in Sunday school that day. There had been 900 the week before and the church's goal is to have perhaps 1,000 Sunday school regulars. There is no doubt that the goal will be reached and possibly surpassed.

Some liberal mainline church members continue to use disparaging epithets, like "Bible thumpers" and "holy rollers." From experience, it is evident that at least these Christians have a real acquaintance with their Bibles. They know the books of the Bible, the content of the books, and how the Old and New Testament Scriptures fit together in the plan of salvation. The standing joke among graduates of liberal theological centers who have come out of these kinds of churches is that they are glad they learned the Bible *before* they got to seminary, otherwise they would not have learned it at all.

Orality and Literacy Issues

Much has been said about the intellectual tone of Grace's formal worship. The worship features written prayers and preaching that is largely discursive, for instance. The University of Chicago's Philip Devenish, a member of my dissertation reading committee, has suggested that one of the keys to the difference between formal and charismatic worship may be the roles of literacy and orality.

Walter J. Ong has written extensively on these issues in his book, *Orality and Literacy: The Technologizing of the Word*.[18] His discussion of the psychodynamics of orality and characteristics of orally based thought and expression seem relevant here.

Ong's argument is that persons from oral cultures—that is, cultures wholly or largely untouched by writing—think and express themselves differently from persons from chirographic/typographic cultures, who are more geared to writing and print. According to Ong, orally based thought and expression involve, among other things, redundancy;[19] conceptualization and verbalization of all knowledge with close reference to the human lifeworld;[20] empathetic and participatory communication;[21] and situational rather than abstract thinking.[22] These contrast with the conciseness that writing demands, abstract thinking, and objective distancing of speaker from audience.

By virtue of education and professional pursuits, Grace's pastor and members are highly chirographic/typographic folk. Members of "Fire Baptized" Assembly of God Church—the other congregation under consideration—while certainly not illiterate, tend to work in positions that require far less preoccupation with the printed word and in-depth intellectual analysis. Its members are more like the majority of African Americans, whose employment and personal surroundings reflect a massive oral residue, to use Ong's terminology.

Thus, while many of Grace's members can tolerate and even thrive on the abstract, distancing nature of much Grace worship content, other Grace members (and also most Fire Baptized members) desire communication that is more orally based. Specifically, survey work and informal conversations with Grace members reveal that a good number want to feel less like spectators and participate more fully in their worship. Fire Baptized members say that these things are already a part of their worship and they appreciate them.

In relating orality issues to community and the sacral, Ong suggests that the spoken word forms human beings into close-knit groups. "When a speaker is addressing an audience," he explains, "the members of the audience normally become a unity, with themselves and with the speaker. If the speaker asks the audience to read a handout . . . , as each enters into his or her private reading world, the unity of the audience is shattered, to be reestablished only when oral speech begins again. Writing and print isolate."[23]

One can perhaps relate these remarks about the isolation created by writing and print to the written prayers of confession that Grace members often read from a printed bulletin. But even more importantly, one can relate them to methods of membership intake—specifically, use of a pew card versus an altar call for those who wish to make a commitment to Christ and/or join the church.

What is the theological or other significance, for instance, of inviting persons to come forward as a public declaration of faith in the midst of the worship service while the Spirit is powerfully touching and motivating by prayer, song, and sermon those who perhaps have been straddling the fence of Christian commitment for some time? Will more persons join the church if allowed to come as the Spirit of God moves them during worship than if they have to go through the formal housekeeping details of filling out a card on the pew to make an appointment with the pastor?

One must ask whether Grace misses a lot of opportunities to bring in new members because the process of joining seems too cold and mechanical, and because some persons just are not geared, culturally or psychologically, to this kind of formality. Are there some persons who would never join a church because of these formal hurdles of a chirographic/typographic society? Does this system of intake "fit" the psychosocial, oral orientation of many African Americans? Specifically, is this system of membership intake too individualistic, too lonesome, too indirect for many African Americans, who tend to have a community orientation?

Recall comments on the African worldview of African scholars like Mercy Oduyoye of Nigeria, who speak of the importance of the human being acting in community, rather than in isolation as an individual. Also consider a commonly held view among sociologists that African Americans generally are slower to complete and return written surveys than other groups. Forms and paperwork generally are a "turn-off." This makes sense given the African roots of Blacks and the heavy emphasis of Africans on oral tradition. A great deal of vital information in African societies is not written down, but rather passed on orally.

At least three key issues are raised here. The first is the matter of spontaneity and ways in which persons might be allowed to respond immediately to the immediate presence of the Spirit in worship. A second relates to methods of membership intake that seem more appropriate for particular cultures or congregations. To see the importance of these two issues, consider a scenario in which someone is touched or convicted in a special way to renew or affirm faith in Christ during worship on a particular Sunday. The formal method of joining puts him/her off, however, and s/he loses resolve after leaving the church building and becomes embroiled in other concerns and temptations. It may be years before the person is inspired in the same way again. Meanwhile, the opportunity to harvest that soul, so to speak, and others like it has been lost. How many likely candidates for membership "get away" in this fashion?

A third issue, which builds on the second, is the overall notion of church growth. Grace members might ask themselves, "How much do we wish to grow numerically and what kinds of people do we hope to attract?" Putting aside the oft-heard complaint that there are not enough youth at Grace, Grace members seem basically happy with their numbers. There is little evangelistic thrust in the worship or the church's life overall.

Would many of the lower- and lower-middle-class African Americans who live in the rather economically depressed neighborhood surrounding the Grace building be or feel welcome at Grace? What changes in worship and attitudes are needed to attract and hold such persons ("people who are not like us" educationally and economically), and how can these be made so as not to repel current Grace members? Grace members might care to wrestle with some of these challenges on an ongoing basis in the future. Many white liberal mainline churches located in racially transitional and racially diverse urban areas also share this same struggle.

Conclusion

Grace's worship is *formal*. It features rather elegant, though somewhat inflexible architecture; formal liturgical vestments for clergy leading worship; formal, written prayers; preaching that is basically discursive; and classical sacred music, alongside spirituals and some gospels. Formal worship is "authentic": It is theologically sound, well planned, and meaningful. At its best, it is even "anointed," to use the Pentecostal term. There is nothing wrong with formal worship, in and of itself.

In fact, Pastor A. and others like him who carefully plan worship so that songs, prayers, and sermon all complement one another offer an important spiritual lesson to those who fail or refuse to plan for fear of putting the

ༀ ༀ

Holy Spirit in a straitjacket. They remind us that the Spirit of God can be just as much at work in the pastor's study during the week as during worship itself on Sunday. Further, planning adds to the richness of the worship experience.

Black worshipers, like any others, have differing personality types, and worship styles and choices often reflect these. Some prefer a great deal of formality, structure, and restraint, while others do not. Further, as Dr. Martin Marty reminded me during my thesis preparation, one cannot assume that restraint in worship is necessarily unemotional. As he points out, many persons have quasi-mystical or profound spiritual experiences that are intellectually based, without engaging in vigorous physical movement or spontaneous worship. There is room for such experiences and persons among black worshipers. The African American community is allowed its diversity of worship expressions, as is any other race of people. Black worship is not monolithic, nor should it be.

At its best, Grace offers formal worship that is extremely well planned, the music is varied and expertly done, the preaching is provocative and tackles important social questions. Yet its most serious shortcoming is *a lack of spiritual vitality*; a formidable flaw for any worship, but especially for black worship.

Worship provides a place for African Americans to be free in a generally oppressive society. Thus, black folks come to church with the expectation that worship will be joyful and celebrative, an expectation that has integrity. This expectation often is not fulfilled at Grace, however—its worship resembling traditional African American worship only to a limited extent.

The strengths of Grace's worship are the other side of its weaknesses. It is well planned, but some might say that the pastor and minister of music have done so much planning that they have in effect planned *out* the Holy Spirit. The spontaneity and free movement of the Spirit—which one experiences in most black churches in prayer, preaching, and singing—are missing from Grace's worship. People stand up and sit down on cue, and the congregation is always dotted with people sleeping. Perhaps this is due to the age of the congregants, and the combination of limited energy and medication may cause drowsiness. But not all those dozing are elderly.

Outwardly at least, worshipers seem basically detached and uninvolved—

elements quite uncharacteristic of black worship. Worshipers at Grace seem to constitute an audience viewing a performance rather than actively participating to actually help shape worship.

Blandness and cultural capitulation to Eurocentric liturgical preferences are serious flaws for Grace's worship. If the church is to grow rather than decline, the worship must be enhanced along the lines suggested here. The church must come to grips with its identity crisis, which may largely be an issue of socioeconomic class, and must answer an important question: What kind of church do we want to be, and what kind of members do we hope to attract?

If the answer is, "We don't want to change the basic face of the congregation—we want to continue to attract solely or mostly middle-aged and older professionals with high incomes who like a rather sedate service," then no changes are necessary. If, however, the answer is, "We really want to attract and hold a high percentage of younger families, teens, and children, who can carry on after most of the older members of this elderly congregation have died," major changes in worship tone and content will have to be effected.

Study Questions

1. What is the relationship between worship and architecture? How does your church's architecture either enhance or hinder worship? What changes might be made?
2. How does planning enrich worship? Can planning be overdone? If so, what is the result?
3. What is the difference between experiencing the *transcendence* and the *immanence* of God in worship? How does your church balance these two experiences in worship?
4. Do most members of your church enjoy your current hymnal? If not, how might congregational singing be improved?
5. What is holistic worship? Is your church's worship holistic? Should it be? Can it be? What changes will have to be made to make it so?

~ 4 ~
PRAISING AS SPIRITUAL ECSTASY

I baptize you with water for repentance, but he who is coming after
me is mightier than I, whose sandals I am not worthy to carry.
He shall baptize you with the Holy Spirit, and with fire.
—Matthew 3:11, RSV

Fervent spirit, manifestation of Holy Spirit charismata, spontaneity, enthusiasm, Bible-centeredness, and emphasis on the immanence, or closeness, of God—these are the prominent features of the ecstatic worship to be experienced at the black Assemblies of God (AOG) church under study. The congregation will be referred to as "Fire Baptized" Assembly of God Church, a fitting appellation, given the fiery, almost frenzied nature of services there.

Surely John referred to the spiritual experience of these Christians and others like them when he spoke of Jesus coming to baptize believers "with the Holy Spirit and with fire." For without question, reflection on this worship readily calls to mind the fiery colors red, orange, and yellow. Vivid mental pictures come to mind of "Fire Baptized" members rejoicing excitedly over their salvation in Jesus Christ and over the immediate, healing, comforting presence of the Holy Spirit.

Quieter moments in the service, such as a "holy hush" in anticipation of a message in tongues, interpretation of tongues, or a word of prophecy, conjure up cool, refreshing shades of green and blue. But there is nothing gray or bland about this worship ever—as the uninitiated will soon discover and as those who have had experience with Pentecostal worship already know.

We will attempt to capture the flavor, color, and *feeling* of "Fire Baptized" worship in this chapter through consideration of its liturgical structure, "tone" of the service, and specific strengths and limitations in much the same way as we examined worship at Grace UCC in chapter 3. This chapter concludes with specific suggestions to heighten the appeal and effectiveness of the worship.

"Fire Baptized" Assembly of God Church: General Description

"Fire Baptized" began as a five-person Bible study in the home of the current pastor and has grown in just two years to 125 members. The initial five members came from the disbanded Hyde Park Fellowship Assembly of God Church.

Several months after its founding, the group began holding services in the fellowship hall/auditorium of a black United Methodist church located in Chicago's Hyde Park–Kenwood area. Worship services I observed during my six-month research period were all held at this facility, but the group has since purchased its own building—a former banquet facility further south and east of Hyde Park in the city's Marquette Gardens area.

Pastor B. is thirty-five years of age and leads an equally youthful congregation. Median age for members of this all black congregation is twenty-nine. Median yearly income is $23,000 and the median level of education is twelfth grade.

Fire Baptized members include real estate agents, nurses, administrative assistants, teachers, grocery store cashiers and stockers, and small business owners, among other white collar professionals and entrepreneurs. Alongside these are some fast-food workers and others in similar low-paying jobs.

For the most part, then, these are not the older, established lawyers, doctors, and judges with household incomes above $70,000 that one finds at Grace. But neither are they poor, illiterate persons. They are mostly young families trying to get ahead in life. Pastor B. suggests, too, that the congregation's statistics are dynamic, that median age, income, and level of education are all rising.

These socioeconomic facts may shatter the preconceived notion of some that Pentecostals are mostly poor, uneducated persons of pariah status in society. If this was true in the past, increasingly it is no longer the case. My experience as a Pentecostal church member for five years, and my visits to middle- and upper-middle-income Assemblies of God churches for this project, convince me that Pentecostalism knows no socioeconomic bounds. It is as attractive and meaningful to persons of middle and high incomes as it is to those in lower income groups.

Assemblies of God historian William W. Menzies explains:

> Prior to 1941 the Assemblies of God grew at a prodigious rate, draw-
> ing chiefly from the distressed classes of society. . . . Since World War
> II, the urban congregations have been engaged in a steady exodus to
> the suburbs. The clientele of the church can no longer be easily stereo-
> typed, for in addition to the lower social classes there has been an
> accession of middle-class people to the fellowship. There are marked
> indications of upward social mobility, strongly linked to the economic
> effects of World War II among the working classes, and the enlarged
> horizons of the [people] who returned from the military service.[1]

In terms of educational background, Pastor B. has had some training at Chicago's Moody Bible Institute in addition to a brief period of study in a junior college. He also did some course work at the School of the Art Institute of Chicago during a period of his life when he had hoped to become a commercial artist. He recently left the security of a managerial position with Illinois Bell (now Ameritech) to take on the full-time pastorate of his flock.

He is an attractive, energetic man of medium height and build, and light complexion. Good humor and a sprinkling of contemporary African American jargon are ever with him, whether he is sermonizing or relating to persons on an informal basis.

Worship Space, Architecture

Again, during my research period, the group rented space in a black United Methodist church erected in 1925. The large fellowship hall/auditorium used for worship probably would get above-average marks according to James White's criteria of utility, simplicity, flexibility, and intimacy.

There are no pews in this large room, only folding chairs to seat approximately 160 persons. A center aisle separates two sections of chairs, each section containing about ten rows of eight seats. The walls are creamy and trimmed with heavy, dark wood. Beams overhead are of the same wood. Dim lighting fixtures are placed intermittently along the side walls. The floor is a dark linoleum.

At the front, a stage concealed by heavy burgundy drapes stretches the length of the auditorium. It is never used during Fire Baptized worship. Clergy and worship leaders are not situated on a higher level, "railed off and raised up away from the congregation."[2] Rather, all ritual/worship action by clergy and congregation occurs on one level.

A lectern of carved wood is centered at the front of the sanctuary, close to the first rows of worshipers' chairs. It is used for preaching, Scripture readings, and choir solos. A small organ is seen at the left of the preaching/altar area, where a guitarist and drummer also usually sit, and a grand piano is situated at right. (See Exhibit 3 on page 95.)

In all, this is flexible space which can be easily arranged for any purpose. At the time of the altar call, for instance, the lectern is removed so that all the space in the preaching area may be used by those who come forward for prayer, to receive Christ as personal Savior, and/or to receive the baptism of the Holy Spirit.

The lectern is also removed when the children put on Christmas or Easter productions and when guest musical groups are present. Folding tables, draped with lace tablecloths, are added to the altar area on first Sundays to hold the communion elements.

The space is useful, simple, flexible and *intimate*. There is no sense of sound or self being swallowed up as in Gothic cathedral-type worship spaces. The auditorium is not particularly elegant, light, or airy. Yet the dark wood and dim lighting do not seem to hinder effervescence of worship.

Order of Service

Liberal mainline Christians are often heard to remark, "I couldn't worship at a Pentecostal church because I need something with structure." It is a common misconception that there is no order or orderliness in a

Pentecostal worship service. Participation in these services suggests that the opposite is true.

Fire Baptized uses no *printed* order of worship, and members there often note this fact with a great deal of pride and pleasure. Nonetheless, there definitely is an order or structure to worship, which after several Sundays' attendance was easy to discern. Fire Baptized worshipers do the same kinds of things in basically the same order each Sunday. Yet worshipers do not perceive the service to be routinized or ritualistic in a negative sense, because spontaneity is built into the order, which is not set in concrete.

Although there are some basic elements and a basic order of ritual action, worship flows with the dynamic movement of the Holy Spirit. Often, the order of some elements of worship is switched or elements added and deleted as the Spirit leads the pastor. Structure is there, but *flexibility and spontaneity* in response to the movement of the Spirit are of the highest priority. It is safe to say that no one at Fire Baptized, or at any other Pentecostal church I know of, cares to be slavishly tied to a printed, prescribed order of worship.

AOG churches typically seem to forgo a printed order of worship. I visited five other AOG churches in the Chicago area for research purposes—one racially integrated, two black, and two white congregations. Only one of the five—a medium-sized black church—had a very simple order of worship, which took only about six typed lines on a four-page bulletin featuring church announcements.

Even an upper-middle-income south suburban AOG church, which boasts 1,300 attendees each week, was without a printed order. The suburban church in question offered a rich variety of slick brochures and other printed materials detailing the church's weekly schedule of services, its central doctrines, its many ministries, and a church bulletin containing announcements and the lyrics to the contemporary scripture songs to be sung during worship. Yet, no printed order of worship was used.

Some of the other AOG churches I visited also offer various printed materials, but no printed order of worship. Clearly, AOG churches give a high priority to the leading and guiding of the Spirit in worship. While many liberal mainline denominations offer a suggested order of worship for churches to follow, the Assemblies of God denomination offers no such guidelines. Thus, all AOG churches structure their worship services in different ways. It is apparent during visits to these churches, however, that each church does have a discernible pattern of worship.

Worship Ritual: The Therapeutic Value of "Shouting" or "Acting Out"

Regular Sunday worship at Fire Baptized begins somewhere between 3:00 and 3:15 P.M. This is to accommodate the church organist, who plays for another church on Sunday mornings, says Pastor B. The service follows the Sunday school period, which begins at 2:00. The service is simply structured and has relatively few elements. But it is quite lengthy—usually three hours, sometimes longer.

The pastor's wife usually acts as "liturgist," or she may be more accurately called "devotional leader" in this context. As worship begins, she invites the congregation to stand for the entrance of the choir.

Choir members, numbering about fifteen, proceed down the aisle, clapping and swaying rhythmically as a unit to the music. The same processional is always used—a contemporary black gospel piece entitled, "O Magnify the Lord with Me." They wear no robes, but generally sport color-coordinated clothing each Sunday.

For instance, the women may wear red blouses, cream-colored skirts, and cream-colored shoes. On the same Sunday, the men would wear black slacks, white shirts, red ties, and red suspenders. Or the colors might be turquoise and black, or some other combination. Generally, they look smart and youthful.

The singers file into the first three rows of chairs at the left front as they continue singing. The congregation enthusiastically sings and claps along with them. As choir members conclude the processional song, spontaneous praise breaks out and Mrs. B. leads the congregation in a time of devotion, praise, and singing—the first segment of worship.

Congregants clap, cheer, and lift their hands in adoration and surrender to Christ, whom they consider the honored guest at worship, present by way of the Holy Spirit. One hears as much cheering and applause as might be experienced at any major sporting event.

Mrs. B. often suggests to worshipers that they are "getting in practice for what we will be doing when we get to glory [heaven]!" The comment is often made that if Christians cannot praise God enthusiastically here on earth, they will be unable to do so in the after life in the ways described in the book of Revelation. Tears stream down the faces of some. Mrs. B. exhorts and encourages the people, her hearty, amplified voice barely audible over the din.

As she offers what may best be described as "spiritual pep talk," worshipers can be heard speaking in tongues, others praising God in English. Some worshipers dance in the Spirit. After seeing parishioners break into what Pentecostals call a "holy dance" (initiated by one person, a few, or several), the organist adds accompaniment to make for what one Pentecostal pastor calls in good humor a "Holy Ghost hoe-down."

After an unspecified amount of time, Pastor B. may signal the organist that the praise has gone on long enough. The musician then alters the music to something softer, slower, and more meditative. But usually it is the Holy Spirit, without aid of the pastor, who signals the end of the praise.

Sunday after Sunday, I watched with wonder and amazement as a "holy hush" would fall over worshipers, ending the loud praise as spontaneously as it had begun. Usually, no one gave a signal. No one said, "It's time to quiet down now." Yet, everyone seemed to have some sense of when it was time to be quiet before God. It is as if the Holy Spirit bodily stood in front of the congregation with a baton, indicating crescendo and diminuendo in the level of praise. This is a phenomenon common to the worship of many Pentecostal churches, and it is fascinating to watch and experience.

During these quiet periods, during the "holy hush," there is dead silence. This is perhaps a poor choice of words because the silence is very much alive with anticipation as all wait for "a word from the Lord." This might be prophecy—that is, an inspired declaration of divine will or purpose from one or more persons moved by the Spirit, or a message in tongues followed by interpretation of tongues in English.

If a spiritual message for the congregation is in the form of tongues/interpretation of tongues, the message of tongues bursts forth from whomever the Spirit has touched for that special purpose, shattering the silence. When he or she has finished speaking, there is another silence as all wait for an English interpretation. It might come from the person who spoke in tongues, or it might be given by someone else. In the event of a fairly lengthy message in tongues, two or three persons may be inspired to interpret a portion of the message.

For example, I present below the transcript of a three-part interpretation of a message in tongues, heard one Sunday. The length of the original message in tongues was thirty-five seconds. The interpretations lasted a total of twenty-seven seconds.

> *Interpreter 1*: "Believe on the Lord and his healing power. He will continue to bless as we [are] obedient."

> (Silence)

> *Interpreter 2*: "If you would only believe. He will bless you if you would only believe. Just believe on the Lord. If you would only just believe. I love you, and I want to bless you. If you would only believe."

> (Silence)

> *Interpreter 3*: "Yea, my people I have loved you with an everlasting love. I have called you to abundant life, to prosperity and wealth, even as your souls prosper. Amen."

> (Silence)

When it seems clear that no more messages are forthcoming, worshipers offer thankful applause to God for the visitation of the Spirit in this fashion. Certainly, there is no way to prove the accuracy of the interpretations. Perhaps all or none of them were accurate. But these interpretations or inspirational messages are believed to be a "word from the Lord" and, as such, always serve to *edify* or spiritually encourage and build up the body of believers present. The messages typically remind worshipers of God's provision, loving-kindness, desire to bless the faithful, intention to give victory over Satan in difficult life circumstances, and the like.

For those unfamiliar with the gift of tongues, in 1 Corinthians 13:1 and 14:1–14, the apostle Paul describes two varieties—the tongues of men

ꙮ

(earthly languages) and the tongues of angels (heavenly languages incomprehensible to humans without aid of the Spirit). Often, the messenger does not know the origin (heaven or earth) of the language he or she utters. But I am aware of cases when a listener from another country recognized his or her own language and later informed the messenger of this. This calls to mind the day of Pentecost described in Acts 2, where visitors from other lands recognized Galileans speaking their own languages when the Holy Spirit descended.

For instance, I once heard a Pentecostal pastor report during a worship service that his wife was inspired of the Spirit to give a message in tongues in the midst of a large regional gathering of Pentecostals. After the service, the wife was approached by an older Asian woman, who said she had not heard anyone speak that particular dialect—her own—of her national language so well in years!

Such experiences, commonplace in the religious life of many Pentecostals, are a challenge to liberal mainline skeptics and others who make light of "xenolalia," as tongues are called in scholarly circles. They also serve to make unshakable Pentecostals' faith in the supernatural edification gifts of the Spirit.

The *order* and *edification* principles Paul suggests in 1 Corinthians 14 with regard to the use of tongues/interpretation of tongues and prophetic utterances in worship are clearly upheld at Fire Baptized. "God is not the author of confusion, but of peace in the churches" (1 Cor. 14:33). There are definitely *order* and *orderliness* in the execution of this portion of the service, as in all other portions of Fire Baptized worship.

Just as it is wrong to suggest that there is no order or structure for Pentecostal worship, it is also an error to assume or assert that there is no orderliness or decorum in such worship. While the uninitiated may view the lively praise periods of Pentecostal and much black worship as pandemonium, it should be noted, as earlier, that worshipers in a spiritually mature congregation seem to know instinctively when to engage in fervent, boisterous praise and when to observe quietness before God.

At Fire Baptized, no one is dancing in the aisles when the Spirit says it is time for quiet praise. No one tries to prophesy while the pastor is preaching. Nor do two or three persons try to give an interpretation of tongues all at once. These abuses can be experienced in Pentecostal worship where human enthusiasm has replaced genuine spiritual enthusiasm. Thus, while the individual elements of some Pentecostal worship may seem uncontrolled, in Pentecostal worship at its best and most mature, each element always has a beginning and an ending, and the elements do not clash with one another.

The choir processional and devotional period may last thirty minutes, and are followed by a responsive Scripture reading. Congregants, still standing, usually read a full chapter of Scripture responsively with the devotional leader. All read from their personal copies of the King James version of the Bible.

The reading of Scripture is enthusiastically punctuated throughout with various affirmations from devotional leader and worshipers—"Amen!," "Glory to God!," and such. After all read the final verse in unison, enthusiastic applause is given God for the enduring Word. The devotional leader then presents the pastor, who comes to the lectern amidst applause.

What follows is something that I like to call "the time of holy hugs." At the pastor's, and sometimes the devotional leader's, instructions, members go around the sanctuary for a few minutes to hug and greet as many persons as they can. The equivalent in liberal mainline churches might be "the passing of the peace," but it was never like this! When many liberal mainline church members "pass the peace," they act as if they are afraid of one another, barely touching one another's hands, quietly murmuring something like, "The peace of God is yours" or "Peace be with you." But the holy hug is a genuine bear hug, accompanied by a hearty "God bless you!" or "I love you in the Lord!," and it is hard to fake a bear hug. Often Pastor B. has to make a forceful effort to bring this portion of the service to an end. If not, it would continue for quite some time.

In the interview for this project, Pastor B. said that touching, a tactile approach to worship, is important to enhance unity. He says he has learned from psychology that if people are angry with one another, if they can hold one another's hands, it helps the reconciliation process. "Touching is necessary for human nurturing," he comments. The more intellectual the worship, the more distant the participants. If there is no emotional attachment among worshipers, there will be no real support for the church overall, he asserts.

Reflection thus far on features of this worship probably cause the reader to focus on things like enthusiasm, spontaneity, the supernatural, the highly participatory nature of the worship, spiritual intoxication or "the high" many experience, and the seeming affection congregants seem to have for one another and their investment in one another's lives. We will revisit these issues in discussing the strengths and limitations of this worship.

The period of greetings is proceeded by announcements by the pastor relating to upcoming events, fundraising projects, and other matters of crucial concern to the congregation. Once monthly he reminds the congregation of the standing "consecration weekend." This is the two-day period preceding the first Sunday of each month, during which members are encouraged to fast and pray for at least three hours each day—longer if they can—to boost personal spirituality and closeness to God. During the announcement period, he also acknowledges any first-time visitors, asking them to stand as a group. Other worshipers are then asked to greet these persons with "a holy handclap."

Next comes the offertory. "Now it is time to lift an offering to God!," Pastor B. announces energetically. Again, spirited applause bursts forth. Nearly every Sunday, Pastor B. reiterates that giving is as integral a part of worship as study of the Scripture, the ministry of song, and general praise and devotion. He suggests that God does not really have a person's devotion until God has received from that person obedience and generosity in giving to the church's work.

Enthusiasm for giving in this congregation is fed by these exhortations, frequent biblical teaching on tithes and offerings, and testimonies by members of how God has blessed them materially and in other ways—with good health, peace of mind, divine protection, etc.—as a result of obedience and faithfulness in giving. Frequently during the offertory, Pastor B. will call on a faithful tither to testify.

Such a person typically shares how they have "planted seed" in giving and then realized a "yield" in blessings that was many times their initial gift. The words of Malachi 3:10 and Luke 6:38 seem very much alive in the hearts and lives of these persons, who along with the pastor, often quote both passages: "Bring ye all the tithes into the storehouse, that there may be meat in mine house, and prove me now herewith, saith the Lord of hosts, if I will not open you the windows of heaven, and pour you out a blessing, that there shall not be room enough to receive it" (Mal. 3:10, KJV). "Give, and it shall be given unto you; good measure, pressed down, and shaken together, and running over, shall men give into your bosom. For with the same measure that ye mete withal it shall be measured to you again" (Luke 6:38, KJV).

Before ushers collect the offering, Pastor B. often asks members to stand and physically lift their offering to God during the offertory prayer. He then gives thanks for what is being received, fervently prays that God will help the church use the funds properly and that, in accordance with the promises in the Bible, God might return severalfold to each person gifts that s/he has shared with the church in faith that day. As ushers, all male, pass the offering buckets, the choir and congregation sing a contemporary gospel number, "What Shall I Render (unto God for all these Blessings)?"

Two choral selections follow the offering. Choir members file up to the pulpit area and face the congregation. Prior to each song, the soloist or a choir member reads a portion of Scripture which biblically undergirds the song to be offered.

All selections are contemporary gospels and are rendered well. It is clear that the youthful organist/minister of music and choir members work very hard on performance considerations. The singers blend well and are quite disciplined, closely following the director.

But more than this, choir members sing with conviction and spiritual power. There is no spiritual/emotional detachment from the words they sing. Each choir member sings as if s/he is singing his or her own personal testimony. The impact on singers and hearers is powerful. To use the Pentecostal term, the singing is "anointed."

Generally, the music is relatively soft at the beginning so that the words of songs might be fully understood. Soon, the levels of both song and music rise, sometimes to a fever pitch. During lively numbers, one by one, members of the congregation rise to clap and sway along with choir members, affirming a song's message as their testimony also. Soloists often make full use of all the space in the altar area while singing, making expressive gestures while moving from one end of the altar to another. (Recall Leon Forrest's description in chapter 2 of soloist Melvin Smothers during worship at Christian Tabernacle Baptist Church.)

Choir members often try to end a selection, but find the congregation's response and their own spiritual leading is to start up again and keep singing. Often, spontaneous praise breaks forth as a result of the singing. As a number ends, and sometimes while it is still in progress, worshipers may dance in the aisles or by their seats. Some speak in tongues; others yell, cry, or scream; others flail their arms or fall to the floor as if having convulsions. Without batting an eyelash of surprise, worshipers move chairs aside to accommodate the dancing and falling. When quiet has been restored, the chairs are placed neatly in rows once again as if nothing had happened. (See Exhibit 3 for an illustration of the worship space at Fire Baptized.)

A related aside: Pastor B. comments that black Pentecostal churches and white Pentecostal churches use folding chairs, rather than pews, in the sanctuary for different reasons. African Americans use them because they tend to be frenzied in physical praise. Whites use them because their sanctuaries are often multipurpose spaces that double as gymnasiums and the like during the week. Visits to different AOG churches for this project prove him right on both points. First, it does seem that white worshipers often are not as physically "violent" during worship as African Americans. (Although, if I could have observed the praise responses/behavior of whites mingling with African slaves during the revival camp meetings in this country during the Great Awakening of the 1800s, I probably could not have made this assertion.) Second, a white south suburban AOG pastor admits that, as his local church membership grew, it was not financially feasible to build a separate gymnasium for the church school held during the week. Therefore, the sanctuary was constructed specifically as a multipurpose space and contains folding chairs with nicely cushioned seats and backs rather than pews. Pastor B. objects to using a church's sanctuary for anything other than worship and prayer.

Returning to description of worship ritual action (see Exhibit 4 for the order of worship at Fire Baptized), lively praise has erupted in the Fire Baptized worship service as a result of the choral selections. Pastor B. remarked one Sunday after such a time of praise, perhaps for the benefit of startled visitors, "I do not apologize for the way we carry on. At a Chicago Bears game, they never apologize for carrying on. If I get carried away praising God, I refuse to apologize." His comments were greeted by a loud, "Amen" from worshipers. Here Pastor B. echoes the sentiments I expressed in the discussion at the end of chapter 3 about the seeming irony of Christians' willingness to cheer mortal sports figures enthusiastically while appearing embarrassed or reluctant to praise God with similar enthusiasm.

Exhibit 3. "Fire Baptized" Worship Space

Stage (never used)

Guitarist

Drums

Organ

{ Choir members stand in this space when choral selections are rendered }

Piano

Preaching lectern

Chancel/Altar area

⬤ Floral arrangement

Rows of folding chairs

꙳ ꙳

Exhibit 4. "Fire Baptized" Assembly of God Church: Order of Worship

- Choir Processional
- Period of Devotion/Praise
- Responsive Scripture Reading
- Time of Holy Hugs/Love Fest
- Announcements
- Offering
- Choral Selections (A & B)
- Sermon*
- Altar Call
- Benediction

Children dismissed to Children's Church just prior to the sermon.
Length of service: Three hours

The reader will recognize this praise behavior as "getting happy" or the "shouting" described by James Cone and others. For those unaccustomed to it, it appears as chaos—bizarre and even frightening. Yet some scholars acknowledge its psychotherapeutic value, even as Cone has lifted up its spiritual validity. It may be helpful at this point to explore this phenomenon a bit more fully, since it has been reported as occurring at two points already in a typical Sunday worship service at Fire Baptized.

Colby College's Dr. Cheryl Townsend Gilkes, in an article on the black church as a therapeutic community, takes an in-depth look at this phenomenon she calls "acting-out" in black worship.[3] She suggests that because of the emotional release many experience in black worship, rates of mental illness and hospitalization in mental institutions are lower for African Americans than for whites.

These rates are also lower than would be expected given the stress African Americans experience as an oppressed minority in a white-dominated society and the concentration of Blacks in lower socioeconomic strata.

Research by scholars like August B. Hollingshead and Frederick C. Redlich indicates a higher rate of mental illness for those in low socioeconomic classes. Gilkes explains that "Recent developments in radical therapies for dealing with mental disorders bear an overwhelming similarity to some of the instrumental and expressive aspects of the black religious experience" and she enumerates four possible therapeutic functions of black religious activities: "the *articulation of suffering; the location of persecutors; the provision of asylum for "acting out"; and the validation of experiences.*"[4]

Articulation of suffering has to do with speaking and singing about suffering through prayer, song, and sermon. Insults, scorn, and difficult life circumstances (which Pentecostals often label as attacks from Satan) are all lifted up in the group, and this provides therapeutic release. Gilkes refers to Thomas J. Scheff's work in labeling theory. Scheff suggests that "Speak Bitterness" sessions held in the People's Republic of China, and similar social forums to be found in fundamentalist and black churches in the United States, allow persons to confess not their sins but their sorrows. He indicated that there is therapeutic value in doing so:

> Such meetings "stimulate *collective catharsis in such a way that the needs of individuals to release tension or distressful emotion are* met. At the same time, this collective catharsis gives rise to heightened solidarity and a sense of cultural community within the group. As long as this form leads to genuine and spontaneous emotional release, it serves a vital need for the members and develops an extremely cohesive group."[5]

Gilkes notes that in many black churches, this type of session occurs in midweek prayer meetings, during which members recount sources of suffering in their lives and ask for prayers by the membership to alleviate their suffering. "They ask for help in bearing their burdens in the same manner that Jesus did in order not to be crushed by them."[6]

I recall an example of what Gilkes describes from a Thursday night prayer service at Fire Baptized. A young woman stood up and told those present that she and her husband had separated and that she was very broken as a result of it. Immediately, the entire congregation directed its prayer attention to her. All stretched their hands toward her as if to direct all the healing, comforting energy of the Holy Spirit present in the sanctuary onto that one young woman. All prayed quietly to themselves, while the pastor's wife prayed aloud for this member. "It is this ability to collectively talk about their troubles within the context of the church that may account for the low rates of depression found among black psychiatric diagnoses," says Gilkes.[7]

In black worship experiences, Gilkes remarks that participants also:

o Locate their persecutors, or account for the causes of both personal and collective suffering (e.g., an arrest, a lost job, a drinking problem, even adultery).

o Use the church as an asylum (defined by Gilkes as an inviolable place of refuge and protection, a place of retreat and security, a shelter for "acting-out" or "shouting").

o Validate black experiences. This has to do with redefining and reinterpreting societal events and issues that adversely affect African Americans, which whites and white media either seriously misrepresent or dismiss as unimportant.

As we have seen, Fire Baptized worship experiences do enable participants to articulate suffering and locate persecutors, and they do provide asylum for acting out. They do not do a good a job, however, at validating collective black experience. This matter will be explored in the discussion of worship limitations.

Generally, recognizing the therapeutic healing provided by black religion is important both because of the financial and cultural inaccessibility of therapy for African Americans and because of the cultural differences in black and white approaches to handling suffering that it points up. Gilkes observes that because of the "overall economic status" of African Americans, "therapy is an expensive solution to private troubles with a limited availability." Furthermore, "cultural factors, such as language barriers, divergent life experiences, and family background are also countervailing forces limiting access to therapeutic facilities."[8]

Gilkes continues by discussing white embarrassment over personal troubles versus black openness in discussing these in the safety of the church:

> a major factor in the labeling process is the society's overall view
> that having a psychiatric personal trouble is shameful. . . . Besides

mental illness, other aspects of personal disorganization such as alco-
holism, illegitimacy, criminal involvement, and marital troubles are
also considered shameful and the "fault" of the person involved. In
middle-class America, seeking help for personal troubles, therefore
holds socially punitive overtones. *Suburban ministers, when counseling their parishioners, sometimes exchange offices with ministers in
another town so that the neighbors of the church member will not
know that he or she is seeking help.* William Ryan . . . has shown how
the inability of blacks to hide or disguise their personal pathologies in
the same manner as whites has led to the *distorted view of the black
population as pathology-ridden and therefore somehow inferior.*[9]

All of this provides food for thought on the relationship of worship to
pastoral care, psychotherapeutic aspects of black worship, and other issues.
Further comment and discussion on these questions will be offered in later
sections of the chapter.

Before leaving the question of "acting out," another issue for research
this type of praise raises for me is the relationship of sexuality to black and
Pentecostal worship. Often, I am struck by the sensual, almost sexual,
nature of much of the audience participation and of the overall worship at
Fire Baptized and other black churches with similar worship. The bodily
swaying, the flailing on the floor, the crying out, the rising of music (and
response to it) to fever pitch, the general frenzy, and the resultant "high" or
sense of spiritual intoxication derived from this worship all seem, for lack
of a better term, almost orgasmic.

Like the best intercourse, the worship experience at Fire Baptized and
other churches like it is at once totally exhausting and totally exhilarating—
a totally satisfying experience. This is something that many African Americans in pastoral care talk about quietly among themselves, but this author is
not aware of any serious research having been done on the subject.

In musing over this matter, some of these caregivers theorize informally
for instance, that, in Pentecostal churches, where celibacy for the unmarried
is stressed and secular dancing frowned on, often the most fervent
"shouters" are those who are abstaining sexually or older people who live
alone. The dancing and other movements serve, then, not only as a vehicle
for praise to God, but also as a vehicle for release of sexual tension, an

outlet for repressed sexuality. No one proffers a judgment as to whether this may be good, bad, or simply a logical feature of worship which tends to be *holistic.* There seems to be a gap in the scholarly literature on this point. These issues warrant serious academic study, reflection, and publication of materials of help to those attempting to understand all the psychotherapeutic aspects of black worship ritual.

To return to the worship ritual itself, once the congregation has quieted down following choral selections, the children are dismissed to children's church and the sermon is given. The sermons, often lasting an hour, are extemporaneous and perhaps best classified as biblical teaching-preaching. They are decidedly practical and Bible-centered.

Pastor B. wears a business suit, the preference of many Pentecostal pastors, as opposed to a formal liturgical robe. Pacing the altar area with Bible in hand, Pastor B. rambles and digresses quite often as he uses sketchy notes, if any, to discuss the topic or theme announced at the beginning. Sometimes, after announcing the sermon topic, Pastor B. will ask members to stand and repeat a spontaneously devised positive faith confession suited to the topic. These can be lengthy.

Members are told to say things like, "What God says, I say. What I say, God says," "My faith is stronger than ever before," "I and the Creator are one," "When I pray, something happens in heaven." The confessions are designed to bolster faith, to serve as encouragement, and to heighten interest in the sermon he is about to deliver.

Sermon content and digressions include lots of storytelling from his own life, as well as from the lives of others, references to any number of Scriptures from both the Old and New Testaments which strengthen the points he is making, much humor, and a great many black colloquialisms. His humor and black folkways of speaking appeal strongly perhaps to the teens and young adults present, if not to all those regularly in attendance. They make Pastor B. seem approachable, human, down-to-earth, and lacking in pretenses of any kind. Indeed, based on my personal contact with him, Pastor B. is all those things.

The rambling and length aside, the worshipers say they enjoy the preaching because of its practical thrust—its relating of biblical stories, concepts, and principles to everyday life situations. Catchy titles, when Pastor B. thinks to offer them, reflect the encouraging bent and common Pentecostal themes of most of these sermons. Sermons have included: "You Can't Touch Me, I'm God's Property," a message on Christians' victory over Satan in the spiritual warfare they face daily; "Put the Pressure on God," a reminder to the "saints" to pray the Word of God, to remind God of divine *promises from the Bible* (for health, prosperity, protection from enemies, etc.) when these seem unfulfilled; "Something like Jesus: Or Jesus, the Counterfeit," discussion of *false doctrines and beliefs* about Jesus as taught in various other Christian denominations or circles.

Sermons also touch on such practical matters as Christian marriage and family life, forgiveness of sins/salvation through Jesus Christ, the fruit and ministry gifts of the Holy Spirit, the power of the spoken word (saying the positive things the Bible promises and watching them be manifest, rather than creating negative circumstances with negative "confessions"), and the like. Those who listen via Christian radio and television to Pentecostal Bible teachers—the so-called Word-faith teachers like Kenneth Hagin, Marilyn Hickey, Frederick K. Price, and Kenneth Copeland—will be familiar with the gist of such teachings. These broadcast ministries and others like them, of which many Fire Baptized members say they enjoy a steady diet rather than partaking of "secular" radio and television, bolster and confirm Pastor B.'s teaching during the week.

Many worshipers bring paper and writing implements and take notes as the pastor is preaching. The word *indoctrination* occurs to me. Members are given specific ways of thinking about Christian concepts and biblical principles. Doctrines of Christian and other faith groups are specifically lifted up and shown as inconsistent, inadequate, or erroneous in light of Pentecostal interpretation of the Bible. There seems to be little room for ambiguity or debate about what the pastor says or how he interprets the Bible.

Pastor B. encourages listeners, nearly all of whom faithfully bring their Bibles to worship, to turn to the various Scriptures to which he refers and allows time for them to do so. The speed with which most people find the passages gives evidence that they, unlike many of their liberal mainline counterparts, are well acquainted with their Bibles. They know which books are in the Old Testament versus the New Testament, and where they are located.

A glance at the Bible of the person either to one's left or right is likely to reveal a book of many dog-eared pages, marked heavily by felt-tip marker and/or ballpoint pen. Undeniably, the Bibles are well used, both in worship and in personal devotion time away from church, as members will testify.

To be sure, one would not consider the sermons intellectual. There are no heavy theoretical treatments of complex theological ideologies, no quotes from famous theologians or the writings of famous African Americans, and no brilliant elocutionary techniques, as in preaching at churches like Grace. Yet, a great deal of rational, cognitive activity is involved, for both preacher and participants.

Chiefly, frequent congregants are steeped in biblical content. This enables them to quote chapter, line, and verse (from the King James version, of course) of beloved Scripture passages anytime and anywhere, and, again, to relate biblical stories and admonitions to situations in daily living. Without doubt, this strengthens personal spirituality and provides members enough sound Bible knowledge, and hopefully enough spiritual maturity, to encourage one another from the Scriptures during the week. This lightens the minister's overall pastoral-care duties.

The sermon is always followed by the altar call. Each Sunday, opportunity is given for those whose hearts have been moved to repentance to come forward—not to join the church, but to accept Christ as "personal Savior" and to begin anew their relationships with God. These persons may or may not officially join the church at some point in the future. After being "saved," they may even go on to membership in another Pentecostal church.

The thrust is not on church membership; it is on saving souls. A white Assemblies of God pastor reports, for instance, that regular worship attendance at his church is thirteen hundred each Sunday, and Sunday school attendance more than nine hundred. The church rolls, however, contain only six hundred names. This contrasts markedly with liberal mainline churches which, as Pastor A. noted in chapter 3, typically have only one-third of the recorded members in church on any given Sunday.

Pastor B.'s appeal to the "unsaved" in the congregation communicates both an evangelistic burden for souls to be saved and a tremendous sense of urgency that they be saved today. "Sinners," who may include even those who attend worship regularly but have not received Christ, are reminded that tomorrow is not promised to them, that once they leave the church building that day, there is no guarantee that they will reach home safely or live until the following morning.

While such words are frightening, Pastor B.'s appeal is not primarily one of scare tactics. Many Pentecostal ministers seem solely to use fear of death and of hell to persuade persons to receive Christ. While the issue of "hell" as a literal place is not ignored, Pastor B. focuses more on what the "sinner" will gain, rather than escape, as one of Christ's fold.

Hearers are told that the secular vices they may be enjoying so much at present, and which they find so hard to relinquish, cannot compare to the spiritual riches to be had in a relationship with Christ. Their inheritance as a true child of God is a life of joy and victory, despite the trials that come, he remarks. Further, these persons are reminded that they will not have to struggle in their own strength to give up bad habits or vices. The Spirit of God will take away the appetite or desire for these things and provide desires for godly companions and habits instead.

While the pastor encourages the "unsaved" to come forward in this manner, church members sit praying audibly, but quietly—some in tongues—asking God to move by the Spirit to touch forcefully and convict the hearts of the "unsaved" so that they might commit their lives to Christ that afternoon. On most Sundays, one or more persons come forward. A deaconess also comes forward, bearing white cloths. These will be used to cover the legs of any women who may fall under the power of the Spirit during prayer at the altar. The consideration here is one of modesty, in the event the hem of a woman's dress is raised above the knee as she falls.

As each "unsaved" person comes forward, there is applause and great rejoicing. The words of Jesus in Luke 15:7, that there is more rejoicing in heaven over one lost sinner who repents than over ninety-nine righteous persons who need no repentance, comes to mind. Many cry and rejoice fervently, too, because they have been praying for years that a particular loved one or coworker might yield his or her life to Christ. To see the husband who has been struggling with drug addiction or the mean-spirited wife or coworker accept Christ is answered prayer and simply incredible in many cases.

The saved testify that weeks, months, and even years after receiving Christ as personal Savior, the "conversion" or transformation of their lives has been real and lasting. The drug addict has recovered and no longer desires drugs. The wife of twenty years—once cantankerous, irascible, and intractable in pressing for divorce—is now sweet and loving. Perhaps practitioners of the various psychotherapeutic disciplines may have other explanations for these "conversions." But Fire Baptized members credit these dramatic life changes to the transformative power of the Holy Spirit. They only know that, although their loved one or friend is not now perfect, whereas s/he once made life at home or at work a living hell, s/he has changed dramatically for the better.

The pastor lays hands on and prays quietly with each person, who then goes back to his or her seat. At other Pentecostal churches, "personal workers" or "counselors," men and women armed with Bibles, then lead these persons out of the sanctuary to another room, where they attempt to answer questions of the newly saved, distribute evangelistic tracts (such as "The Four Spiritual Laws") and other devotional literature, and offer prayer to get these persons off to a solid start in their new relationship with Christ.

After the call for those who wish to be saved, usually the pastor calls forward three other groups of persons: those who wish to receive healing, the Baptism of the Holy Spirit, or prayers of consolation. This is time-consuming business, as often nearly everyone in the sanctuary will line up single-file down the center aisle of the church; the pastor then prays fervently, though briefly, with each one for his or her special circumstance.

Those remaining seated in the congregation, as well as those in line for prayer, pray quietly to themselves that God will minister powerfully to the needs of all those present. At the front, the pastor is assisted by the deaconess(es) with cloths, a male deacon holding a bottle of olive oil, and other male deacons who stand behind each person prayed for, prepared to lower him or her slowly to the floor in the event that he or she falls under the power of the Spirit. The forehead of each person desiring prayer is anointed with a bit of the oil, representing an infusion of the healing and comforting power of the Holy Spirit.

Eventually, all who desired special prayer have been attended to and the pastor gives the benediction from the front of the sanctuary. Three hours have passed at least, yet members are in no hurry to get home. Frequently, Pastor B. or one of the deacons must blink the lights in the worship space on and off to force persons to end their protracted informal conversation.

Worship Strengths

Spontaneity, Congregational Participation

As with the worship at Grace UCC, the positive features of this worship are many and obvious. Chief among these, most mentioned a bit earlier on, are its spontaneity, the enthusiasm of worshipers, their intense participation, and the holistic nature of the worship.

The existing order of worship—again, not printed but practiced—has spontaneity built in, both because the order is not believed to be set in stone and because the Spirit is allowed time and room to minister to people as the Spirit wills. The Pastor and worshipers are also free to express themselves spontaneously, making for a service that is highly participatory, rather than one that resembles a performance by pastor, choir, and worship leaders with very little input from congregants.

There are any number of points in the service when active participation is required of worshipers. These include the offering of praise and adoration to God during the devotional period, the "time of holy hugs," the greeting of visitors with applause, the physical lifting of the offering to God during the offertory prayer, the reciting of a positive faith confession before sermons, praying for the unsaved and the unconsoled during the altar call, not to mention the freedom of people to act spontaneously, standing, clapping, dancing, speaking in tongues, singing along with the choir, and offering verbal affirmations during choral numbers and at other times during the service.

This worship is *fun,* as members often verbalize as they leave: "We had a good time in the Lord today" is the expression often heard. There is little time for anyone to become bored, and worshipers are hardly uninvolved. Their enthusiasm shows in their intense participation. This is the worship's main strength from Pastor B.'s perspective—that it involves the whole person. Further, it requires an intense emotional response to God and to God's Spirit. No one goes away without having had to experience and respond to God in some profound way. Even the "sinner" who does not go forward to the altar to be "saved" at the end of the service has been given the opportunity to say yes or no to God that day.

Obviously, this same strength of high participation can be a drawback for the elderly and/or the handicapped, who sometimes have little agility and/or inclination to stand and move about a great deal. Again, this worship, while exhilarating, is also exhausting. Thoughts on this issue will be shared more fully in the section on limitations.

At least in its *form*, then, Fire Baptized worship is definitely black worship, as James Cone, Nathan Jones, and others have described it. The spontaneity, the Spirit-led and holistic nature of the service, the contemporary black gospel music rendered with much improvisation and conviction, the informal call and response between pastor and hearers, the inductive rather than deductive approach to sermons, the spiritual "high" and sense of exhilaration derived from the service—these and the other features discussed in chapter 2 are all present.

While the style and form are black, in some respects, the content of the worship is another matter. This will be addressed later.

Role of the Supernatural

Another distinct feature, related to its Spirit-led nature, is the manifestation of and attention given the *supernatural*. As with all religions, Christianity is based on supernatural concepts and personages. The concepts described in the Bible on which the Christian faith hinges—the virgin birth, the immortal soul, the resurrection, the Holy Spirit, heaven and hell, God and Satan and their respective opposing realms of light and dark, to name but a few—are all supernatural concepts.

Yet, much Christian worship, particularly liberal mainline worship, seems bereft of any *discussion* of supernatural concepts (e.g., spiritual warfare of good and evil forces in the world and in the lives of individual Christians) and also of any *manifestation* of the supernatural. Rarely are the words *devil* or *hell*, for instance, heard from the pulpit in a church like Grace. These seem to be outmoded notions for many liberal mainline ministers and parishioners.

Yet, the existence of what some call radical evil in the world gives one pause to consider very seriously the ways in which evil is described biblically.

Human history and human present are full of examples of radical evil, including the practice of slavery in America, the events of the Holocaust, and widespread starvation in war-torn countries where great stockpiles of food exist but, for political reasons, are not disbursed.

Even contemporary developments, such as recent discoveries of devil worship in some rock lyrics, have caused alarm in the wider "secular" society among parents who perhaps do not even consider themselves religious at all. It seems that the wider society may give more credence and attention to supernatural concepts and manifestations than many Christians who own a biblical faith.

No Christian worship is without supernatural aspects. To be certain, the Spirit of God moves at least quietly in *all* worship where the name of Christ is lifted up in sincere adoration. Yet, it would seem that worshipers come away with a heightened sense of personal spirituality, of God's activity in the world, and of God's activity in their own individual lives, when they can experience dramatic movement and presence of the Spirit in worship, and when pointed, direct, and explicit attention is given to supernatural concepts and personages. Worship like that at Fire Baptized seems more compelling, powerful, and spiritually thought-provoking than other varieties of worship that seem indifferent or even hostile to the idea of the supernatural with a capital "S."

Pastor B. and his wife, the devotional leader, get high marks for their frequent explanations of what is happening in worship. Many Pentecostal pastors do not take the time to explain to those unfamiliar with Pentecostal worship what the various Holy Spirit manifestations are all about, why worshipers rejoice as they do, the Scriptural bases for these gifts and lively praise, the meaning of receiving Christ as personal Savior, etc. In nearly every worship service, those present are helped to understand what is happening in the worship and why.

Bible-Centeredness, Relating the Bible to Everyday Life

The Bible plays a very large role in congregations like Fire Baptized. There is a very literal approach to the text, and all the furor of the last century over things like biblical historical criticism and the debate over the Christ of faith versus the Jesus of history are unknown to pastor and congregants at Fire Baptized and many churches like it. Indeed, if these persons were exposed to such issues, they would brand them as unimportant and nonsensical, if not blasphemous and therefore anathema.

Pastor B. spends a great deal of time looking at practical issues, like marriage, money management, child-rearing and such, and what the Bible has to say about them. Grace's Pastor A. tends to act as if his parishioners do not need any help, as if they already know what God would have them do in their marriages, money management, or other practical, down-to-earth matters. Of course, that is not true at all. Perhaps Pastor A., in his study of the Bible, would not say the same things Pastor B. would say about any of these practical issues. But it seems *something* should be said.

Liberal mainliners often berate fundamentalist and Pentecostal Christians like those at Fire Baptized for their literal approach to Bible content, but, as was said earlier, Fire Baptized members are at least very well acquainted with Scripture content. Whether one is liberal or conservative when it comes to beliefs about the origin, infallibility, inspiration, and authority of Scripture, no one would argue that, aside from personal experience of the three personages of the Godhead, the Bible is the Christian's major source of information about the faith. Therefore, while Christians of various theological bents can dicker until the second coming of Christ about Bible *interpretation,* knowledge of its *contents* is crucial.

It has already been stated repeatedly that worshipers at Fire Baptized surpass worshipers at Grace UCC and other similar churches in knowing what is in the Bible, where to find it, and how to apply it to everyday life situations. This is a decided strength. Helping and encouraging worshipers to become intimately acquainted with Bible content enables them to encourage and nurture themselves during the interval between worship services.

When one combines the emphasis on Scripture study and application with emphasis on other spiritual disciplines, like prayer and fasting, the result is vital, vibrant personal spirituality for a large percentage of worshipers in a congregation. When I encounter Fire Baptized members during the week at the grocery store or in other settings, Scripture and positive words about what God is doing through spiritual disciplines are the centerpiece of their conversation.

Some may say these persons are too narrow and too fanatical to relate to persons on a normal, human basis. They seem only to talk about God and the Bible. In some cases, that may be true. But many Fire Baptized attendees are finding something compelling enough in their Sunday worship to keep a sense of personal worship going throughout the week, and that is to be applauded.

Further, the worship at such churches is probably so "charged" with spiritual energy on Sundays because many of the worshipers come "charged" as a result of spiritual disciplines. Most of us have probably heard Christians in a variety of churches say at one time or another at the conclusion of worship something to the effect of, "I didn't really get anything out of the service today." Pastor B.'s question would be, "What did you bring to the service spiritually yourself? How did you *prepare for worship* during the week?" Comments that nothing of spiritual benefit was gained from a worship service reflect an "Entertain me. I'm part of an audience" mentality about worship, rather than an attitude of active participation in worship and of spiritual preparation before worship. Fire Baptized members are to be emulated in their spiritual preparation for worship through frequent attention to spiritual disciplines at home during the week.

Evangelistic Thrust, Burden for Souls

One of the greatest strengths of this worship is its evangelistic thrust. Fire Baptized members take very seriously the Great Commission—Jesus' instructions to the disciples, given at the time of His ascension, to go and make more disciples: "Go ye into all the world, and preach the gospel to every creature." (Mark 16:15, KJV) The church cannot increase itself and continue to exist without evangelism. Yet, many Christian churches pay no real attention to issues of "soul winning," and individual members often are at a loss as to how to "win" others to the faith.

Often, ignorance of Bible content and basic concepts of the Christian faith make it impossible for many Christians to say anything concrete to unchurched persons on a one-on-one basis about what it means to be "saved" and why being a member of Christ's body is important, for example. This will become painfully evident as we consider survey results from Grace UCC members in the next chapter. In many instances, spaces allowed on the survey sheets for a sentence or two about fundamental Christian concepts, such as God, salvation, Holy Spirit and so on, were left blank or the answers given were unscriptural and generally muddy theologically.

Grace UCC members are not alone in the inability to do personal evangelism. In his book on church growth, American Baptist Ralph H. Elliott, senior pastor of North Shore Baptist Church in Chicago, says that when he suggested to his congregation recently that "'everyone win one,' there was a great deal of surprise expressed, as though this were most unusual and certainly highly unlikely. Such a sharing of the faith on a one-on-one basis may always have been inherent in the church's mission, but it is not a pattern for much of contemporary Christianity."[10]

At Fire Baptized, vibrant spirituality leads to a desire to share the faith with others, and Bible knowledge provides something specific to say. Each worship service is evangelistic, in that time and encouragement are provided for persons to make a decision about Christ.

Members pray earnestly for souls to be saved during the service, pray for the salvation of loved ones and friends during the week, and "witness" to persons about the faith informally away from church. They have a sense of their own individual responsibility to bring others to the faith, rather than leaving this role solely to the pastor, a board of deacons, or an evangelism committee. There is a real burden for souls, a real concern that the unchurched and the churched unsaved become "converted," transformed, and that they better the quality of their lives through a meaningful, personal relationship with God. This is admirable.

Christians of other churches in other denominations often are so comfortable with the "sinfulness" that stains us all, so at home with the "we're only human" approach to religious life, that no one tries to be any better or believes that it is it actually possible, with God's help, for people to live "kinder, gentler" lives (to borrow a phrase from former President George Bush). There is a kind of apathy, resignation, even defeatism with regard to the human condition of sinfulness. This is not the case at Fire Baptized. Hope always abounds that persons' behavior and lives can be dramatically changed for the better by the power of God.

Pastor B. stresses the importance of the new convert coming forward publicly in the service to declare faith in Christ the instant he or she decides to receive Christ as personal Savior. He says that the extreme psychological encouragement given by other worshipers to those who make a public show of their commitment both bolsters the converts' confidence that they have made the right decision and helps them keep the commitment they have made. This contrasts greatly with the Grace practice of having persons fill out a card to be collected by an usher and processed through the church office. The person, not necessarily considered a "convert" to the faith but a church member, joins the church publicly weeks later.

Persons availing themselves of either system may do so for all the wrong reasons or for all the right reasons, clearly. However, one practice seems more evangelistic, the other more administrative and somehow less spiritual. The altar call is more explicitly geared to personal spirituality and bringing persons into a "saving knowledge of Jesus Christ" and the universal family of Christ. The use of a pew card may do the same thing implicitly and actually, but seems more focused on bringing members into a particular local church, than into the faith of Christ.

Liberal mainline churches that are very concerned about and involved with social justice issues but which fail to pay serious attention to evangelism should consider that there will be no troops to carry out future prophetic social ministries and tasks if no one is evangelized in the present. Evangelism has become a dirty word for many liberal mainline Christians, who view the approaches of some evangelical Christians as too heavy-handed and somehow repulsive. There is no need for liberal mainliners to imitate such approaches, but there is a need to develop some of their own, for use both in worship and away from worship.

Personal Attention, Affection of Members, Investment in Lives

The final strength to be highlighted is the amount of personal attention available to persons in worship at Fire Baptized. The service is lengthy in part because of the time spent on individuals. Individuals are prayed with to receive Christ or consolation; individuals greet one another warmly during the time of "holy hugs"; individuals who fall under the power of the Spirit are cared for by ushers, deacons, and deaconesses, etc. This is hands-on worship.

In a large urban city like Chicago—where persons can become terribly isolated and alienated from others, where the pace moves quickly and the climate (both in terms of the elements and emotional attachments) can be quite cold—worship that is so personal is a tremendous blessing and boost for many. Spiritual and human warmth and the unconditional acceptance of persons, which can be enjoyed at churches like Fire Baptized, are very attractive to many. This is particularly true of African Americans, who often are badly beaten up emotionally throughout the week as they struggle against subtle and not-so-subtle forms of discrimination and rejection in the work place and elsewhere.

It would be safe to conjecture that if persons were not attracted to any other aspects of Fire Baptized worship, they might be tempted to come back again and again just to experience the love that seems to flow so freely there. The profound sense that members have of being loved by God seems to spill over as warm affection for and acceptance of others.

Anyone would feel welcome and at home here, emotionally and spiritually as well as practically. The reference to practicality has to do with wardrobe. It is probably not news to any black churchgoer that many African Americans on limited budgets who would like to attend church often refrain because they say they do not have the "right" clothing. The fact that most African Americans who attend church go "dressed to the nines" every Sunday is well known and readily apparent to everyone in the black community. Hence the frequent protestations from many unchurched persons that church is "nothing but a fashion show."

In contrast to a great number of black and other churches of various denominations, then, where the unwritten dress code is ties and coats for men, and elegant dresses, suits, and hats for women, the implicit rule at Fire Baptized and churches like it is, come as you are. The hymn "Just as I Am, without One Plea" is taken very seriously, both in terms of spiritual neediness and physical appearance. Attendees at Fire Baptized sport everything from the most casual to the most elegant of attire. The implicit, and sometimes explicit, message from pastor and members is that God is not concerned about how a person looks on the outside. Rather, it is important that the soul be "dressed up" and beautified by salvation.

No one can escape the sense of investment these church members seem to have in each other's lives. Their willingness to share and hear each other's pains and to pray for one another, both in worship and away from worship, is one indication of this investment. The church has a "Someone Cares Ministry," which makes phone calls to members. Each week, different persons are designated as callers. Callers and those called share prayer requests and pray together by phone.

Most in the church seem to know many other church members, what they do for a living, how many children they have, the names of these children, and other tidbits of information that reveal a true sense of *community* at the church. Size is probably a factor. Pastor B. admits that the church's greatest challenge will be to keep this quality of communal spirit when the church has grown from 125 to 1,000 members.

Worship Limitations

Lack of Planning

As is the case with worship at Grace UCC, the worship strengths of Fire Baptized worship are often also its limitations. In looking at the first of these limitations to be identified, the reader is forced to wrestle with that ever-present issue for liturgists and planners of worship—the delicate balance between *discipline* and *freedom* in worship.

Pastor and parishioners of Fire Baptized often note with pride that they are not slavishly tied to a printed order of worship and that spontaneity at the leading of the Spirit is of the highest priority. Yet, a tiny bit of additional planning, particularly around themes, would only enhance the meaning of services there and not put the Holy Spirit in a straitjacket as is feared and supposed.

First, glaringly absent from the church's informal order of service for any churched person are the Prayer of Jesus (commonly referred to as "The Lord's Prayer") and congregational singing. These are meaningful inclusions in most brands of Christian worship. While many Pentecostal churches do not sing classic hymns, contemporary Scripture songs are used. Often the words of these spiritual songs are projected by transparency in front of the congregation, where they are visible to all. Sometimes they are printed on a bulletin insert.

There would appear to be already plenty of congregational participation in the worship at Fire Baptized, but congregants need the opportunity to lift their voices in song as a body in praise to God. The only time Fire Baptized members sing is when they spontaneously join in on choral numbers and when the offering is lifted. If *leitourgia* is at least in part humans' service to God, it is entirely appropriate that Jesus' Prayer and hymns or contemporary Scripture songs be sung. The Assemblies of God does have a hymnal, *Hymns of Glorious Praise*,[11] which is used in some AOG churches. As Fire Baptized grows in finances and membership, this resource and others might be purchased.

Also, if the church is trying to attract, among others, the churched unsaved (that is, those from other churches and denominations who have not received Christ as personal Savior), it might help these persons feel a bit more at home if these familiar items were included in worship. In terms of the book's aim to promote ecumenical unity, nearly every Christian knows the prayer Jesus taught. It is universally, ecumenically recited and cherished by Christian believers of all theological bents and national origins.

With regard to hymns, as was stated earlier, there seems to be a body of church music or hymns common to the black religious experience, regardless of denomination. Inclusion of some of these cherished hymns can only heighten the meaningfulness of worship for participants. Much of Pentecostal worship is strange, even frightening, to those unaccustomed to it. The evangelistic *message* of such worship might be enhanced and more readily received if the *medium* or *media* for conveying it were a bit more familiar.

Over the years, I have been astounded, too, by the numbers of youth growing up in Pentecostal churches who are what I call "hymn illiterates." There is an entire generation of youngsters growing up in many of these churches who do not know the words of beloved Christmas carols and other hymns commonly sung by nearly every other Christian in the world. Their parents, who may have come originally from other denominations, know them—often several verses of some of these songs. But the children and grandchildren are at a loss.

This appears to represent an impoverishment of faith and further limits common ground that might be shared between these and others of authentic Christian faith. Some Pentecostals (indeed some liberal mainline Christians as well) say that the theology presented in certain classic and familiar hymns is at odds with their own theology. For instance, some legalistically refuse to sing songs like, "Pass Me Not, O Gentle Savior." Critics of this song argue that since Jesus promised never to leave us or forsake us, these lyrics reveal a lack of faith.

While I would beg to differ with these perspectives on hymns, the point is that the worshiping body should sing hymns of some kind—hymns these Christians can live with theologically—to heighten meaning and impact of worship services. Careful planning would involve the selection of hymns that relate to the particular season of the church year (Easter, Pentecost, etc.) or a particular sermonic theme to enhance the cohesiveness and richness of the worship experience.

Again, this can be done without hindering spontaneity and the movement of the Spirit during worship. Further, it is theologically inappropriate to assume that the Holy Spirit is at work only during the worship service itself. As was stated in chapter 3, the Spirit can be just as active in the pastor's study during the week when worship is shaped through sermon preparation and hymn selection.

When I asked Pastor B. why the worship service failed to include Jesus' prayer and hymns, Pastor B. reminded the researcher that the worship is not yet matured. The congregation is only two years old and is still developing in many ways. Hymnals likely will be purchased in the future, he says.

Length and Impact of Service: Long and Exhausting

When and if Pastor B. begins to pay serious attention to the issue of planning, he must consider the length of the service and seek ways to shorten the worship without losing its spiritual impact. There are several places in the regular Sunday worship where time can (and must) be saved without ruining overall effectiveness.

The choir processional time of thirty-plus minutes, for instance, must be shortened. This is too long for parishioners to stand, particularly any elderly persons who attend worship. This is largely a young congregation, but older and sometimes handicapped persons—both members and visitors—do worship at Fire Baptized. Members have the freedom to sit and stand as they wish during lengthy periods of praise, but I usually feel guilty sitting down for a moment while many others continue to stand. I am sure I am not the only one who has felt such guilt.

Perhaps the altar call, which includes laying on of hands by the pastor for almost every kind of spiritual need, might be only for the unsaved who wish to receive Christ. Those wishing special prayer to receive the Baptism of the Holy Spirit, for healing or for other needs might be asked to stand briefly as a group and/or be invited back to the church for a regular Friday night deliverance service, for example. Now that Fire Baptized has its own worship facility, everything need not be done in the context of a single Sunday service.

The sermons can be tightened considerably. Often, it seems that Pastor B. could make the same point in half the time if he planned his notes more carefully or (God forbid) prepared a manuscript.

Pastor B. might be able to come up with other strategies to trim the service's length but he must do so. Again, while exhilarating, the service is also exhausting.

Spiritual benefits aside, this type of holistic service, which demands members' intense participation, is extremely taxing physically. Members are on their feet more than off, standing for protracted periods to sing, clap, dance, hug, pray, lift hands of adoration, etc. The notion of *leitourgia* (worship as the work of the people) is stretched to the limit here. Further, the idea of the Sabbath as a day of rest is made a mockery. Speaking from my own experience, members often begin the work week with an energy deficit.

I worry for the pastor as much as for parishioners. Pastor B. talks of having two services each Sunday when the membership moves to its own facility. If each of the two services is as emotionally and physically intense as the current Sunday afternoon service, the pastor will soon suffer burnout.

I suspect the new 9:00 A.M. service will be quieter and more meditative in tone. It will be almost impossible to have two Sunday services like the current one on a single day unless someone other than Pastor B. leads one of the two services and a different choir sings for each.

Lack of Attention to Church Year Seasons, Special Black Observances

It was striking to this observer that no attention whatever is paid to the major seasons of the church year in Fire Baptized worship. Many black churches that are not liberal mainline churches do not observe the church year calendar or use the lectionary that guides many Christian pastors' sermon theme preparation. They, for instance, do not observe the season of Advent; or, more accurately, while focusing on the birth of Christ on the

Sundays leading up to Christmas, they do not refer to these Sundays as constituting the Advent season. Most, however, do pay attention to the season of Lent, which precedes Easter.

I waited in vain during the Lenten season for Pastor B. to say something about the meaning of Ash Wednesday and Lent, about why and how many Christians choose to observe this season, and why many Pentecostals ignore it. I also waited in vain during the months of January and February, which feature the nationwide celebration of the birthday of Dr. Martin Luther King Jr. and recognition of African American Heritage month, for some serious discussion of how God has moved in the history of black Americans. What has the black pilgrimage from slavery to contemporary times of affirmative action retrenchment meant religiously? How has God been active in the collective past of African Americans as a people? What biblical themes or motifs seem appropriate sources of reflection and encouragement for those who continue in the living nightmare of second-class citizenship and discrimination in every sector of society?

While Christians need help in relating the Bible to practical issues of family, money, and living out the Christian witness on a day-to-day basis—which Pastor B. often provides—many Christians also need help in understanding how the gospel relates to some of the larger social questions. I often found myself mentally asking questions that no one else at Fire Baptized was asking, let alone attempting to answer. While one may not necessarily agree with the religious perspectives of Grace's Pastor A. on various social questions, at least he does wrestle with these issues and consistently provides some theologically faithful ways of considering them.

Black in Style but Not in Content: Lack of Theological Grounding for Addressing Societal Issues

This leads to discussion of perhaps the most crucial limitation of Fire Baptized worship: while it is definitely black in style and flavor (as Cone et al. have described the tone and feel of black worship at its best), it is questionable whether this is black worship with respect to its *content*. For it fails to help congregants *validate collective black experience* à la Gilkes. Specifically, it does not provide them the necessary theological tools for redefining and reinterpreting societal events and issues that adversely (or positively) affect African Americans, in the light of the Christian gospel.

(See page 98.) I would levy this critique against most black Pentecostal worship I have experienced.

Many Pentecostal and evangelical denominations and fellowships to which black people flock for comfort and spiritual development these days do not seem to take seriously the particular struggles and needs of African Americans as oppressed persons in America. This is mirrored in most of the preaching and other content of worship at Fire Baptized and other churches like it.

In some respects, it is a plus for ecumenical unity that almost any Christian of any persuasion could come to Fire Baptized and be blessed by the biblical teaching and preaching to be heard there. In another way, however, it is a keen loss to these African American Christians that they are not given some ways of thinking about what God has done for them specifically and particularly as a people. This would not constitute a denigration of others, only an affirmation of what God has wrought in them, to borrow from Clarence Rivers.

Building on this fact, that African Americans are not given ways of appreciating what God has done for them as a people, Fire Baptized worship is limited in that it fails to provide *religious meaning for action in spheres outside the church.* Thinking of Christian experience as having a vertical dimension (relating to love of God and inner personal piety) and also a horizontal dimension (relating to love of neighbor—the neighbor being the starving Ethiopian across the globe as much as the person who lives comfortably next door), it seems that inadequate attention is given to the horizontal dimension of Christian existence in its broadest, fullest sense in preaching, prayers, and other elements of worship in Fire Baptized and similar churches.

So much attention is given to issues of personal piety and nurturing the individual that attention to larger, global issues or even social issues in the economically depressed and crime-ridden neighborhood where Fire Baptized is located are ignored.

Arthur E. Paris comes to the same conclusion about a Boston black Pentecostal church in his work, *Black Pentecostalism.* Paris's work provides an in-depth look at worship and communal life in three black Pentecostal congregations in Boston, all affiliated with the Mount Calvary Holy Church of America, Inc. He describes in detail the ritual life of these congregations, giving the reader insight into the regular Sunday worship, midweek worship, prayer meetings, and other ritual demanding members' time about three or four nights a week. Yet, for all the time Pentecostal believers spend in church, many seem unable to grapple at church with various sociopolitical problems that affect the neighborhoods in which their congregations are located or that impact their churches directly.

In his chapter "The Church in the Social World," Paris offers an excellent illustration. He tells of a series of events that arose during his field work with the three churches. The Boston Redevelopment Authority (BRA) wanted to appropriate the church property of one of the congregations (designated by Paris as Alpha Church) and raze the church structure in order to make way for neighborhood renewal. BRA notified the pastor, who after some discussions with the authority, held a business meeting for church members to explain BRA's intentions.

> Generally, the pastor took a quietist attitude in presenting the case to his parishioners. He showed a willingness to accept the BRA position on the matter and suggested that the membership begin canvassing possible sites to move to and/or build on. He asked for members' opinions, stating, "I feel that if it's the Lord's will, then they'll get it; if not, then their plans will be interrupted. They will give us someone to help us find a place. We can take the settlement they give us and make a down payment on a building and then renovate it. They will pay us to move, and we can do that ourselves and add the money to it. If we get a mover, you know he'd charge us what they give us." He also noted that whether the membership agreed or not, the BRA would take the property by the right of eminent domain.[12]

Paris comments that the pastor's remarks conform to his church's theological heritage, to the idea of "putting oneself totally into the hands of God and acting on one's own behalf to conform oneself to the probable outcome, which is seen as the will of the Almighty." Further, the pastor's remarks show a realistic assessment of the situation and an acceptance of the threatened loss of the church. Yet, the members' responses were not quietist and, as Paris notes, with a single exception, they had no religious referent.

The pastor's wife opened the discussion on a historical note, reminding the congregation that her family had had dealings with the BRA before and that they had literally been "taken." "It set us back twenty years." She counseled against being willing victims again. The rest of the membership took still stronger positions. It was suggested that another church (not in Mount Calvary) had fought the BRA successfully and that Alpha do the same, that otherwise they were not putting [God] to the test; another member objected that the church was to be replaced with a playground and that the church was of more value and should not be given up; others rejected the proposal on grounds that to move the church would inconvenience them, that the church was not a blight on the community, and that it was more than ever necessary to the health of the community with all the new housing being built. The basic thrust of sentiment was a rejection of the BRA take over attempt and a willingness to fight. The pastor accepted the sentiments and agreed to inform the BRA of the membership's rejection of its offer.[13]

Paris comments on "the almost complete absence of a religious rationale for the congregation's opposition in this case." The pastor's initial sentiment, suggested by tradition, was an acceptance of the chain of events and a consignment of the future "to the Lord in prayer," Paris notes. But in the face of direct personal threat, the members did not accept this quietist solution but rather decided to fight.

They did not invoke the religious framework within which they understood their lives, because, Paris says, "their religious understanding was largely irrelevant to their effort to deal with a concrete social and political problem."[14]

The political "blind spot" of the religious world view held by these Christians is clear in this instance. This is where quietism becomes manifest. It is not that these Christians are politically reactionary but rather that their religious world view gives them no handles with which to deal with secular events, other than prayerfully accepting them as the working out of God's plan. This is not simply an acceptance of events, however; it *ignores responsibility for them.* These people have no framework as Christians within which to understand their own political action. Thus, although they may act politically, they do so not as Christians or as a Christian community but simply as concerned individuals. Their action has no significance within the religious framework within which they understand their lives and the world. It is this dichotomy between accepting (or ignoring) events as the inevitable working out of God's plan and being unable to see that plan as meaning and justification for their own secular action that is to blame for the political quietism of these Boston congregations and of the churches of the Pentecostal-Holiness tradition generally.[15]

Grace's Pastor A. and Pastor B. of Fire Baptized present a true study in contrasts when it comes to views and experience related to social activism. Pastor A. marched with Dr. Martin Luther King Jr. in the sixties. He views the civil rights movement as having been very effective in helping African Americans make remarkable progress in every aspect of life and work.

Meanwhile, Pastor B. was a member of the Black Panther Party and a disciple of Malcolm X during the sixties. He says his experience was negative, frustrating, and ineffective, and he never changed one single person's life for the better through such involvement. "I've gone the civil disobedience route, including advocation of a violent overthrow of the government, all of which got us nowhere as a people," he says.

For Pastor B., the only way to make an impact on social issues is to let Jesus make an impact on the persons who deal with those issues. "This may be very simplistic, but if we can get those people saved, we can impact issues. I personally feel we can accomplish more if we emphasize the vertical [dimension of spirituality] and let God deal with the horizontal," comments this pastor.

Pastor B.'s remarks validate Paris's comments about Pentecostals ignoring responsibility for certain social problems. No member of Pastor B.'s church would sit by and let Satan attack their finances (through loss of a job, for instance) without a spiritual and practical fight. Yet, the spiritual vision is not broad enough to see that often the loss of a job is tied to a much larger issue—discrimination in the workplace, which also requires a spiritual and practical fight. To not fight, either on the level of individual problems or of social problems, means we have ignored the problems and implicitly condoned the evil by not taking action against it.

Civil rights officials often suggest that the legacy of the Reagan years has been to make discrimination, both on the basis of race and class, acceptable once again. Through affirmative action retrenchment and deep cuts in the social programs that most help minorities and the poor, during the eighties the Reagan-Bush administration sent the message that it is okay to dismiss the needs of minorities and low-income persons while catering to large corporations and the military.

Given this state of affairs, Pastor B.'s approach to activism is too limited in scope. It involves individuals being saved *one at a time*; learning the tools of spiritual warfare *one at a time*; and having their prayers for food, shelter, and a decent income answered *one at a time*. I think the God who created the whole universe from nothing except the spoken word can do better than that. It is not good enough or fast enough for one person at a time to pray and find another job, or one person to pray and escape homelessness by one more paycheck, or one person to pray and find some food to eat this week when no one is sure about next week. God has given humankind the tools and know-how to develop programs and legislation that can help millions of people at once.

Some evangelical and Pentecostal Christians already believe this, lobbying feverishly in Congress for pro-life legislation and legislation to end pornography. God is just as concerned about discrimination and poverty as abortion and sexually explicit film and literature. (Some discussion of the Religious Right's involvement in politics is offered in chapter 6.)

Pastor B. commented during the research interview that his small congregation could not make an impact on any particular social issue by itself. I suggested that if Fire Baptized were to join forces with other churches in the Assemblies of God denomination as a whole, the collective probably would have a significant influence. He said that the vision for this kind of activism is not there. But he hopes to hold some important posts in the denominational structure in years to come and will attempt to raise spiritual consciousness in this regard.

Pastor B. might begin by raising consciousness in his congregation. His members may be saved, but unless the Sunday worship provides them a theological rationale for social action, they will not understand the need for such action or its spiritual validity.

Sexism at Fire Baptized

Another weakness of Fire Baptized worship is that it is too male-dominated. Women are frequently seen and heard, but not in leadership roles. The pastor's wife usually serves as devotional leader for the service. Though she can also preach, she rarely does.

Women worship assistants handle minor tasks at the altar, like draping cloths over women who fall under the power of the Spirit. But they do not serve communion or take up the offering. Of course women sing in the choir, teach children's Sunday school, and exercise the spiritual gifts (like speaking in tongues and interpreting tongues). But the roles of spiritual authority and leadership are left to the men.

Literal interpretation of Scripture relating to the role of women in the church, usually from the King James version of the Bible, is often the cause in churches like Fire Baptized. But feminist scholars are aware that the King James translation of certain key Bible passages relating to women is not particularly honest or accurate. The translation of 1 Timothy 3:11, for example, obscures the fact that there were women deacons in New Testament times. While many Pentecostal ministers teach women to keep silent in the churches (1 Cor. 14:34) and not usurp authority over men in church (1 Tim. 2:12), few preach about Phoebe the pastor, or the apostle Julia (Junias), both mentioned in Romans 16. Pastor B. could benefit from in-depth study of the Scriptures in the original Greek and study of the women's question in general.

To be fair, Pastor B. is not dogmatic about the conservative texts mentioned. Males are prominent in the leadership roles at Fire Baptized mostly for sociological reasons, he comments. Noting that black churches are heavily populated by women, Pastor B. says he wants the young boys who grow up in the church to realize that men serve God, too, and "not just Mama." While not wanting to stifle the women, he does encourage the men to be as visible as possible, he says.

What of the young girls growing up in the church? Shouldn't they see that women preach and lead at church, too, and not just men? Over the years, how many women in a variety of churches have squelched their own God-given ministry gifts because there were no mentors or role models to encourage them?

While the AOG does ordain women, Pastor B. is hard-pressed to name any ordained women in the Chicago area. One person comes to mind—a Sister Lydia, who has planted several AOG churches; but her last name escapes him. It seems as if it would be very difficult for a female ministerial candidate to get the necessary mentoring and support at a church like Fire Baptized. Love and affection would likely abound if she were clearly "saved and Spirit-filled," but true understanding of her struggles, aspirations, and needs might be hard to come by.

Pastor B. might do well to wrestle with the role of women in his congregation. Indeed, as I conclude my work on my thesis, it is clear that having thrown light on this matter has altered it a bit. More will be said in chapter 6 about changes in each of the two congregations.

Pastoral-Care Issues

While affirming Cheryl Gilkes's suggestion that black worship is highly therapeutic, Fire Baptized worship can make improvements in this regard. While much care is given to individuals in various ways throughout the service, both the pastor and the pastor's wife seem impatient with persons in crisis who do not, in rubber band–like fashion, "snap back" emotionally immediately after prayer or exhortation.

One Sunday during the devotional period, the pastor's wife chided unnamed members of the congregation for appearing spiritually "high" on Sunday, then coming to the pastor's office for further counseling on Monday. "I don't want to hear about your problems," she told them—saying in so many words, if not outright—that if these persons had faith in the prayers that had been lifted up for their situation, they would not need further counseling.

It is clear that there is no appreciation of the grief process at Fire Baptized. Thanks to the work of Elisabeth Kübler-Ross[16] and others, students of pastoral counseling are aware that any type of loss—loss of a job, the end of a marriage, or the death of a loved one, for example—

involves serious grief, which has several stages that must be worked through for complete emotional healing.

Even minimal training in pastoral counseling, perhaps one term of Clinical Pastoral Education, would help Pastor B. and his wife to understand that just because a Christian needs day-to-day encouragement for a time after a significant loss, does not mean that s/he lacks faith. Further, labeling or naming one's fears and troubles by speaking of them robs them of their power. The process may be likened to Jesus naming the demons and calling them out. In the Mark 5 account of the Gadarean man in the tombs, Jesus asked the name of the demon spirits before allowing them to enter the swine. "What is thy name?" Jesus asked. The response was, "My name is Legion for we are many."

The intolerance one experiences at Fire Baptized of prolonged sadness or complaining of any kind is characteristic of what one finds at many so-called Word-faith churches. It is a reaction (perhaps an overreaction) to a perceived lifestyle of complaining, manifest by liberal mainline and other denominational Christians. They are perceived as often being "down in the dumps," or continually having a "pity party." When asked how they are doing, many describe some type of suffering or need while failing to acknowledge blessings present in their lives at that same moment in time.

Members at Fire Baptized and similar churches have been indoctrinated to do just the opposite—to lift up the positive things God is doing and to gloss over what Satan is doing, if they mention it at all. Typically, then, a Fire Baptized member who is asked, "How are you today?" (either at church or away from the church) will respond, "The Lord is blessing," then describe whatever good is happening in his or her life. If experiencing a spiritual trial, the person will express in a few sentences what is happening or has happened, then rush on to affirm that God is in charge and will make or has already made good out of the situation: "Someone broke into my house last week and took about $3,000 worth of belongings. But thank God no one was at home at the time. If we had surprised the robber, maybe someone would have gotten hurt, even killed. We can replace things, but not people. I thank God for divine protection, which did not allow any of us to be home at the time."

It would be more beneficial in terms of emotional healing if members had permission to wrestle with some of the things that have happened to them and to ask some hard questions of God, even as Job did. It is ironic to have someone thank God for divine protection after their house has been robbed. Where were God and God's divine protection while the house was being robbed?

Some would perceive in this question irreverence or a lack of faith in God. Quite the contrary, wrestling shows extreme faith in God. Such questioning comes from a Christian who is aware that God is strong enough and understanding enough to take our tough questions. These struggles come from a believer who is not afraid to be emotionally naked and totally honest with God.

From my own perspective, to pretend that all is well when one's heart is breaking represents a serious form of spiritual dishonesty. If I may share from my personal experience in this regard, my father was murdered during a robbery attempt away from home in December 1984. For nearly two years afterward, I was still living with a great deal of emotional pain and perplexity because I had never worked through and resolved my acute grief.

For the first few months, Pentecostal friends offered typical words of consolation, "The Holy Spirit, who is Comforter, will help you during this time." Emotionally, these usually soothing words felt like clichés. Soon, nothing more was said about this huge tragedy. People did not know what to say; some seemed to assume that if I had true faith, I would not continue to be depressed about this event. So I went on smiling with these friends— indeed, with the whole world—as if all were well.

I had just joined the liberal mainline (United Church of Christ) congregation to which I currently belong when my father died. Most of these church members did not know about the murder, and, of course, with my warped or limited sense of what it means to live a life of thanksgiving before God, I never mentioned it to anyone. So, the liberal mainline members, just getting to know me, had no opportunity to offer care because they were not aware that I needed it. The pastor did know about the death, but neither offered counseling nor made a referral for counseling. It seems many liberal mainline pastors do not do a good job of helping parishioners work through grief, either. They are present during funeral week; some even check on members on the one-year anniversary of a death; but often, that is the extent of it.

A year-long residency in Clinical Pastoral Education during 1986–87 finally brought needed healing in my case. I believe firmly that Christians should have a predominant lifestyle of thanksgiving. However, I also believe that if one's spiritual life is to have any integrity, there must be room to be emotionally honest with God without feeling that God will zap us from on high if we show the least bit of sadness, dissatisfaction, or perplexity over life's troubling circumstances.

This is not to deny the real power and work of the Holy Spirit as Comforter. I believe I was able to cope with my father's death better because of this work than I would have if I had not had this spiritual resource. Still, Fire Baptized worship leaders need some real training in pastoral counseling if the worship is to be as effective as it can be for church members healing emotionally after trauma and losses. Fire Baptized is not unique in this regard: Worship leaders in many types of denominations could benefit from the same training. During survey work, one member complained that the worship at Fire Baptized is too geared to families, and that as a single person she feels left out. Training would sensitize worship leaders to this and other pastoral-care issues.

Music and "The High"

I described earlier the strengths of the worship music. Its weaknesses are chiefly three.

First, while loud praise is prescribed in Scripture, the music is often too loud to be comfortably enjoyed. The volume should be lowered a bit.

Second, the music should be varied. Only contemporary gospel music is sung. The minister of music says that the choir is not capable of singing anything else at this point in its development and training. As the choir grows in its ability, it should attempt other types of music—hymns, Negro spirituals, anthems by black composers, even some sacred classical pieces on occasion. These will only enhance the quality of music and, as Wendell Mapson points out, ensure that black forms of religious music from our history do not die.

Third, the children's choir should sing music appropriate for its age. The adult members of the congregation get a kick out of seeing the little ones perform contemporary gospel just as the adults do. But their voices are not mature enough to do the runs and other vocal improvisational maneuvers of adults, though they often try. Also, when they sing lyrics like "The Lord will a make way out of no way," the testimony does not ring true, because they really do not understand what the words mean. While teenagers should not sing songs that are too juvenile, "Jesus Loves the Little Children" and similar selections are more appropriate for small children.

In the context of earlier discussion about the worship ritual, I mentioned how the music and level of praise often rise to a fever pitch. Some members thrive on the kind of "high" the service gives, and Pastor B. acknowledges that things can easily get out of balance if worship leaders are not careful and church members are not mature. If the service is less effervescent than usual, some may go away feeling they have not adequately worshiped that Sunday because they did not get the high. This frame of mind leads some liberal mainliners to accuse recovering drug addicts and alcoholics in Pentecostal churches of having replaced one high with another.

Somehow, worshipers must be taught that a service in which the Spirit of God nourishes people quietly can be just as beneficial as one where much loud, demonstrative praise is experienced, and that such meditative services are needed from time to time. There is no need to have a spiritual hootenanny every Sunday.

In the next chapter, we will hear the voices of church members of both Grace and Fire Baptized as they express satisfactions and dissatisfactions with their worship through their completed surveys. Attention will also be given to what they learn about basic theological concepts from their worship.

Study Questions

1. Is there order and/or an order of worship in Pentecostal worship? Explain.
2. What are Pentecostal "charismata," and what are the scriptural bases for these spiritual gifts? What is their purpose? What cautions did the apostle Paul give regarding their use in public worship? What manifestations of the supernatural have you witnessed in worship at your church?

3. What are the advantages of flexibility and spontaneity of the Spirit in worship? Can these be problematic in worship, and how? How does liturgical discipline relate to this matter?

4. What are the purposes of an altar call? Does your church's worship include one? Does it need one?

5. What is "shouting" in black worship? What are its meaning and therapeutic value?

~ 5 ~

PRAISING AS EXPERIENCED THROUGH THE EYES, EARS, AND HEARTS OF WORSHIPERS

And with all you have gotten, get understanding—discernment, compre-hension and interpretation.
—Proverbs 4:7c (Amplified Bible)

In previous chapters, we examined views on worship of "experts"—practicing liturgiologists, various scholars, pastors of the two study church-es, and my own views. It is both fitting and important to give full consider-ation now to the opinions of the worshipers themselves.

What do *they* feel worship should be and do? Do members of the two contrasting churches reveal any unity or consensus of opinion, or only diversity, concerning their worship needs and preferences?

I distributed a three-part survey instrument in both churches to supple-ment my own observation and scores of informal conversations with worshipers. Respondents were informed that the survey responses would be treated confidentially, and signing their names to the survey was optional.

The initial section asks respondents to provide demographic information in order to enhance understanding of how socioeconomic factors affect worship. Worshipers were asked their age, gender, race, marital status, fam-ily size, years at the church, occupation, and yearly gross income (optional).

In the second section, worshipers were asked to share their theological understandings of the following basic Christian concepts: God, Christ, the Holy Spirit, sin, salvation, the body of Christ, the world, and the Bible. Next respondents were asked to identify the sources of their religious understandings (e.g., sermons, Bible study, Christian radio/TV ministries, books, etc.). Worshipers were also asked to describe briefly their spiritual pilgrimage.

In the final section of the survey, participants were asked to evaluate and describe the strengths and weaknesses of their worship services, to compare their church to other churches they had visited, and to make any comments they would like regarding their worship.

Analyzing these survey responses will help us to address three issues: (1) What makes for a fulfilling worship experience from the perspectives of these laypersons, and how do their expectations jibe or not with those of the experts heard from in earlier chapters? (2) What are worshipers learning theologically in worship; what kind of *understanding* are they getting regarding basic Christian concepts? (3) How do theology and other factors, such as socioeconomic status and pastoral leadership style, impact worship?

I am not a trained statistician, so my data analysis is more qualitative than quantitative. Still, the survey results are both revealing and instructive. After some general remarks about survey response, we will examine survey material from each of the two churches in turn.

Pastoral Leadership Styles, Socioeconomic Factors, and Survey Response

Thirty-eight persons completed surveys at Grace. This represents roughly 10 percent of the 350 persons who might attend worship on any given Sunday. The relatively low response rate points to at least three things: a pastoral leadership style which is largely nonauthoritarian, a membership accustomed to making up its own mind about matters large and small, and also disgruntlement about the handling of a previous survey conducted in the congregation roughly two years before.

In keeping with his gracious, priestly style, Pastor A. allowed the survey to be enclosed in a regular Sunday bulletin. A notice was printed in the bulletin about the survey, and the pastor briefly mentioned it during the announcement period on the Sunday the instrument was distributed in the congregation. While he did not downplay the matter, Pastor A. gave his members freedom of choice. The survey would be considered optional, then, by most if not all members. Given such freedom, relatively few persons opted to respond.

On the other hand, Fire Baptized's Pastor B., who is typically prophetic and authoritarian in pastoral leadership style, gave the survey a big push personally from the pulpit, and asked me to join him in doing so. Parishioners were told point blank that they needed to fill out a survey. Furthermore, they were reminded that because the duplicating of the survey had cost me money, a member should not take a survey unless he or she meant business! By sheer charisma and force of personality, he convinced nearly half the active members to respond.

In *The Sociology of Religion,* Max Weber talks of *priestly* and *prophetic* pastoral leadership styles. In chapter 4 he states that "the personal call is the decisive element distinguishing the prophet from the priest. The latter lays claim to authority by virtue of his [or her] service in a sacred tradition, while the prophet's claim is based on personal revelation and charisma."[1]

Parishioners in both churches studied received the same survey and the same written instructions. Yet, only about 10 percent of the regular attendees (5 percent of the seven hundred active members) at Grace responded, while thirty-two persons, or 20 percent of the regulars (43 percent—approaching half—of the core membership of seventy-five), responded at Fire Baptized. Weber's distinctions between priest and prophet seem significant here.

While Pastor A. does have a strong sense of personal call à la Weber's "prophet," and is socially prophetic, those who know him best would probably classify Pastor A. as basically gracious, nonauthoritarian, and "priestly" in pastoral style.

For Pastor B.'s parishioners, who are generally accepting of his authoritarian, prophetic leadership style, his promoting the survey made participation almost mandatory. There was little freedom of choice. Personable as he is, Pastor A. does not seem to enjoy the same persuasive force over his flock.

Socioeconomic factors certainly make a difference here. While members of Fire Baptized are neither illiterate, nor unemployed for the most part, generally they are not the highly educated managers and executives one finds at Grace—persons who are largely accustomed to giving orders, not taking them. For Grace's members, the freedom and thoughtfulness exercised in the secular work world in the making of decisions and choices is carried over into church life to a great extent.

In addition, during the research period, Grace Church was fractionalized, with some diehard supporters facing off against virulent opponents of

Pastor A. One of the primary divisive issues was the style of worship.

A year or two before I distributed my survey to the congregation, another survey had been issued—perhaps by the board of trustees—to determine how well members believed the pastor was doing. The pastor fared much better than some had hoped. Thus, the survey was held hostage by opponents of the pastor who were members of the issuing group, and the results were never released to the congregation. With a bad taste in their mouths from this prior survey experience, many chose not to participate in this latest one.

Grace Church

While relatively small, the Grace sampling is rich and meaningful. All respondents were African American (black). Most respondents were female (thirty-one of thirty-eight). The average age of respondents was sixty-one. With the exception of two visitors who filled out the survey, most respondents said they had attended and/or been a member of the church anywhere from five to thirty-five years.

The church transitioned from a mostly white to a black congregation in 1953. Seven persons classified themselves as charter members, having been around since the beginning or even a few years prior to the transition. The average number of years at the church for respondents is high—twenty-seven.

In terms of occupations, respondents included a senior advertising manager, a retired investment officer, a professor of nursing, many primary and secondary educators, a Chicago Housing Authority field supervisor, a sales representative, a retired businesswoman, a retired nurse, a carpenter, an engineer technician for the Bureau of Electricity of Chicago's Department of Streets and Sanitation, a surgical technologist, a secretary, a few retired homemakers and widows, and one college student. A number of persons simply described themselves as retired but did not specify from what field of work.

Twenty-four of the thirty-eight respondents rated the service as good to excellent, while the remaining fourteen rated it fair or poor or gave no rating. Regardless of the rating given, at least three points were hammered home as worshiper responses were considered as a group.

꒳꒳

First, members said the pastor should pay more attention to issues of personal spirituality and less attention to matters of global, social, political, and economic importance. Second, with respect to music, while the choir is superior in its performance, congregants said they wished to sing familiar hymns from the black religious experience and not the "strange" hymns contained in the UCC hymnal.

Finally, members gave rather "fuzzy" or nebulous answers in response to the theological questions, especially when asked to talk about the meaning of the Holy Spirit and the body of Christ. It seems that members were getting little concrete information about basic Christian concepts from their worship services and were thus ill-equipped to explain what it means to be Christian doctrinally.

Let us go on now to consider the survey responses. I remind the reader of the earlier author's note on the issue of inclusive language. The caveat will need to be taken to heart for this chapter in particular as we, in humility and a spirit of openness, hear worshipers speak about their worship in the ways most comfortable for them.

Sermon Content: A Plea for Attention to Issues of Personal Spirituality

In chapter 3, much attention was devoted to the pastor's sociopolitical thrust in preaching. In the words of one member, "I like to hear about civil rights, but not every Sunday." We will now hear the voices of other members who concur and plead for more attention to practical issues of spirituality.

In response to the question about worship strengths and weaknesses, a sixty-seven-year-old male who had been a member of the church for twenty-nine years said, "One strength that still remains is our choir and its music. A weakness is the sermons, which in the recent past have been loud and more like lectures and mostly on subjects such as racism, politics, the economy, etc."

An eighty-year-old man who was a charter member of the church said that "weakness is in poor and tasteless sermons not based on religious teachings. Too much emphasis on race and sex. . . . Sermons leave me empty and unsatisfied spiritually. I need more interlacing of religious thought and practices with everyday living and practices. The music is the outstanding feature of the worship period."

"The strength of the service is the music. If I could change something it would be the sermons. Often at the end of the sermon, I do not know what the message was," said one forty-nine-year-old woman, a member of Grace for nineteen years.

A sixty-year-old woman who had been a member of the church for thirty years said, "The length of service is satisfactory. I'd not want it to be shorter. The music is better now with the new minister of music. It could be, as far as hymns are concerned, more soulful and joyful. The main thing is the lack of real preaching."

For many, real preaching has little to do with intellectual or socially activist treatises which seem only remotely related to spiritual things. "The minister should preach and not lecture," said one female charter member. "I receive a lot of substance and spiritual uplifting when I hear a beautiful sermon." She also asked the minister to stick to his subject and not digress so much.

"I come to church more as a long-standing habit (for the) fellowship/singing—I get absolutely nothing from the sermons," comments one seventy-two-year-old female charter member. This woman also mentioned how much she had enjoyed the sermons by the two previous African American pastors before Pastor A.

"Stick to the Bible in the sermons," advised one woman, a twenty-five-year member at Grace.

Another woman said, "I like the choir. I would change the sermons. Length of service is fine. I wish for sermons concerning Christ, the dominion of God, the Christian faith. I would wish for less social and political doctrine." This respondent had worshiped at Grace for thirty-one years.

The crucial issue for many seems to be expressed best by two other members, one female, one male. "The sermons are often not spiritually uplifting enough. I have nothing to think about that next week," complained a seventy-five-year-old woman. Her tenure at the church was thirty years.

"Worship is religious reverence and homage to God; a well (from which) to draw refreshing water that should bring joy and strength for revival and survival. It has slipped," said a man who had been a member of the church for thirty-one years. He continued, "One should be able to carry that song or that thought throughout the entire week. Then and only then would one be able to go out and help or minister to others."

The resounding message for Pastor A. was to be more spiritual and less activist, to get closer to home in his sermons. Members pleaded to hear Bible-based, spiritually enriching messages which would equip them with truths, perspectives, and strategies they could apply in their everyday lives.

Members said they wanted and needed encouragement and joy to get through the week, and the socially activist messages or "lectures" given by Pastor A. simply did not provide these. While choir music adds beauty to the worship, they indicated, it cannot do it all. Members felt that the sermon is of supreme importance in a worship service.

There was a minority contingent who loved the sermons. This is a highly educated congregation, after all, and many of the worshipers had chosen Grace precisely because of its intellectual ministers and the stately tone of the services. One fifty-four-year-old woman who had been at the church five years said, "I chose this church because the minister is an intellectual, and it is close to my home."

A woman from a Baptist church wrote, "I am a frequent visitor but truly enjoy the quiet during worship and the beautiful music rendered and the eloquent preaching." A few others also seemed to be former or current Baptists running away from what they perceived as loud, disorderly worship to find something quieter and more intellectual in tone. "Being a Baptist for the first thirty-one years of my life, I always wished for a quiet service and order," said a fifty-six-year-old woman, a member of Grace for twenty-five years.

From the woman who wished for sermons related to Christ and the dominion of God, "I like the structure of service. No screaming, quiet. . . ." Another woman, aged sixty-six, said, "I like a quiet service—no clapping, etc." She had been at Grace for thirty-two years.

In other instances, members said that the quiet, intellectual worship was what they had been accustomed to for some years prior to coming to Grace. "I like a worship service that is quiet, dignified, and spiritually satisfying in both sermon and song. . . . Worship [at Grace] reflects educated leadership more than some others. Fellowship—about the same," said a fifty-three-year-old woman who had been at Grace for thirty-one years.

"I chose this church because I attended Talladega College, where I sang in the college choir and enjoyed the quiet, intellectual service. . . . I like the program of the church and the fact that people here are educated or generally intelligent and *thinking* versus simply *feeling* people," commented a sixty-year-old woman who indicated that she had been at Grace for thirty-four years. She added, "All of my needs are met at this church. I need beautiful music, quiet worship, intellectual sermons, study, growing youth who participate, and new worship ideas. I also feel that (Pastor A.) is superior in caring for our needs in life and death."

More accolades were heard for the quality of Pastor A.'s sermons: "I like current issues discussed in sermons," said a fifty-five-year-old respondent, a twenty-year member of the church. One sixty-two-year-old man said, "Minister delivers sermons with an in-depth approach to everyday life. Intellectual interpretations. . . . Lectures and sermons delivered by pastor are the strengths."

"Strengths (include) sermons. Excellent preacher. . . . The minister tries very hard to stimulate the people. Sometimes you wonder what do they really want. I don't think we need the emotionalism that some want," said a seventy-two-year-old woman who had been at Grace for twenty-six years.

"Sermons encourage reaching out to others," said another woman, aged sixty-eight. She had been at Grace for twenty-eight years.

Clearly, Pastor A.'s sermons do not lack fans. But if this small research sampling is any indication, the detractors far outnumber the fans. Far more persons shared the point of view of a twenty-six-year-old woman student who had been reared at Grace. She said, "My primary unmet need of the service is not leaving feeling uplifted—which I attribute to the very serious tone of the services. I feel uplifted when the sermons are structured to make me leave comparing them to everyday life. Many times I feel the sermons are too technical and difficult to absorb."

By and large, members seemed to bear out my own thoughts regarding sermonizing by Pastor A. As I suggested in chapter 3, Grace's congregation is not a seminary-trained audience. Pastor A. must be sensitive to the fact that while some of his hearers grasp almost every idea he tries to express, much of the thoughtful intellectual material he packages as sermon goes right over the heads of many, leaving them spiritually empty as he concludes and worship ends.

While these members are highly educated and partial to an educated minister, their needs are more than intellectual, they said. Sermons need to be closer to home and to touch them spiritually, emotionally, and practically. In the words of the one respondent, "Then and only then would one be able to go out and help or minister to others."

Music: The Need for Additional Hymn Resources

When asked to talk about strengths and weaknesses of worship, worshipers usually talked about sermon content and music in one breath. This makes sense, since these are the two most important elements of worship for many.

As is probably evident from parishioner comments above, the congregation was very pleased with its professional choir for the most part. Some survey respondents asked for more spirituals and more gospel music. As was mentioned in chapter 3, contemporary gospel music is rarely rendered by the Chancel Choir.

But for those who spoke of music, what most concerned them was congregational singing and the fact that the hymns that the pastor selected for worship were often culturally, rhythmically, melodically, and spiritually alien. In the words of an earlier respondent, the hymns needed to be "more soulful and joyful."

"I do wish that we would sing more of the old songs that we know and are uplifting. . . . Bring back the old songs that mean so much to our race," said a seventy-five-year old Grace member. She had been at the church for twenty-five years.

Said one woman, "Sometimes if the sermon is political or ethnic in content and unfamiliar songs are used, I leave church unsatisfied spiritually."

In listing weaknesses of the church worship, one gentleman cited "Lack of warmth expressed by members. Lack of communication between minister and congregation. Hymnal selections very poor and unmoving spiritually."

One respondent went so far as to type up a suggested order of worship. It was largely the same as that currently in use, with the major change being the inclusion of a "Songs of Praise" devotional period between 10:15 and 10:30, following the candle-lighting ceremony. The respondent, a sixty-five-year-old woman who had been at Grace for thirty-one years, underscored the words familiar songs on her suggested order of worship.

The message for Pastor A. is easily summed up by a seventy-five-year-old respondent who advised, "Include the standard songs more (e.g., 'Amazing Grace'). Let the whole church sing songs that warm the soul, along with (those from the UCC) hymnal."

It should be noted that "Amazing Grace" is in the UCC hymnal, but

Grace worshipers may not be aware of that, as it is rarely—if ever—sung. The main point, however, that the church should sing hymns that warm the soul, is worth noting.

These sentiments dovetail with my own comments in Chapter 3 about hymns for African Americans. Again, there seems to be a body of religious music that black church folk sing across denominations. Not only blacks sing these particular songs, but the songs have become standards or favorites over decades of black historical experience. Any worship of African Americans which ignores this body of musical literature is spiritually impoverished in the minds and hearts of the worshipers involved.

Grace worshipers will be heartened to know that the United Church of Christ has published a new hymnal, *The New Century Hymnal*,[2] which is more sensitive to all the various cultural and ethnic groups that comprise the UCC total membership. Grace members might consider purchasing it and/or other musical resources to supplement the UCC hymnal in worship. Suggestions of specific hymnals which carry a large number of the musical offerings Grace members crave include *Songs of Zion*[3] and *Lead Me, Guide Me: The African American Catholic Hymnal*.[4]

Theological Understandings and Blindspots

What is most striking as the surveys are considered is the inability of respondents—many of whom have worshiped at Grace and other Christian churches for twenty to fifty years—to discuss basic Christian concepts intelligently. In the verse from Proverbs 4, quoted at the beginning of this chapter, the biblical writer is speaking of the importance of getting spiritual understanding; of comprehending and being able to interpret spiritual matters.

Generally, the survey responses point to a highly educated congregation which is woefully ignorant when it comes to things spiritual. What this suggests is that evangelism for this congregation is nearly impossible because members do not seem to have a firm enough grasp on what the Christian faith is about to explain to an unchurched person why he or she should be churched.

In the second section of the survey, respondents were asked to describe briefly in their own words the meaning of eight central concepts: God,

꿍 쒜

Christ, the Holy Spirit, sin, salvation, the body of Christ, the world, and the Bible. In some cases, the respondent did not describe at all two or more of the concepts. In one case, the respondent chose not to respond to any of the eight. Those who did respond often gave nebulous or outright incorrect responses. In evaluating the responses, I did not consider a particular response incorrect because it was theologically "liberal" or "conservative," but only if it had no sound biblical basis and would be challenged by both liberals and conservatives.

Nearly every church has at least a few people who know the Bible very well and can talk intelligently about spiritual concepts. Grace is no exception. A few of the surveys showed a good understanding of Christian basics on the part of respondents. Incidentally, some answers from respondents in this generally theologically liberal congregation could have come from members at Fire Baptized. In a very few instances, the theological understandings of some Grace members mirrored those of persons at Fire Baptized.

By and large, however, responses were extremely brief, consisting of only a few words or a phrase or two, and showed a real lack of clarity about basic Christian beliefs. Most inadequate were the responses describing the Holy Spirit and the body of Christ.

The basic traditional Christian notions of the Holy Spirit as the third person of the Trinity and as the Comforter, for instance, seemed to escape most, though certainly not all, Grace worshipers. One respondent said the Holy Spirit is "that which manifests God's presence in our lives at all times." It is not clear what that really meant.

One man said of the Spirit, "(It) deals with our conscience," perhaps getting at the idea that among the many functions of the Spirit are convicting of sin and causing sinners to repent. But the member did not express this fully.

Perhaps thinking the concept to be described was the Holy Trinity or perhaps working with the idea of the Trinity, one respondent described the Spirit as, "God in three persons."

A few persons described the Spirit as the "benefactor" that Jesus said would come after his death. I am not used to seeing or hearing this term in connection with the Holy Spirit. Usually *benefactor* denotes a financial sponsor. I am not sure whether this term comes from a particular translation of the Bible, or whether it is simply a bad choice of words.

"The Spirit of God in all humankind," is how one woman described the spirit. Similarly, another woman said the Spirit is, "an extension of God and is inside each person." These types of responses were vague, as they gave no suggestion of what this Spirit does in or for humans.

Also a bit vague were responses about the Spirit as "guide". The scriptures talk of the Spirit as one who guides us into all truth. Respondents described the Spirit as "a guiding force of mind and body" and as one who "guides us through life"—not really touching on the idea of truth at all.

Most prominent were descriptions of the Spirit as a "feeling": "The feeling that overcomes one when you are moved in a profound manner by a religious and/or loving experience." "The feeling you have about God." "The elated feeling of happiness and fulfillment." "The special feeling that one receives when worshiping the heavenly Father." "Inner feeling of satisfaction."

Other responses included: "The invisible force for good." "The divine Spirit of God." "The power source from God that allows man to do things beyond his own human power." "God Himself and His presence being felt everywhere." "Interaction with God." "An unseen, yet always present, Being. The same as God. He (It) watches over me." "Gift of God." "Living by the Scriptures." "Is with me every hour." "The force which lives within us, perhaps more specifically, the part of God within us."

Looking at responses on the question of salvation, it is also the case that only a few people seemed to have the traditional, basic two-part understanding of this concept as redemption from sin through God's grace so that one might have eternal life.

While a couple of persons responded with fundamentalist/evangelical language related to being born again or having received Christ as one's personal Savior, others responded variously as follows: "Means the act of saving." "Doing the will of God and eternal life." "Being saved to do good." "Deliverance, healing, blessing." "Helps me through on life's path." "Finding the truth." "Believing in the promises of Jesus Christ." "Forgiveness of sins through prayer." "The feeling that one has atoned for their sins and is ready to meet their God." "To believe in Christ's teachings and embrace them." "The spiritual awareness of the dominance of the presence of God within (Holy Spirit); and the practice of godly ways." "The means of being saved or protected." "Being saved and the hope of being raised from the level at which we now are to a higher one."

With respect to the concept of the body of Christ, I was expecting responses having to do with the community of Christian believers, however people chose to flesh that out. Of course, a few people did describe the body of Christ as the local and/or global church of believers. Many Grace members, however, often left response space for this term blank. Many also connected the body of Christ with the communion elements or Christ's physical person which hung on the cross. Or they gave responses that were either irrelevant or biblically unsound, including the following: "Those things that concretely represent Christ in our everyday world." "Christ offered himself for our salvation." "A symbol of God's love." "Uplifts me." "A belief that Christ lives within the Christian's soul." "A sacred presence that brings about salvation."

Compare these responses, and lack of responses, about the Holy Spirit, salvation, and the body of Christ, to those of one of the Baptist visitors who completed a survey:

> Third person of the Trinity. Comforter and brings conviction of sin. Baptizes believers into the body of Christ and imparts new birth.

> God offers salvation to all but it must be accepted by us. It is a free gift. Salvation is deliverance (from) sin by the manifestation of God's grace.

> Christ is the head of the Church. Believers are to be members of Christ's body. Many members but only one body.

Clearly, the visitor from another tradition had retained something concrete about salvation, about the body of Christ, and also five crucial theological characteristics about the nature and many functions of the Spirit from life in her worshiping community (or from somewhere). Her descriptions for the other five concepts were equally rich.

This exercise of listing responses regarding three of the concepts points up certain theological blindspots in the congregation. Judging from limited survey results (and we assume the surveys came from the most committed persons at Grace), members did not seem to have grasped the idea of the body of Christ in the same way that Pastor A. described it in his survey: "The people of God gathered for mutual support and service to others."

Nor did they have a firm handle on the matter of salvation.

Most importantly, however, members seemed to know little about the vital third person of the Trinity. That will become even more apparent when we consider Fire Baptized responses on the matter of the Spirit in the next section of this chapter.

Ignorance about the Spirit can be seen in many ways throughout the United Church of Christ as a whole. Perhaps the most important place to detect this ignorance of, or at least this lack of attention to, the Spirit is the United Church of Christ Statement of Faith:

> We believe in you, O God, Eternal Spirit, God of our Savior
>
> Jesus Christ and our God, and to your deeds we testify:
>
> You call the worlds into being,
>
> create persons in your own image,
>
> and set before each one the ways of life and death.
>
> You seek in holy love to save all people from aimlessness and sin.
>
> You judge people and nations by your righteous will declared
>
> through prophets and apostles.
>
> In Jesus Christ, the man of Nazareth, our crucified and risen Savior,
>
> you have come to us
>
> and shared our common lot,
>
> conquering sin and death
>
> and reconciling the world to yourself.
>
> You bestow upon us your Holy Spirit,
>
> creating and renewing the church of Jesus Christ,
>
> binding in covenant faithful people of all ages, tongues, and races.

You call us into your church

to accept the cost and joy of discipleship,

to be your servants in the service of others,

to proclaim the gospel to all the world

and resist the powers of evil,

to share in Christ's baptism and eat at his table,

to join him in his passion and victory.

You promise to all who trust you

forgiveness of sins and fullness of grace,

courage in the struggle for justice and peace,

your presence in trial and rejoicing,

and eternal life in your realm which has no end.

Blessing and honor, glory and power be unto you. Amen.[5]

Including the two introductory lines, there are twenty descriptive lines about God and one line of praise to God in this statement. This contrasts with nine lines about or mentioning Jesus Christ and only four lines about the Holy Spirit.

The lack of attention to the Spirit in the statement is especially glaring in contrast to the constant emphasis on at least seven of the Spirit's functions one experiences at Fire Baptized and other churches like it. In these churches, one hears often that the Spirit:

1. Equips believers for evangelical witness (Acts 1:8).
2. Imparts certain spiritual "fruit" and empowers believers to live godly, wholesome lives (Gal. 5:22, 23).

3. Is teacher and guide, and gives wisdom, discernment and direction (John 16:13; 14:26).
4. Is Comforter in times of pain and perplexity (John 14:16–18).
5. Is intercessor, i.e., intercedes for believers in prayer before God (Rom. 8:26, 27).
6. Works to edify or build up the body of Christ, the church, through spiritual gifts (1 Cor. 12).
7. Brings unity of purpose and equality in the body—unity across gender, racial, ethnic, and national lines (Acts 2:1; Gal. 3:27).

When Fire Baptized survey responses are evaluated shortly, these functions will be lifted up by members time and again.

If extended to the other five concepts listed on the survey, the exercise of examining Grace members' responses also points up a general lack of basic biblical teaching during worship. The pastor seems to assume that parishioners already have a basic understanding of Christianity, gained during childhood in Sunday school classes or elsewhere, and that members have retained such vital information. Clearly, they have not. This fact is clear despite members' citing, in the second section of the survey, myriad sources for their religious understandings (sermons, Bible study, Christian radio/TV, books, and devotional literature). Somehow, they have not internalized what they have heard, perhaps because these key concepts are not packaged simply enough for people to grab hold of them. Perhaps many of these members' personal spiritual experience is so shallow that these academic theological concepts have not yet come alive in their hearts. Or the answer may lie somewhere else.

All in all, Grace members often have to supplement their worship by attending services and/or Bible study at other churches in order to gain basic knowledge about the Bible and matters of personal spirituality. One woman, a member at Grace for thirty-three years, who did admirably well on the conceptual questions, said as much in her survey: "[Grace] worship enhances my spiritual well-being because I went out to take some Bible classes at other churches. There I learned to read and meditate daily. From reading I learned what is expected of me as a Christian, about stewardship, etc. I didn't learn that at [Grace]."

Indoctrination and Evangelism

In light of the reality that many Grace members do not seem to know or retain basic Christian doctrine, one is forced to wrestle with the idea of "indoctrination." The term's generally negative connotations spring from the lessons of history, in which millions of people at times have been victimized as a result of bad doctrine or philosophies touted by political or religious madmen and their zealous followers. Hence, no one cares to be "indoctrinated" in any way these days. Americans especially treasure freedom of thought and ideas.

But the term needs to be "redeemed" (excuse the pun) and its true neutral meaning restored to people's consciousness. While the word *indoctrinate* can mean "to teach to accept a system of thought uncritically," it more simply means "to instruct in a body of doctrine."[6]

Without being unduly harsh, many of the responses of Grace members to the conceptual survey questions are theologically muddy. This state of affairs is distressing and particularly jarring for one who comes out of a Pentecostal background, where basic Christian doctrine is drilled indelibly into the minds and hearts of parishioners Sunday after Sunday, and at other times during the week as well, through Bible-centered teaching.

Further, this situation constitutes a grave indictment of preaching and Christian education at Grace and suggests the possibility of Grace becoming extinct in the not-too-distant future. How is the church to grow and replace itself as the oldest generation of members dies if parishioners cannot explain basic Christian concepts to the unchurched?

The average age of Grace respondents is sixty-seven, and Pastor A. says two-thirds of the members are sixty-five years of age or older. In other words, most of Grace's current members probably will not be around in ten to fifteen years.

Grace members need to begin to ask themselves if they really care about spiritually "winning" and nurturing the unchurched. These members must begin to wrestle with their image as a "black country club church," to use the language of some Grace insiders and outsiders. Are they only concerned about gaining new members from among persons who are already churched, hold the same high socioeconomic status, and speak the same "language" as they themselves do? Do they wish to continue as a church that basically attracts only high-status African Americans for reasons which have nothing to do with spirituality? Or do they want to be a church of true spiritual integrity? These are tough questions for people to consider emotionally. But the inability of many members to give a reasonable account of their faith after decades at Grace forces one to ask them.

Grace members must have basic Christian beliefs presented to them in a way in which they can receive such information. Since attendance at adult Sunday school classes is low, Pastor A. must find some creative, interesting ways of conveying basic Christian concepts in his sermons. Of course, Bible classes at the church must be enhanced as well so that members want to come and gain knowledge. Further, increased attention must be given to matters of personal spirituality.

Other Comments on Grace Worship and Fellowship Life

It may be of interest to hear some of the other suggestions and concerns raised in the Grace surveys. Members touch on a variety of matters, from the mundane to the sublime. Comments can be divided into four broad categories: (1) praise, blame or suggestions related to specific elements of the Sunday worship service; (2) applause for the pastor's nonauthoritarian leadership style and of UCC congregational polity; (3) debate concerning the quality of communal spirit and interaction between members; and (4) the need for outreach to the surrounding community.

On the Worship Service. At least two members said the trustees are too noisy as they exit the service to count money after the offertory; they suggested that the trustees all sit together as a group and exit the sanctuary quietly. One of these two persons commented that she feels like a spectator at worship. This affirms my own thoughts, offered in chapter 3, relative to the lack of congregational participation in Grace worship. Another person said she liked the fact that communion is "all-inclusive"—open to any Christian believer from any denomination. Some members applauded both the pastor's use of children in worship and the warm recognition of visitors he gives during the announcement period; it seems the previous two pastors did neither. Others commented that since everyone in the congregation can read, there is no reason to read the printed announcements aloud during worship. One person asked for a more refined printed order of worship, referring in part to frequent typing errors.

Leadership Style and UCC Polity. Members raised issues which point to Pastor A.'s nonauthoritarian leadership style and the UCC's congregational polity, which vests most power in the local congregation, rather than in episcopal jurisdictions or national headquarters. One member said, "I chose this church because of . . . the mature manner in which members were treated," apparently commenting on the fact that members are not brow-beaten from the pulpit in an authoritarian manner about beliefs, conformity in lifestyle, or anything else. Another woman agreed, stating, "The doctrine is not dogmatic or a pretense of absolutism. Freedom to seek a strong spiritual life and to help others is not condemned, but encouraged." A male member said he joined Grace because of, "the freedom of the congregation, its method of organization, its worship practices, its independence from superior bodies, its confession of faith," and its right to control the affairs of the congregation, including its ability to select a pastor.

Communal Spirit. Probably most interesting were the mixed reviews on communal experiences and good-will at the church. While many respondents seemed to have found a comfortable niche and were well pleased with the way members interacted with one another, just as many bemoaned the lack of love and courtesy among members, particularly in church business meetings. One woman called for more togetherness. Citing an undercurrent of coolness and resentment among members, she slammed the egotistical approach to church affairs of some who carry on as if to say, "I am the church." "No, *we* are the church," she stated emphatically. In the same vein, one man said, "I would like to see all organizations coordinate their efforts better. . . . I think there could be a little more team effort."

Community Outreach. There were challenges to the membership to offer programming to help those in the surrounding neighborhood and to be a part of the wider UCC church. On this latter point, the member in question commented, "Sometimes I feel people tend to think the church doesn't have need for growth and change because members are isolated and uninformed."

As a whole, the survey responses pointed to a church that must come to grips with a variety of identity crises. These are liturgical, spiritual, and socioeconomic in nature.

Liturgically, some want a livelier, more soulful worship service, closer in style to that of their roots. Others are running from their roots.

Spiritually, the church members need to decide if they really want to reach the unchurched. If so, they must equip themselves to talk in intelligent spiritual terms to unchurched persons about Christian doctrine.

In terms of issues of socioeconomic class, the church must decide if it cares to reach all unchurched persons, including those who live in the inner-city neighborhood where the church is located, as well as the unchurched who are like them.

To be certain, major changes in tone of worship and socioeconomic make-up of the congregation may drive some Grace members away. The church must be open to the dynamic movement of the Spirit, which brings change. Perhaps a radical refashioning of Grace that takes place gradually over time is what is needed for Grace to become what God intends it to be and for the spiritual needs of both the churched and interested unchurched to be met fully.

Fire Baptized Church

The youthfulness of this congregation is reflected in the average age of the thirty-two respondents—thirty-one years. The average tenure at the church was two years and four months, meaning that most had been there since the church was established or became affiliated with the church when it had existed previously under another name and was headed by another pastor.

All respondents were African Americans. All but two said they attended services very frequently. Of the remaining two, one did not answer the question and the other said s/he attended frequently.

Respondents reported their occupations as: marketing specialist, nurse, student (twice), secretary (several times), administrative assistant, trading floor clerk, clerk and senior clerk (no fields specified), meter reader, real estate salesman, insurance salesman, telephone company employee, cashier, grocery cashier, grocery dairy man, janitor, fast-food service worker, management trainee, electrician, and skilled worker. One person was unemployed, and two classified themselves as housewives.

By and large, these are not the highly educated managers, executives and decision makers one finds at Grace, but the occupations do require intelligence. For the most part, these are young people trying to get a start in life.

A much larger percentage of males responded from the Fire Baptized congregation than did at Grace—eleven men, or 34 percent of respondents. Of course, the women respondents still outnumbered the men two to one.

Like Grace members' surveys, Fire Baptized survey responses also place a spotlight on three important issues when considered as a group. First was the matter of indoctrination; responses to the theological questions reflected thorough acquaintance with Scripture and/or frequent biblical teaching related to each concept, and also homogenization of thinking in the congregation. Second, I was struck by the Damascus Road–type experiences that each member described in the section on spiritual pilgrimage. Third, notable as well were the love members felt toward one another, the loyalty they expressed toward Pastor B., and the church's approach to things spiritual.

Lay Theologians

The thoroughness of responses to the theological questions on the survey was impressive, as was the depth of understanding. Many members attached separate sheets to the survey in order to give adequate treatment to the concepts. In addition, without being instructed to do so, many persons provided supporting Scripture references for the information supplied. In a few instances, a respondent left a concept blank or gave a response that did not seem biblically sound. But generally, theological gobbledygook was rare.

While members would not think of themselves as such, they are excellent lay theologians within the Evangelical/Pentecostal traditions. They seem to have a better grasp on these concepts than most students I encountered during my many years of graduate theological education! Many of the responses were mini-sermons. Rarely did persons respond in terse phrases, like, "Christ—the Son of God."

The first survey I read, for instance, which was completed by a twenty-two-year-old man, carried these words about Christ: "My Lord, my Redeemer, my Savior, God Himself manifested in the flesh, justified in the Spirit, seen of angels, preached unto the Gentiles (which is unto *me*), believed on in the world, received up into Glory." [Unless stated otherwise, emphasis on survey comments is that of respondent.] Perhaps the man had taken notes during one of Pastor B.'s sermons (as members often do) and referred back to them. Perhaps it was more a matter of his having committed the material both to memory and to heart.

Not all the responses were as well fleshed out as this one, but all were exceedingly rich and personalized, containing phrases like "received Christ as *my* personal savior" or identified God as "the one I go to with all *my* needs, wants, expectations, desires and troubles."

Consider some of the other responses regarding the meaning of Christ. A forty-nine-year-old woman wrote, "is the Savior, Son of God (only begotten), Redeemer of mankind, was born of a virgin, died for our sins and rose again in three days. He conquered death."

"The Son of God born by the Spirit of God. Lived without sin. Savior, Redeemer, advocate, high priest, lamb of God, etc., etc.," wrote a twenty-six-year-old-male. Christ is "my Redeemer, Elder Brother, Righteousness, Sanctification, Justifier and Friend," said a thirty-six-year-old male teacher/salesman.

A twenty-six-year-old male wrote that God "is the creator of the universe, my Father. He is the only self-existing being. He is wisdom (spiritual and natural). He is understanding. He is knowledge. He has created *all* things and nothing could exist without Him, not even *Satan* himself."

Another said that "God is infinite, without a beginning or end. He is love, all powerful, the Lord of the universe, the ultimate Creator."

As is evident, respondents often gave a long list of descriptive phrases for each person of the Trinity, showing they knew far more than the basics about each. To be certain, the Holy Spirit was given full treatment by these Pentecostal believers. They defined the Holy Spirit variously as:

o "The Comforter. The Holy Spirit has a seven-fold ministry— comforter, counselor, intercessor, helper, strengthener, standby, and advocate."

o "The very Spirit of God that moved over the face of the deep in Genesis 1 and that now is with and in believers today for empowerment over sin, Satan, the world, and works of Satan."

○ "God in the Third Person. He convicts us (the world) of sin, baptizes us into the body of Christ when we receive Jesus, and leads and guides us into all truth. Through Him we know truth from error."

○ "The part of Jesus that he left for us when he died, was resurrected, and ascended into heaven. The Holy Spirit is the third person in the Trinity. He lives within men who welcome him and empowers them to do the will of the Lord."

○ "The very presence of God that resides in me, leads me, teaches me, and corrects me."

○ "The divine life-force and power of God's personality who indwells born-again believers and who is at work in this earth realm to bring man to an awareness of the need for Christ."

○ "My helper, Encourager, Intercessor. The one who lives in me. He speaks the Father's words to me and guides me in everything I do."

○ "The Comforter that Christ spoke of sending after he left the face of the earth. A helper that the Lord has provided me with."

○ "Our Guide, counselor, comforter, sent here for us by God when Jesus died."

○ "The Spirit of truth. He is the one who reveals the truth of God's Word to my spirit, and I walk and live a victorious life in Christ as a result of Him."

○ "The Spirit of God. Also the Holy Ghost. When it comes over your body, you have no control."

This last response relates to the issue of spirit possession, a prominent feature of much African worship. It may also be related to responses from Grace members who spoke of the Spirit of God as a feeling.

Simpler responses about the Spirit included: "The Comforter, my guide"; "dwells in one's body to help change or convict you of your sins"; "my Comforter, Deliverer, Healer"; "dwells within me"; "the power"; and "teacher, guide, spiritual power." There were other responses, but this sample conveys the overall flavor of the remarks.

For the sake of further comparison, it might be helpful to share some of the responses for "body of Christ" and "salvation." Grace members had difficulty with these two concepts, along with the idea of the Holy Spirit. While a couple of people connected the body of Christ with the physical body that hung on the cross ("what God used to carry our sins," in the words of one respondent), most elaborated on the notion of the body as the church or community of believers. Respondents defined the body of Christ as:

- ○ "A group of born-again, Holy Ghost-filled, saintly believers striving for perfection in Christ Jesus our Lord."
- ○ "Those who are serving God, living their lives for Christ. The Church is the body."
- ○ "The Church, not the building, but those that are Christ's."
- ○ "Every person who has received Jesus Christ as their personal Lord and Savior, asked Jesus to come into their heart and life. They make up the body of Christ, and Jesus is the head of the body."
- ○ "Term used to describe believers as functioning parts of a body."
- ○ "The aggregation of believers earthwide, regardless of race, denomination, or other barriers of distinction identifiable by the eye."
- ○ "All (regardless of denomination) who believe Jesus was the Christ and repent of their sins and live obediently to God's commandments, laws, and will, including forsaking not the assembling of yourself with believers."
- ○ "Those who have received Jesus as their Lord and Savior and are walking in holiness and righteousness."
- ○ "The local body of saints called by the Lord Jesus Christ."
- ○ "The church, the people I can depend on, who pray and intercede for me. My heavenly family. I thank God for them and our body throughout the world."
- ○ "The individuals (people) who make up the Church, united in fellowship to the head (Christ)."
- ○ "The church with all of the gifts in operation."

Shorter responses included: "the people of God"; "the Church"; and "all who accept Jesus as their Savior."

It is readily apparent that, for these believers, the body of Christ includes not just any old person naming the name of Christ, but only Spirit-filled believers who have accepted Christ as Savior and who do the will of God. Such persons can be of any denomination, race, or nationality, Fire Baptized members said.

It is hard to separate comments about this concept of salvation from comments about the body of Christ and the world in particular, for members often talk of salvation as that which results from receiving Christ as personal Savior and of the body of Christ as comprising those who have done so. In the next breath, when asked to talk about the world, Fire Baptized members stated that those who have not received Christ Jesus and are opposed to him make up the secular world. A few sample remarks will be representative of many.

A forty-one-year-old woman said salvation involves "acknowledging that Jesus is the Son of God, repenting and openly confessing to others that he is God's Son, who died and rose and forgave your sins." For her the world is "nonbelievers."

One forty-nine-year-old female defined salvation as "being saved and delivered from sin or evil," and referred to the world as the aggregation of those who are "out of relationship with God, against God, and under the sinful guide of Satan."

The body of Christ is, "all who accept Jesus as their Savior," while the world is composed of "all who have not accepted Jesus as their Savior," said a twenty-two-year-old male.

A thirty-five-year-old woman described the body of Christ as "all persons who have received Jesus Christ as Lord—Jesus being the head and the believers making up the parts of the body." She explained that the world refers to "anyone who has not received Jesus as Lord—putting themselves under the authority of Satan."

For Grace members, the world is something neutral—God's creation, including the entire universe. For Fire Baptized members, the world is a spiritual battleground in which "saints," or Spirit-filled believers, are only to evangelize nonbelievers, nothing more.

A theological blindspot for Fire Baptized members is to be so focused on the evil of the world and the idea that it is Satan's realm, that they neglect God's overwhelming love for it—a love so great that God gave for it God's only begotten Son. This theological oversight has serious consequences with respect to social action.

If one believes there is no hope for the world, that Jesus will return any minute now for the church, and that one's only responsibility to the world is to evangelize, one will take no action to make the world a better place—to pray about and work on larger social issues like discrimination, homelessness, the nuclear arms race, cuts in federal social-service budgets, etc. A broader vision is needed for Pastor B. and his members to see that often their day-to-day struggles for survival as African Americans are a direct result of some of these larger social issues.

To pay no attention to these issues or to fail to work on them is to give Satan free reign over God's property (the earth) and the fates (economic and otherwise) of God's people. It takes a broader vision to recognize that what the liberation theologians call "structural" or "institutional" sin has a far more devastating impact on far more people than the individual sins of one person against another.

Furthermore, pastor and members need to wrestle with the fact that God loves and cares about the well-being of all of creation, regardless of whether or not individuals have the "right" beliefs about Jesus. God wants every person to have adequate clothing, shelter, and dignity, as well as a healthy spirituality.

It is hard for a homeless person to concentrate on the life-giving message of salvation when his or her stomach is grumbling so loudly that he or she can hardly hear the words spoken! Some basic needs of humanity—physical and psychosocial—have to be taken care of, alongside the dispensing of the good news about salvation. Indeed, some will be drawn to the message of salvation because the church has met their practical needs.

Damascus Road–type Conversion Experiences

Personal testimonies of conversion experiences like Paul's on the Damascus Road (Acts 9) are inescapable in responses to the question in the second section of the survey related to spiritual pilgrimage. Grace members typically responded in one of two ways: "I can't recall myself ever being anything but a Christian," or "I was baptized around age twelve or thirteen and later joined Grace Church because it was (is) near my residence."

In contrast, Fire Baptized members made distinctions between being churchgoers and being truly Christian; between being Christian and being a saved Christian. They often spoke of leaving Baptist and liberal mainline churches, even UCC congregations like Grace, to find that "something missing" spiritually. The watershed moment for most was the receiving of Christ and/or of the Baptism of the Holy Spirit, moments which came once they moved on to "full gospel" churches.

Stating that she had been a Christian for ten years, one woman said, "I received Jesus at twenty-five, and my life drastically changed, especially my mind and my thinking. Then on April 23, 1980, I received the Baptism with the Holy Spirit and my life has never been and will never be the same."

Said one woman who was saved seventeen years ago, "I received Jesus Christ as Savior when I was nineteen years old as a result of my fiancé's father sharing the gospel with me. In 1980 at age thirty I received the Baptism with the Holy Spirit, thus empowering me to more fully live for Christ. This experience was the turning point in my walk with the Lord."

A sixteen-year-old girl described the negative reaction of a liberal mainline pastor when her watershed moment came. "I've been a 'Christian' all my life. But I've been a saved Christian for about three years. I went to a UCC church that was dry and nice, and I never learned anything. Our Sunday School teacher got saved and used the Holy Spirit to teach and minister to us. Our whole class accepted Christ. The pastor gave us problems because we wouldn't go to his sermons. We had a youth group. He took away our money. Told us we couldn't pray in tongues and shook the faith of some. Everyone left. But I go to two churches now because I have to go to the UCC one. (I don't enjoy it but the Lord told me to obey my parents.)"

A twenty-two-year-old man said, "In 1982, I received the Baptism of the Holy Spirit while on vacation (to Chicago from Louisiana). When I returned to Louisiana, I didn't like being in the Methodist church anymore, so I started looking for a church that believed in the Holy Spirit. In February 1985, I found one that I was comfortable with."

Another rejected the denomination of her early spiritual roots—in this case, a Baptist church: "I have been a born-again Christian for a little more than three years. I had been in church all my life before I got saved, but none of the Baptist churches I ever belonged to seemed to clarify salvation. Through a friend, I found my way to a full gospel church."

The two most dramatic testimonies related to deliverance from drugs and other serious vices. A thirty-three-year-old woman confessed, "All my life I attended various churches. As a teen in college I got involved in drugs. I returned to church and attended a UCC church because their denomination was very liberal. I continued to do drugs. I found through Bible study and attending other churches I wasn't saved. I repented and gave my life to

Jesus. He delivered me from drugs, alcohol, nicotine, healed my body, and filled me with the Holy Ghost."

A thirty-seven-year-old man testified, "I've been saved one year and eleven months. I called myself Christian for thirty-seven years. I'm a twice-wounded Vietnam vet, a former drug user, drug pusher, thief, extortionist, arsonist, fornicator, adulterer, armed robber, liar, and murderer. I've been shot through the head and hand in Chicago during my service to Satan.

"I had a suicide spirit. I was shooting cocaine one day in 1984, with the thought in mind of killing myself. As I increased the dosage of the drug repeatedly, the Lord showed me a vision of myself dead on the bathroom floor. This disturbed me. The Lord led me to a saint, who led me to the Lord, who led me to [Fire Baptized]."

Personal enthusiasm about conversion is ever present in these testimonies. The same vibrant personal spirituality is also evident in these members' discussions of the sources of their theological understanding. Many of them said that their personal devotion time of prayer and Bible study was an important source.

An illustrative remark came from a thirty-five-year-old woman. "The most powerful and primary source utilized is prayer and the study of God's word. In these one is able to be in tune with the Spirit of God which gives the understanding." Of note, not one Grace respondent listed personal devotion as a source of theological understandings.

Loyalty to Pastor B., Fire Baptized Approach to Worship and Things Spiritual

The surveys reveal overwhelming satisfaction with the worship as currently shaped and with the overall quality of communal feeling at the church. Many said they came to the church by divine leading—"God led me here." Apparently, they were not disappointed after obeying the Spirit's leading.

Twenty-three respondents (72 percent) gave services an overall rating of excellent. Another seven persons, or 22 percent, rated the service good to excellent. In all, 94 percent of respondents rated the service good, close to excellent, or excellent. Only one person gave the worship a fair rating, while one other person failed to supply a rating.

Members applauded the spontaneity of the service, the fact that the Holy Spirit has free reign. "I love the worship here because of the freedom we allow to have the Holy Spirit move in our midst and minister to meet the individual needs of the people here," said one woman. She commented that the service provides a weekly spiritual recharge.

A young man agreed that the worship "meets the need of fellowship after a long hard week of Devil-busting. Charges up those spiritual batteries," he said.

"I like the freedom of everyone to minister (men and women) in the laying on of hands, use of the 1 Corinthians 12 gifts, praying in one's own heavenly language," said one respondent.

Many noted with pride that the church has no printed bulletin. "I don't think the Holy Spirit should be on a program and told when to move and when not to move," wrote one male respondent. "I prefer not having a printed program, because it tends to leave out the free moving of the Holy Ghost. God may at one time or another want to do something different, something that is not on the program. I believe in structure but not in putting God in a box—plus it saves money!"

Along with the Spirit's free movement, members spoke excitedly about the impact of such movement. "The worship enhances me spiritually because it gives me a chance to get under a *corporate anointing*," said one woman (emphasis mine). This member seemed to indicate that more than individual ecstasy was being experienced in Fire Baptized worship. Even though each saved person present has an individual experience with the Holy Spirit, there seems to be something even more powerful about all of the "saints" coming together. In other words, when assembled for worship, two saints plus two saints would seem to equal five or six saints. There is the sense that Jesus himself is there, stepping down the aisles and between the rows of seats, healing infirmities and uplifting discouraged hearts as he goes.

Next most often praised was the Bible teaching enjoyed during the services and in Sunday school—practical sermons and teaching that relate biblical truth to everyday situations and struggles. "I like the teaching by Pastor in Sunday school, because it deals with everyday situations and what the Lord wants us to do about them," said one woman.

"I like the teaching ministry that goes on in a full gospel church and all the gifts working in harmony," remarked another. Judging from the quality of responses to the theological questions on the survey, it is clear that Pastor B.'s Bible teaching is both enjoyed and absorbed.

Said one person, "I chose [Fire Baptized] because they aren't afraid to worship in spirit and in truth and because they teach the Word and not just the parts people want to hear. Its worship is a whole lot deeper than that of the UCC church I've been at all my life. Here, we get answers and needs met. There they say a morning prayer and call that worship." One young man wrote simply, "This church believes in the whole Bible."

Also mentioned frequently was the genuine love members show to one another and their love for God. "There is so much love here," said one man. "I like the closeness that the members have, the sermons, the praising of the Lord, the loving atmosphere that the church has," said another.

Still another said, "I have chosen this church as my home because it is full of the love of God. The pastor and elders of this church preach the pure unadulterated Word of God, which has transformed my life. The fellowship here doesn't compare to any other I have ever been in before because the love for God and desire to be in obedience at all times to Him is so great. There is help here for all those who need it."

Members also praise the humility and anointing evident in Pastor B.'s life, saying that in other churches, "ministers lift themselves up. This church lifts up the name of Jesus, and goes only by the leading of the Holy Spirit," said a forty-six-year-old woman.

One woman said she liked the fact that the youngsters have children's church and that Fire Baptized has a good nursery. "This lessens distractions," she said. Two persons were thankful for the monthly periods of consecration (prayer and fasting) the weekend before communion Sunday.

One member neatly summed up the sentiments of many in assessing the worship's strengths and impact when he said, "Since I've been here, my whole life has changed."

Other Practical Suggestions

While most were extremely satisfied with the worship as currently shaped and often said that none of their spiritual needs were unmet, a variety of suggestions were offered for enhancing the services.

Chief among the regrets about the service was the lack of a permanent facility. One woman spoke for many when she said, "Because we are renting, sometimes our time is limited and we are rushed because of time commitments. There are times when the Holy Spirit starts ministering to the people and we have to be aware of the time." "We are constantly reminded that we are not in our own building," another said.

More than a few people wanted the service to start a few hours earlier. Others wanted longer Bible study before service and/or during the Thursday night communal gathering. One man even wanted Pastor B. to preach longer than the one hour he currently preaches! Someone else wanted even more freedom of movement of the Spirit in the services.

One divorced woman protested that the focus was too heavily on the needs of married families and couples. She wanted more attention paid to the needs and struggles of single Christians. Echoing a complaint that I voiced earlier, one member criticized the volume of the music, saying, "I would lower the volume of the speakers during praise."

There was not universal agreement on the issue of a printed bulletin. While some felt that to have one would put the Spirit in a straitjacket, others said that it would be helpful to visitors. "I would only change the way a visitor does not know what is going on. Because the order of church is always different, and it needs to be explained," suggested one woman.

Her thoughts were affirmed by another who said, "I'd like to have the words of the praise and worship songs printed and available in a bulletin or handout sheet so visitors that aren't familiar with the songs could more easily join in the praise and worship portion of the service."

"I wish we had a printed program sometimes," the sixteen-year-old said, "and I think if maybe the service were shorter, my parents would come. But the length is fine for me."

This brings up another issue, which I raised earlier, about which some members also expressed concern—the lengthy duration of the service. Most agree with one man who suggested that because worship "is all we will be doing" when Jesus comes back for the church, believers may as well become accustomed to protracted praise. However, a few wondered if there were not ways to shorten the service a bit.

"Sometimes I feel the services might be a little lengthy, but when I look back, I can never see anything that wasn't necessary or that didn't minister," one woman said. Without knowing it, she was wrestling here, at least in part, with the issue of balancing liturgical enthusiasm and liturgical discipline.

Only the sixteen-year-old complained about the physicality of the worship. She said, "Sometimes the people falling out or bumping into me bothers me, but I'm not the Holy Spirit and that's how He chooses to work."

Experts versus Laypersons

Do the expectations of worshipers jibe with what experts (liturgiologists, scholars, psychologists, and others) say makes for authentic worship? In large measure, the answer is yes. Remarks of scholars highlighted in earlier chapters had two common threads—that worship must be the work of the people (*leitourgia*) and that it must be emotionally satisfying.

At both Grace Church and Fire Baptized, members said they welcomed the opportunity to participate actively in worship. At least some Grace Church members said so by calling for hymns from the black religious experience that they could sing with gusto. Fire Baptized members expressed pleasure repeatedly in the fact that their worship allows them to be able to minister freely to God in praise and to one another, through things like the laying on of hands and use of charismata during worship.

In a united voice, I also heard members at both churches say that worship must be emotionally satisfying; specifically, it must give one tools for relating biblical truth to everyday situations, and it must impart joy and spiritual energy that last through the week until it is time to "recharge" the spiritual batteries in worship again the following Sunday.

In the next (and final) chapter, I will offer concluding thoughts and recommendations relative to these two worship forms, one formal, one ecstatic.

Study Questions

1. Which comments or testimonies of members at either study church excited you spiritually? Frightened or puzzled you? Angered you? Gave you food for thought?
2. Consider the eight Christian symbols or ideas listed in the survey (God,

Christ, the Holy Spirit, sin, salvation, the body of Christ, the world, the Bible). Are you comfortable enough with these concepts to evangelize—to explain the basics of the Christian faith to others in a compelling enough fashion for them to become seriously interested in improving their spiritual lives and/or in joining your church? If not, how can worship improve your knowledge of these basic concepts? Should it? What is the relationship between your ability to evangelize and the future of your church?

3. Review the third section of the survey instrument (on the worship and communal life of the church) below and use it as the basis for discussing the worship life at your church. What desired changes cited by parishioners at either Grace or Fire Baptized are also needed at your church to improve its worship?

Section III. Worship and Communal Life of the Church

A. Why have you chosen this church as a church home? How does its worship and communal life compare with that of other churches you know of, have visited, or have been a member of?

B. Describe specific strengths and weaknesses of the current worship service. What do you like? What would you change if you had the opportunity? Give attention to structure, tone, or feel of the services, length, music, preaching, printed program (or the lack of one), etc.

C. Please make any other comments you would like about the worship life at the church and how it enhances or detracts from your general spiritual well-being. What needs does the worship meet? What needs remain unmet that you expect worship to meet?

D. Based on your assessment above, please give the worship an overall rating of excellent, good, fair, poor, or failing.

E. How often do you attend Sunday worship? Circle one:

Very Frequently (4–5 times/mo.)

Frequently (2–3 times/mo.)

Somewhat Frequently (about once/mo.)

Infrequently (6–10 times/yr.)

Very Infrequently (1–5 times/yr.)

~ 6 ~
KEY ISSUES OF PRAISING REVISITED

For as many of you as were baptized into Christ have put on Christ.
There is neither Jew nor Greek, there is neither slave nor free, there is
neither male nor female; for you are all one in Christ Jesus.
—Galatians 3:27–28, RSV

But as it is, God arranged the organs in the body,
each one of them, as he chose.
—1 Corinthians 12:18, RSV

Shedding light on any subject often alters its appearance. Thus, since I completed the original research in 1986, there have been some important enhancements to worship ritual at both Grace and Fire Baptized. Notwithstanding these changes, the major limitations described in earlier chapters still exist in these churches and continue to hinder their overall effectiveness.

In this final chapter, then, we discuss these changes and offer expanded treatment of three key issues raised earlier in the context of discussions of worship strengths and limitations at the two study churches. Specifically, these are: evangelism and church growth; the gospel and sociopolitical activism; and the "women's question." In keeping with the central aim of this work, which is to enhance ecumenical unity and cooperation through the promotion of appreciation of these two broadly defined worship forms (formal and charismatic), we will summarize elements to be celebrated in the worship of each of these two churches.

Finally, I will present an original worship evaluation form. This may be used as a basis or guide for dialogue around matters of worship in any congregation.

Grace's Continuing Identity Crisis

Since 1986, Pastor A. has taken a church in another state. Subsequently, an interim pastor served the congregation. The next pastor died after four years of service. Another interim pastor followed. Recently, a permanent minister has been installed. All four successors to Pastor A. have worked hard at bringing more soulful feeling to the worship service and have made (mostly) gradual changes without destroying the overall beauty and order of Grace worship.

Some of the changes include purchasing the *Songs of Zion* hymnal[1] as a supplement to the UCC hymnal to allow for weekly inclusion of cherished hymns from historical black religious experience, and the addition of an altar call for those who wish to receive Christ as personal Savior and to join the church. Members and others often comment on the warmth they experience from others at the church. The Spirit is indeed moving and working quietly at Grace.

Nonetheless, the hard questions and tough issues raised in this book for Grace still remain. For instance, while none of Pastor A.'s successors have tended to focus on sociopolitical activism in sermonizing, it seems members still are not grasping basic Christian concepts from worship to a degree that allows them to give a reasonable account of their faith and evangelize one-on-one with others. In a sermon about eternal life, one of the four men commented on "the stuttering" of Grace members when someone from another tradition asks them how they know they are saved. In others words, members are not able to talk intelligently about the concept of salvation. Generally, members are still theologically fuzzy; there is still no real emphasis on the spiritual disciplines.

While there are more youth at the church than in years past, there still is not enough numerical growth annually to keep pace with the number of deaths in this mostly elderly congregation. Sometimes there are two or three funerals in a single week. This demographic profile makes evangelism even more important.

Outreach to the surrounding community is still minimal, though there have been some recent projects related to women in prison, collection of coats, clothing and toys for poor adults and children at Christmas, and adopting a local school.

In the wake of the church school being displaced from the main edifice to the remodeled former parsonage next door, many youth have expressed the feeling that they are "out of sight and out of mind" even more than before. The newest minister's attempts to bring children back into congregational focus by, among other things, including a children's moment in the worship service, have met with some resistance. Those who are more concerned about the length of the service than the spiritual benefits one derives from worship complain that this is one place the new longer worship service could be cut. Given this congregation's need to gain and retain younger members, eliminating the children's moment as a centerpiece of the worship seems to me like cutting off one's nose to spite one's face.

The major challenge that remains for Grace is the need to resolve its liturgical, spiritual, and socioeconomic identity crises—all related to whether the worship will be more Eurocentric or more Afrocentric in tone and feel. Some members have objected to the more soulful worship that Pastor A.'s successors have crafted.

For example, members of the Gospel Mass Choir of New York City worshiped at Grace one Sunday morning. The occasion was like a black Baptist revival service in tone. A number of the refined, usually subdued Grace members stood to their feet and clapped and swayed to the music just like Fire Baptized members! It was as if many had been dying for an opportunity to "let loose," and so they did on that Sunday.

No reader will be surprised to learn that the pastor received letters of complaint about that service from the old guard, who essentially said that they did not want the worship changed from its generally quiet, meditative tone, and that those who wanted that kind of uncontrolled worship should go somewhere else to get it! Thus the liturgical identity crisis reared its head again: some members wanting to get back to their black worship roots, others running from their roots.

Grace's old guard eventually will have to get over its phobia of contemporary black gospel music and incorporate it into the worship if church members are serious about attracting and retaining young people in particular. Many members feel that although Grace's professional Chancel Choir renders the anthems and Negro spirituals beautifully, it has been rehashing the same material for the last forty-plus years since Grace's transition from a white to a black congregation.

During the church's fortieth anniversary celebration, the white minister who was in place at the time of the transition came back to be a part of the festivities. He said that he was surprised that the church had continued in the tradition he had established back in 1953 of including a European classical sacred piece and a Negro spiritual in the worship. He thought that surely the church would have let go of that scheme of things by now and developed something else. What Pastor A. said about indebtedness to the American Missionary Association may be true. But time is long overdue for letting go of what was inherited from other traditions and of what Grace did forty years ago, and to grab hold of African Americans' own very rich musical resources.

Is this an issue of socioeconomic class also? Many view the current repertoire of music as "high brow," and it is generally not welcoming to the persons in the community surrounding the church. Grace needs to wrestle seriously with who it is, who it wants to attract, and whether it is as open to all as the gospel requires. The comments of Methodist pastor Carlyle Fielding Stewart seem more than apropos here, when reflecting on Grace's openness (or lack thereof) to "folk who do not worship like us," musically or in other ways:

> The church has experienced a paradoxical relationship with many of the disillusioned and unchurched. On one hand, the church utilizes the language of caring and invitation. It postures hospitality to the public by claiming to be open to everyone, without regard to race, ethnicity, or national origin. It proclaims an open door policy to any and all who would come: "Whosoever will, let him [or her] come." Yet, in thinking about the churches with which we've had personal experience, we usually find only closed doors. What we painfully discover is a "country club" attitude, an "only for the initiated" mentality,

which doesn't really stand for what it professes. For this reason many people consider the church highly hypocritical. It says one thing but actually does another. It proclaims that all are children of God, worthy of God's grace as long as "they look and act like us." The same deception and duplicity characteristic of the larger society has infested the church, and many people are highly irritated by it.[2]

The changes in Grace's worship thus far are insufficient to rid it of its country club, silk stocking, black-church-trying-to-be-a-white-church images, which it carries both internally and in the community. Experiences with many other black churches suggests that Grace can still retain much of its rich, meaningful formal style and quality while simultaneously incorporating the best of the black religious tradition. It only needs the will and vision to do so.

Continuing Sociopolitical Myopia at Fire Baptized

Since moving to its new location, a remodeled banquet facility, Fire Baptized now holds two services each Sunday, has more than doubled its regular attendees to some four hundred, and has quickly outgrown these quarters. A new printed bulletin featuring church announcements, song lyrics, and a monthly calendar of events (but no order of worship) is packed with notices of activities relating to the enhancement of personal spirituality and the execution of evangelism.

The service is not nearly as male-dominated as before. Women are visibly assuming more substantive sacramental roles in the altar area, such as distributing the communion elements. This is a real step forward and a sign that Pastor B. is perhaps reflecting more deeply on the words of Joel 2:28, 29, which state that God's Spirit is poured out on men *and women* to exercise gifts of the ministry: "And it shall come to pass afterward, that I will pour out my spirit on all flesh; your sons *and your daughters* shall prophesy. . . . Even upon the menservants and *maidservants* in those days, I will pour out my spirit" (emphasis mine).

The 9:00 A.M. service is no less lively than the afternoon service; and, despite my concern that the pastor might suffer burnout under such circumstances, he outwardly shows no such wear and tear. The quality of communal feeling is still very warm, and members are just as satisfied and loyal as previously. Some members have even "graduated" to start their own churches.

Like the previous facility, however, the church is located in an urban community with all the usual urban problems. Members gladly escape from these problems, and also problems at home, through ecstatic worship in the safe shelter of the church.

However, worship points believers back to the world—not simply for evangelism, but also for social action. Is God not concerned with the high percentage of unemployment, the crime rate, the police brutality and other ills of the neighborhood in which Fire Baptized is located? Fire Baptized members would probably answer yes if they thought about it. But that is the trouble—no one is thinking about it. That is to say, Pastor B. is not giving members conceptual, theological tools to ponder and undertake Christian political action. As was stated earlier, this is unusual for a black church, given the history of African Americans as a religiously activist people.

Dr. Martin Luther King Jr. pricked the conscience of the entire nation by lifting up and living out certain Christian principles. Moreover, he mobilized millions of others who helped change the laws of the land for the better. While the *hearts* of many whites have not changed toward African Americans, their *behavior* has had to because of changes in federal law, which are a direct result of King's movement.

Such changes, which have enhanced human dignity and fairness to African Americans in every arena (employment, housing, voting rights, etc.), can be seen as answers to collective black prayers and blessings from God. They are directly related to bread-and-butter issues of daily survival, such as whether or not a qualified African American applicant gets a job or is approved for a lease or mortgage on a nice apartment or home.

During the Reagan years, black leaders decried the loss of civil rights gains made in the 1960s and 1970s through the King movement. The fact that a small percentage of African Americans seemingly have "made it" and have high-paying jobs, drive expensive cars, and own fine homes has desensitized these successful ones, as well as many whites, to the continuing plight of poverty and second-class citizenship for the majority of African Americans. Activist leaders, including the Reverend Mr. Jesse Jackson, seem to say that if African Americans do not wake up and invoke the power of God, coupled with political organization—as they did in days gone by—they will lose even more ground as a people.

Witness recent welfare reform legislation signed into law by President Bill Clinton, which has swept aside six decades of social policy, ending guaranteed cash payments to the poor. While this is not a civil rights bill per se, the changes will adversely affect a far higher percentage of blacks than persons of other racial groups.

Somehow, Fire Baptized members are not making the connection between the many struggles of their personal lives that they pray about and the larger social ills that are responsible for them. They are given neither the tools for such reflection nor the incentive to take action.

I am reminded of a study with college students that the Carnegie Foundation conducted during the late 1980s. Students were asked their opinion of the world's future. Most responded, in essence, that the world was in terrible shape politically, socially, economically, morally, environmentally, and so on. Asked, though, about the prospects for their personal futures, most said that, by virtue of their education and other considerations, they expected their own futures to be exceptionally bright.

This kind of faulty vision—which sees the rest of the world as going to hell in a handbasket, so to speak, but prosperity and health for oneself in spite of it all—is evident at Fire Baptized and Pentecostal churches generally. The attitude is, "I'm saved, I've received Christ as my personal Savior, I'm baptized with the Holy Ghost and fire, and I am living for God. I am living up to what God expects. Why wouldn't God bless me? Whatever happens to unsaved folks is not my concern. I am going to get my blessings regardless of what happens to the rest of the people who are fascinated by the vices and attractions of the secular world and refuse to receive Christ."

This is hardly in keeping with the Bible's suggestion that we are our brothers' and sisters' keepers and that we are to love our neighbors as ourselves. God's love for "unsaved" humanity is no less fervent than the love for the "saints." In fact, God often draws the "unsaved" by loving-kindness and blessings—not only through evangelism, but also through provision of practical needs and answers to prayer.

"I have loved thee with an everlasting love; therefore with lovingkindness have I drawn thee," the prophet Jeremiah wrote to rebellious Israel

(Jer. 31:3, KJV). As the gospels suggest, God causes the sun to shine and the rain to fall on both the just and the unjust. In fact, members of Fire Baptized would be the first to say that God cared for them when they were unsaved, both spiritually and materially, and that God's care for their souls and material circumstances led them to salvation.

Pastor B. must begin to wrestle with the relationship of his flock's troubles to the larger society. Members must be taught to broaden their prayer focus to include more than "us four and no more." If members believe Satan as personage is responsible for their troubles, they need to realize that Satan's approach is far more potent and sophisticated than attacking one individual or one family at a time. The devil works via structural sin and systemic evil (as in institutional racism, for instance) and manifests awesome power—power that cannot be put down until it is at least recognized and called out. These demons must be named and called out just like any others.

Since Fire Baptized is too small to confront these large problems alone and the Assemblies of God denomination does not have the needed vision to do so, members must be given biblical bases for becoming involved in the struggle to ameliorate social conditions by joining hands with those of appropriate organizations who are working on social problems.

The Relationship of Worship to Evangelism and Church Growth

What is the relationship of worship to evangelism and church growth? Statistically, it is clear from resources like the *Yearbook of American and Canadian Churches*[3] that liberal mainline churches like Grace are shrinking in membership, while Pentecostal fellowships like Fire Baptized are experiencing continued dramatic growth.

My own assessment of the decline as being tied at least in part to bland, sterile worship is shared by Stewart in his jewel of a book on African American church growth:

> Churches often don't grow because their worship services are dry,
> lifeless, devoid of the passion and enthusiasm for the celebration of
> life that the Holy Spirit creates. . . . A creative, dynamic worship ser-

vice is essential for reaching the unchurched and winning them to Christ, because it speaks of vitality and aliveness. People need to sense the pulsations, rhythms, joys, and jubilation of life in Christ. Celebrative, exhilarating worship moves people toward positive transformation.[4]

The message for Grace and other churches like it is that, if the church is to grow and thrive, then worship—and particularly preaching in worship— must be alive and exciting, whether the worship style of the church is formal or charismatic.

One cannot help but reflect here on the media's oft-made comparison during late summer 1996 of the ho-hum nature of the Republican National Convention, held in San Diego, with the emotionally riveting quality of the Democratic National Convention, held in Chicago during the same month. The Republican confab was billed by the media as a boring, overly planned, week-long "infomercial" of routine political rhetoric, which many television viewers tuned out.

By contrast, the Democratic gathering spotlighted rousing, if not theatrical, speeches by American heroes, like Christopher Reeve of *Superman* fame, who basically rhetoricized that they personally (and the American people collectively) have benefited greatly from Clinton Administration programs and policies. Apparently the Democratic events, marked by high drama and high energy, produced far better viewer ratings than the GOP offerings.

Again, churches need to take seriously competing events and also both the lessons learned from media convention coverage and the pervasive influence of media in so-called secular society as they shape and plan worship:

> In an era when so many media are contending for the minds and hearts of hearers, it is critical that preaching retain its vitality and attraction as an art form. People today are video-oriented. They not only *listen* to the music, they *watch* it on TV. I remember my father recalling the times as a boy when his family gathered to *watch* the radio. Today children *watch* the music. The audio and visual orientation of people today is much different than it was forty years ago. Preaching must compete in an age of multimedia influences.

> Therefore what is proclaimed is just as important as how it is pro-
> claimed, if people are to be won to Christ. This often means utilizing
> a dramatic medium for the proclamation of God's word.[5]

In other words, in this age of MTV and BET's "Video Soul" programming, even if a church has the most meaningful and socially relevant worship service ever, if it is not packaged in a way that people can enjoy it, they
won't come. Or if they do come, either they won't stay awake or they won't
return.

If God were to give us an Eleventh Commandment, related to the shaping of worship for contemporary times, it would likely be "Thou Shalt Not
Bore—Especially Teenagers." African American churches that have JAM
("Jesus and Me") teen groups, which offer performances of gospel rap
music and gospel steppers dance, have the right idea.

The gospel message must be made relevant to the everyday world in
which teens (and adults) live. It must be proclaimed in a way that hearers
can understand and joyfully receive it. To echo Stewart somewhat, it should
be shared excitedly—with all the color, passion, rhythms, and harmonies to
be experienced in every other aspect of worshipers' indigenous culture.

Efforts to contemporize and indigenize Christ's saving message will
attract many who ordinarily would not even consider going near a church.
In short, if churches are to grow, worship has to be lively. There is no
getting around this. I think even Grace's Pastor A. has come to agree and
has grown through the years in his perspective on the issue of liveliness.
During a visit to his new church in California, I was pleased to experience
the very lively, even soulful worship offered there; this is in contrast to the
worship crafted under his leadership at Grace in Chicago.

The words of the apostle Paul to the church at Corinth seem apropos
here: "Now the Lord is the Spirit, and where the Spirit of the Lord is, there
is freedom" (2 Cor. 3:17). As liturgical planners, we have the freedom, the
liberty, to prayerfully shape worship in some faithful ways that also happen
to be exciting for people to experience.

Worship can only do so much of the job of church growth. The church
members themselves have to be excited about Christ and their church.
Using a metaphor drawn from the business world, Stewart explains that
the preacher is not the only sales representative of Christianity. The laity

have a far more wide-reaching market. All professed Christians are really salespersons for Christ. Whether the church chooses to market itself or not, it does so unintentionally through the lives of its members. Each time a member of a congregation interacts with other people, he or she markets the church.[6]

Contagion for the church spreads from its members' vibrant spirituality, which should be an outgrowth of worship. Members have to be excited enough about what happens in worship and about what is happening in their own spiritual lives to invite persons to church. Once guests arrive, members have to be warm and friendly, not giving the impression that the church is a snobby religious country club, to borrow Stewart's imagery.

UCC officials are aware that their churches are not always the friendliest and their members not always the most vibrant. Self-appellations by these persons as "God's frozen people" often seem justified. Consider this tidbit from a monthly UCC newsletter designed for busy church editors:

> *How to Be a Friendly Church:* UCC evangelism and church develop-
> ment executive, the Rev. Robert Burt, has a great idea to measure
> how friendly your church is. A friend of his, looking for a new
> church home, visited eighteen UCC churches. The person sat near the
> front, walked to the rear after the service, back to the front, and to
> the rear again before leaving. The church's friendliness was measured
> on a point system: ten points for a smile from a church member; ten
> points for a greeting from someone close by; one hundred points for
> an exchange of names; two hundred points for a personal invitation
> to coffee hour; two hundred points for an invitation to return the
> following week; one thousand points for an introduction to another
> church member; and two thousand points for an introduction to the
> pastor. The seeker reports that no church scored higher than two
> hundred points, and half scored less than one hundred points. How
> would our church score?[7]

While Grace members are much warmer now to visitors than in days gone by, they still might not fare that well using this point system for friendliness.

Grace worship places overwhelming emphasis on the gospel's relevance to social issues at the expense of providing members tools for personal spiritual transformation and personal nurture. This is the struggle of many churches in the denomination, as is evident from heated debate at national UCC General Synod meetings over this dichotomy of needs.

When discussions arise in Synod and other settings about the need to lift up personal spirituality as a priority in the denomination's life, some ask whether such focus constitutes a retrenchment from concern for social justice. Those who do so present false alternatives. Clearly, the gospel is not about either/or. It calls for attention to both, and both must go together. If the unchurched and Christians from other denominations feel that UCC worship and church members lack spiritual vitality, they will continue to seek more vibrant congregations and denominations—as many have for the past thirty years.

Says United Methodist Bishop Richard B. Wilke in a Chicago *Tribune* article, "Those of us known as 'mainline' denominations are now called 'oldline,' and we are in trouble. We are wasting away like a leukemia victim when the blood transfusions no longer work." From the same article, "Pentecostals [like the Assemblies of God or Churches of God in Christ denominations] are growing even as we meet here," observed Rev. Emanuel Cleaver, pastor of the St. James-Paseo congregation in Kansas City, Mo. *"They hold no convocation on membership growth. All they will do is go out and get excited in the name of the Lord."*[8]

The remarks by these two ministers came during a conference of clergy, convened here in Chicago for the purpose of developing ways to stem the decline within United Methodism, which "lost two million adherents in the last twenty years and has forfeited its status as the country's largest Protestant body to the Southern Baptist Convention," says former *Tribune* religion editor Bruce Buursma.

As Rev. Cleaver and various scholars would seem to suggest, the decline in mainline membership is due in large part to a lack of excitement, of enthusiasm, in liberal mainline worship and a lack of vital personal spirituality among liberal mainline members. He seems to say that a direct result or natural outgrowth of personal spiritual vitality and enthusiasm is missionary zeal, which manifests itself in evangelistic efforts, both by individuals and churches.

But with regard to evangelism in the liberal mainline churches, Constant Jacquet, a staff researcher for the National Council of Churches, says of declining communions, "These are the up-scale churches and the real problem is they are too well-educated, too skeptical and too committed to other things. When it comes to evangelism, I don't think they have any idea how to do it, frankly."[9]

Both Jacquet's assessment of the inability of liberal mainline Christians to evangelize and Cleaver's astute observation that evangelism flows naturally from vital personal spirituality are instructive for members of Grace Church.

Grace has attempted some social ministries. For example, it has been involved in adoptions of African American children, through the statewide One Church, One Child project, and serves hot meals daily to the elderly in its surrounding community. Pastor A. was a prophetic voice on the board of a UCC-affiliated health care system of hospitals and elderly care facilities in the Chicago metropolitan area. He often urged officials of that corporation to hire more minorities in decision-making capacities. These creative social ministries can be affirmed.

But social ministries—especially what some might call outreach ministries of presence, such as serving hot meals to the poor—cannot substitute for evangelism and the warmth of persons who evangelize with enthusiasm. In the words of Alan Tippitt (quoted by Baptist Ralph H. Elliott in a book on church growth), "we cannot offer a service demonstration as a substitute for gospel proclamation."[10] Comments one female member of a white UCC church in a northwest Chicago suburb, "We have attempted to replace the Good News with good works."

The overall ambience at Grace is not personally and spiritually nurturing in the ways that would produce evangels. There are no prayer cell groups; no well-attended, exciting Bible studies; no special days for consecration (or prayer coupled with fasting); no prayer, praise, or testimony services during which members would have the opportunity to share life experiences and spiritual convictions/insights that flow from these.

No attention is given to spiritual disciples like keeping a spiritual journal or meditation. Nor is any real attention given to the issue of conversion or to the gifts of the Holy Spirit and how they operate. There is no altar call for hurting church members to figuratively place their burdens on the altar and literally receive solace in times of personal trial.

Members come for a brief, often bland, worship service on Sunday and perhaps to a committee meeting or two during the week. And that is the extent of church and spiritual commitment, it appears. Members seem to have very little emotional investment in one another or in things spiritual. Indeed, members often complain (witness survey responses) that there is much gossip, political infighting, and divisiveness at the church.

These issues of vitality and personal nurture are far from insignificant. In their book on church growth, Dean Hoge and David Roozen ask why, since moral values have taken a liberal shift in this country, don't the liberal churches benefit with membership growth. They answer their question this way:

> Somehow the Protestant synthesis [of traditional Christianity and secular humanist values] is not experienced as being personally orienting or sustaining...The wellsprings of Christian church commitment do not seem to exist in/or near the secular humanistic ethos, where intense individualism, relativism, and transient commitments seem to channel spiritual energies in other directions. Church commitment is found mainly in a gradually sinking sector of the culture anchored at the traditional evangelical pole.[11]

In an earlier chapter, Hoge discusses what Dean Kelley (author of *Why Conservative Churches Are Growing*) labels "strong churches," those that grow, and "weak churches," those that decline. Hoge summarizes Kelley's theories about strong and weak churches thusly:

> Strong churches are characterized by (1) a demand for high commitment from their members, including total loyalty and social solidarity. They (2) exact, discipline over both beliefs and life-style. They (3) have missionary zeal, with an eagerness to tell the good news to all persons. They (4) are absolutistic about beliefs. Their beliefs are a total, closed system, sufficient for all purposes, needing no revision and permitting none. They (5) require conformity in life-style, often involving certain avoidances of nonmembers or use of distinctive visible marks or uniforms. Weak churches, by contrast, are characterized by relativism and individualism in beliefs, tolerance of internal diversity and pluralism, lack of any enforcement of canons or doctrine, an

attitude of dialogue with outsiders rather than proselytism, limited commitment to the church, and little effective sharing of convictions or spiritual insights within the group.[12]

For good or ill, I have seen many of Kelley's strong-church characteristics in the growing Pentecostal churches like Fire Baptized and many of the weak-church characteristics at Grace and other liberal mainline churches.

Granted, numerical growth is not the only growth desired for local churches or denominations. To echo Bishop W. T. Handy of St. Louis, "Our main purpose is not simply to add members to our rolls, but to fulfill the basic purpose of the church: to make disciples of Jesus. Not admirers of Jesus. Not scholars of Jesus, But disciples—followers—of Jesus the Christ."[13]

Yet Grace and the UCC must grow, rather than dwindle, numerically if there are to be sufficient troops to carry out the church's various social and other ministries in the future. If Grace and the denomination would reverse the trend of decline and begin to grow, they must give equal attention to issues of spiritual vitality and social action. Visitors who worship at Grace must feel that church members are excited about the God they serve, and they must feel cared for, nurtured as individuals.

UCC historian Louis H. Gunnemann offers helpful insights in this regard when writing about the four denominations that merged in 1957 to form the United Church of Christ. From his perspective, UCC members are sitting on top of a tradition of vital spirituality, coupled with activism.

From the Congregational-Christian side, there is Jonathan Edwards, whose ministry in Northampton is cited as the start of the Great Awakening in New England, a movement of great spiritual vitality in the 1730s and 1740s. Gunnemann says of Edwards:

> His legacy in American Protestantism was a modified Calvinism that incorporated experiential religion (that is, the factor of the experience of God's work in the human soul) into the mainstream of the Reformed faith. In that emphasis Edwards provided a rationale for a dominant characteristic of the Puritan faith, the experience of saving grace. What happened within the human spirit as a result of faith in God's justifying work in Christ is the key to understanding justification. Sanctification, then, as the direct work of God's grace through

the Spirit, assumed a major place not only in the Reformed tradition
of the Congregational churches, but also in much of American
Protestantism.[14]

Grace need only recapture some of Edwards's emphasis on transformation of the human spirit, on experiential religion, to inject a powerful shot
in the church's arm. But Gunnemann notes that Edwards was also
concerned with social transformation. He speaks of Edwards's vision of
"the social redemption of humanity":

> That vision was based on his understanding of God's sovereignty. He
> saw the divine purpose of redemption not in individual terms only
> but in corporate and social terms as well. The Reformed faith had for
> him, as for so many before him, an ultimate focus upon the transfor-
> mation of life and the society. That legacy remains a motivating force
> in the nation's idealism as well as in the churches' commitment to
> active social efforts.[15]

On the Evangelical and Reformed side, there is the activist piety of
Calvin and Zwingli, which coupled a vital private piety (evidenced by the
common historical practice of home instruction in the Heidelberg Cate-
chism) with corporate concern for transformation of society.[16] In effect,
Grace need only appreciate and get back to its UCC roots to achieve the
healthy balance necessary between emphasis on vital spirituality and social
change in its worship and church life.

Gender Inclusiveness: Women in Ministry in the Black Church

In chapter 3, we cited visible inclusiveness of women as liturgical leaders as
a strength of liberal mainline worship like Grace's. While women constitute
the backbone of active membership and execute most of the major programs, many black churches still continue to offer them second-class
citizenship in terms of substantive roles in ministry.

Fire Baptized is growing in its perspective on these issues, but such growth is still needed for clergy and laity in many churches in the histori-cally black denominations. In the words of C. Eric Lincoln and Lawrence H. Mamiya, "Both historical and contemporary evidence underscores the fact that black churches could scarcely have survived without the active support of black women, but in spite of their importance in the life of the church, the offices of preacher and pastor of churches in the historic black churches remain a male preserve and are not generally available to women."[17]

Stewart suggests, and I affirm his viewpoint, that many conservative black churches with charismatic-type worship as defined here are *not* grow-ing precisely because of theologically false and administratively limiting strictures on women:

> The African American church still remains very male-dominated and
> highly paternalistic. . . . Sadly, many black churches struggle with the
> problem of *whether God can call a women to preach,* never realizing
> their true potential because they still haggle over such basic proposi-
> tions. The prophetic black church challenges and denounces the tra-
> ditional reactionary assumption that women cannot lead the people
> of God effectively and cannot be called by God to do so. A climate of
> acceptance of female leadership in nontraditional roles is highly
> needed to create an atmosphere of belonging and participation. It
> will also help grow the church. Women can function as chairpersons
> of finance, trustee, stewardship, and the deacon boards. In fact, by
> encouraging such participation, a church will often experience quan-
> tum growth.[18]

Pastors and others who still hold the false view that women cannot exer-cise positions of ecclesiastical authority in the church are invited to serious-ly study the "women's question." This will have to involve more than sim-ply lifting out of context a few isolated verses of Scripture that seem to pro-hibit women from preaching. Controversial New Testament passages will require study in their original Koine Greek forms; and serious consideration and reflection will have to be given to Christ's relationship to women, the historical and cultural context in which the New Testament was written, and early church history. By approaching such a study with prayerfulness and an open mind, it will be impossible to maintain the same outmoded and errant beliefs about women in ministry.

Some of what I say here will be elementary and review for liberal mainline and charismatic Christians who have long resolved the "women's question" in favor of women having full authority in the church. But for the reader who still wrestles with the question or feels that women should keep their place in the pew and out of the pulpit (and sometimes women are more entrenched in these fallacious assumptions than men, hindering other women from assuming their full place in ministry), the brief remarks to follow may serve as a serious theological eye-opener.

My own in-depth study of the question has uncovered, for instance, inaccurate translations of Scripture in the much-cherished King James version of the Bible—translations that hide important nuances of meaning and, thus, adversely affect interpretation of the Bible around women's issues. For example, in the context of remarks about the proper deportment of deacons found in 1 Timothy 3:8–13 (KJV), verse 11 describes certain qualities required of *wives* of deacons: "Even so must *their wives* be grave, not slanderers, sober, faithful in all things." But in the Greek text, no possessive pronoun "their" is used. The words translated in the KJV as "their wives" should be simply rendered as "the women," as is the case in the RSV: "The *women* likewise must be serious, no slanderers, but temperate, faithful in all things."

In other words, the King James translation obfuscates the fact that there were actually women deacons in the Pauline churches who functioned the same as the men deacons and who had the same spiritual requirements from Paul. Apparently, Paul used no such term as *deaconess,* no feminine form of the word *diakonos.* Instead, he seems to speak of "women deacons," hence the use of the term *diaconate board* in churches like Grace, which have a deacon board composed of men and women who perform exactly the same spiritual tasks.

I also discovered a woman pastor, Phoebe, and an apostle Julia (or Junias) in Romans 16. Investigation of the early house churches—important centers of worship where the early Christians celebrated communion and preached the good news—shows women like Priscilla being as much involved in their spiritual life as men like Aquila. Study of the early Christian church reveals the existence of women bishops, and that later changes in publicly displayed religious art sought to obscure this fact. Says E. Margaret Howe:

Frequently today, the issue of women and church leadership is approached as though women are for the first time in history seeking the right to be appointed to leadership positions. Nothing could be further from the truth. Women are simply seeking to reestablish their claim to leadership positions which were clearly theirs in the early centuries of the Christian era. These positions were wrested from them by circumstances which do not necessarily bear the mark of divine approval.[19]

Howe shares information from British scholar Joan Morris, author of *Against Nature and God* (U.S. edition titled *The Lady Was a Bishop*), which reveals that even the artwork of the first centuries supports the fact that women held positions of leadership in the early churches:

Morris records, for example, that in the church of St. Praxedis in Rome there is a mosaic dating from the fifth century C.E. or earlier. It depicts the head of a veiled woman over which is inscribed the title *episcopa* (overseer, bishop). Written vertically alongside is the name Theodo(ra), the last two letters, which represent the feminine form of the name, have been removed from the mosaic and cubes from a later period have been inserted. Similarly, in the catacombs of Priscilla in Via Salerio Nova in Rome there is a fresco depicting a group of women conducting a eucharistic banquet at a funeral service. The figure to the left is apparently the chief celebrant. The head has been sandpapered down to obscure the feminine hairstyle, though the length of the dress clearly indicates to historians that this figure represents a woman. These stone and mosaic inscriptions show that "women once held a place in the hierarchical service of the church that is now denied them."[20]

My favorite example of taking certain passages out of their proper historical/cultural context is the interpretation of 1 Corinthians 14:33–35: "For God is not a God of confusion but of peace. As in all churches of the saints, the women should keep silence in the churches. For they are not permitted to speak, but should be subordinate, *as even the law says*. If there is anything they desire to know, let them ask their husbands at home."

Obviously, Christians do not operate under Old Testament Jewish law and customs, but rather under grace (Rom. 6:14). That is the first point that must be gotten.

It appears that some black male ministers want to cling adamantly to the law when it comes to the issue of women ministers, but blithely ignore it when it comes to the issue of slavery, for instance. Baltimore pastor Rev. Dr. Vashti Murphy McKenzie discusses this hermeneutical discrepancy, with the help of James Cone:

> James Cone states that some African American male ministers have
> no problem rejecting Paul's commands to slaves "to be obedient to
> their masters" as valid justification of black slavery, but they close
> the door to women with their stance regarding Paul's comments
> about silence and teaching.[21]

In terms of the futility and irrelevance of Christians trying to follow the law, James 2:10 states, "For whoever keeps the whole law but fails in one point has become guilty of all of it." Clearly, subordination and silencing of women, in the ministry or in any other area of life, is non-biblical for Christians today.

Secondly, given the fact that Paul's writings are full of effusive praise for the women who labored alongside him in the gospel vineyard, what is the reason for this statement about silence? It seems that women and men sat on opposite sides of the worship centers of the day. Since women were prohibited from reading the sacred Torah, some would on occasion yell to their husbands on the other side of the sanctuary for clarification of some theological point. In an effort to maintain order in the worship service ("God is not the author of confusion"), Paul cautioned the women not to be silent in ministry (his writings show much respect for his women colleagues), but rather to help the church conduct its worship in an orderly fashion.

Uncovering the full truth of what the gospel brings to us regarding the role of women in the church has made many women resonate with the feelings of Alice Hageman, who declares:

> *No more silence!* say the women who have quietly organized the
> bake sales and bazaars and church dinners while men counted the
> money and planned programs. *No more silence!* say the women

whose intelligence and energies have gone into Sunday schools while men taught in colleges and seminaries. *No more silence!* say the women who seek ordination and full recognition of their capabilities as ministers and priests. *No more silence!*[22]

One could go on and on, as there is a very large body of theologically sound literature addressing some of these hermeneutical mistakes or problems of biblical interpretation related to feminist and African American womanist theology. In addition to the writers already cited, I commend to the earnest seeker of truth on this matter a few works to serve as the beginning of such an exploration, including the writings of Elisabeth Schüssler Fiorenza,[23] Rosemary Radford Ruether,[24] Leonard Swidler,[25] Anne Carr,[26] Letha Scanzoni and Nancy Hardesty,[27] and Jacquelyn Grant.[28]

If African American churches with charismatic-style worship, coupled with second-class ministerial citizenship for women, continue to try to enforce silence and to squelch debate and discussion on this issue, they often will do so at the expense of their own numerical growth. They also will risk losing some of their most talented and spirited women to the predominantly white denominations, which will ordain and place women as pastors. Whether or not ecclesiastical structures affirm women as ordained ministers, I often find it particularly uncanny and gratifying that the Spirit of God has ways of validating women's gifts in spite of the narrowness of perspective of those who want to keep women in their ministerial place. Consider this news item from a 1995 *Christian Century* article:

A week after trustees of Southern Baptist Theological Seminary decided to hire only professors who believe women are not called to preach, women swept the top three awards in the Louisville, Kentucky school's annual preaching competition. This year's Clyde T. Francisco Preaching Awards went to Kimberly Baker of Lincolnton, North Carolina; Mary Beth McCloy of Phillipi, West Virginia; and Dixie Petrey of Knoxville, Tennessee. . . . Recipients of the preaching award were selected by a panel of six students and two faculty members, all male. The initial field of twenty-eight entries was narrowed to three finalists based on a review of written manuscripts which did not identify the author's name or gender. Only after the three finalists

were selected did the judges hear audio tapes to determine first-,
second- and third-place rankings.[29]

All jest aside, there is a serious need for denominations that affirm full
inclusiveness of women in worship to really live this out by placing women
in pastorates—and not just in the smallest, least-viable churches or yoked
parishes. On the surface, women are quite visible in worship leadership at a
church like Grace. UCC seminaries nowadays have student populations
that are 40 to 50 percent female. In reporting trends in seminary education,
the *Yearbook of American and Canadian Churches* said that women consti-
tuted 31 percent of all seminary students in 1993, and that some schools are
reporting women enrollment above 45 percent.[30]

But statistics from the UCC Research Office of the Board for Homeland
Ministries show a very low placement rate of women, and particularly
African American women, in pastorates. Currently, there is only one
African American woman pastor in the entire UCC Illinois Conference, the
Reverend Ms. Mary Parish, senior minister of Lincoln Memorial Congregational UCC in Chicago. There are only ten nationwide, and that figure
includes one co-pastor. Similar statistics for ordained persons in the Assemblies of God also show a low rate of women pastors. No AOG figures were
available by race.

Many ordained women in liberal mainline denominations in communions with congregational polity (where clergy are not appointed, but
churches select their own pastors) face an untenable situation. They acquire
much student-loan debt to meet the rigorous denominational requirements
for theological education prior to ordination. But then they can obtain only
partial or honorary employment in a church, because no search committee
will "call" them as lead pastor. (This is at least partly the fault of the lay-
women who sit on these committees.) The clergywomen thus are forced to
find supplementary employment in another field of endeavor, typically
teaching or social work, in order to pay the bills.

This state of affairs has prompted at least one of my female UCC colleagues in ministry to say in utter frustration, "The UCC seminaries should
just stop taking women students' money if the denomination is not going to
get serious about helping us find suitable ministry assignments after gradu-
ation and ordination. They should just plain stop rippin' us off."

This may appear to some as mere griping. Certainly, male students who come out of seminary with a large amount of educational debt, even when actually placed, also have a tough time making ends meet on the small salaries these dwindling churches offer. They often have to engage in "tent-making" ministries alongside pastoring to survive financially. And there is much bitter discussion at national meetings, by men and women alike, about the huge gap between the salaries of parish pastors and those of denominational executives. However, at least the men usually *are* placed as pastors (sometimes more than once) before the average African American female ever gets to her first pastorate. This is a justice issue—a fairness issue—in some respects, that the denomination must address concretely if its worship, especially its black worship, hopes to do more than superficially reflect full inclusiveness of women's ministry gifts in worship and church life.

The Church and Politics: Is the Religious Right Right?

Much has been said here of the failure of many Pentecostal churches to provide members the theological tools necessary for relating the Bible to societal and sociopolitical issues that ultimately impact their well-being in a variety of areas—housing, employment, toxic-waste management, etc. The attention given in these churches to matters of personal spiritual development almost totally eclipses questions of how God might feel about such issues as public policies that punish the poor while rewarding the rich, and the responsibility of Christians, as caretakers of all creation, to remedy certain injustices and problems in the wider society. In the words of Harvey Cox, "Pentecostalism needs to develop a more penetrating approach to systemic evil, liberationists need to nurture the sense of personal empowerment."[31]

What has *not* been addressed so far is whether all church involvement in the political fray is necessary, helpful, or healthy. From my own viewpoint, much of the activity of the Religious Right in recent years, for instance, seems contrary to what Christianity truly espouses. It flies in the face of Jesus' insistence that we are to be our brother's and sister's keepers, that we are to care for the least of these, and that we are to love our neighbor as ourselves—the neighbor being anyone in the world, and not just people who think, look, act, speak, and smell "like us." Class enmity is also one of the by-products of these groups' activism. Their activities also can have the effect of increasing crime levels, as widespread deprivation of the necessities of life causes more and more people to throw aside conventional morality in order just to survive.

Many legislative proposals crafted by groups like Pat Robertson's Christian Coalition seem terribly misguided, smacking of insensitivity to poor persons in genuine need (what some refer to as the deserving versus the undeserving poor), and of spiritual arrogance and moral jugdmentalism. It is highly unlikely that Jesus would want to have anything to do with these groups if he walked the earth today. In fact, he probably would disavow them, along with many members of the current Republican Congress. Their so-called Contract with America—a package of legislation related to budget cuts, budget balancing, and pocketbook issues generally of the American economy—seems little more than a proposal to be as selfish as possible in meeting the needs of the less fortunate in society and as generous as possible to the individuals and corporations that least need help.

One can almost hear Jesus asking in indignation, "Wherever *did* these people come from—using *my* name to justify inhumane programs and policies that don't reflect my mission and ministry in the least?" It seems a healthy development that counter Christian groups are springing up to offer an alternative viewpoint, maintaining, in effect, that the Christian Coalition's viewpoint is not Christian at all. I concur with the feeling of Herbert Valentine, the chair of one such group, the Interfaith Alliance, who has said, "As religious leaders, we can no longer allow these religious extremists with a political agenda to push that agenda in God's name."[32]

Proposals of this dangerous liaison between the Religious Right and Republican legislators often betray a lack of depth in understanding the intricacy and interwovenness of many very serious societal problems. This ignorance is coupled with a glaring lack of compassion that even other conservative and evangelical Christians discern and condemn. Helen Alvaré, pro-life planning and information director for the National Council of Catholic Bishops, for example, comments that proposals to deny increased benefits to mothers on welfare who have more children threaten to increase the numbers of abortions. She explains, "If you add yet another disincentive—in fact, a punishment—it will only make matters worse. Not to provide food to needy children is a particularly ill-directed way of trying to end teenage parenthood."[33]

While agreeing in principle that rethinking the welfare mentality of the last thirty years is long overdue, San Diego Pentecostal Bishop George McKinney, of the Church of God in Christ, also sees the religious hypocrisy of many of the proposals related to welfare spending cuts, and fears they will go too far in the direction of denying aid to those in genuine need: "What often gets involved in this mix is a mean-spirited, elitist, racist attitude that says the poor are poor because they are lazy, shiftless, and irresponsible, and that people are homeless because they didn't plan properly."[34]

McKinney worries that moral liberalism reflected in Democratic policies has forced many African American evangelicals into the political camp of white evangelicals, even though these same whites have often shone insensitivity to justice issues. In recent history, he says, they have had "more interest in doctrinal purity and maintaining the status quo than in justice and righteousness."[35] That is a good caution for Pentecostal and religiously conservative African Americans who do wish to try to relate their faith to matters of public policy and social concern. African Americans must distinguish between public policies and programs that conform to true Christian values while helping to enhance our well-being, on the one hand, and political stances that seem to conform to Christianity but are actually contrary to biblical tenets of love and communal responsibility, on the other.

In the words of the Interfaith Alliance's Joan Brown Campbell, general secretary of the National Council of Churches, "A nation that treats its poor callously must live with the consequences."[36] One civil rights leader has asked, in the context of the whole Contract with America phenomenon, if a bomb goes off in the basement of society, what will happen to the rest of the house? In formulating policies to punish those who some feel have made poor moral or lifestyle choices for which they must now suffer, the judgmentalists forget that one person's destiny is tied to the destiny of all of us.

Unfortunately, it often takes a wake-up call of a traumatic, personal nature for many to come to grips with others' suffering, hardship, and needs. The highly paid executive who is mugged outside his posh down-town office while heading home after working late one evening may at first call on legislators to be tougher on crime. However, true spiritual reflection would yield the understanding that building more and bigger prisons is not the real solution. Crime is only the symptom and not the real problem.

Solving problems of joblessness, hunger, and homelessness, and ensuring that all in the society acquire a quality education and have enough to live on with dignity and without discrimination, is the only way to truly "get tough on crime." As the Rev. Mr. Jesse Jackson, head of Operation PUSH, often points up, it costs far more to keep someone in prison than to provide that same person with a solid primary education and send him or her to college so that s/he might contribute positively to society.

Jackson expressed this idea very colorfully as he addressed a cheering convention crowd of members of Delta Sigma Theta Sorority, Inc., one of the nation's foremost African American women's public service organizations, at the San Francisco Civic Center Auditorium in July 1988: "A four-year scholarship to a university can cost less than $30,000. A full penitentiary scholarship costs between $100,000 and $160,000. We must choose childcare and education on the front side of life rather than welfare and jail care on the backside of life."[37]

This is not to preach my own political views, though I am sure those come through. It is in the spirit of McKinney's remarks that I urge religiously conservative African Americans, like those at Fire Baptized, not only to relate their faith to social issues, but to be careful to examine closely the political agenda of religious extremists to be sure that it is truly Christian. I urge all to be aware of the tension that can sometimes exist between giving loyalty to authentically Christian *principles* and values and giving loyalty to Christian *groups* whose public-policy stances would have the long-term effect of keeping African Americans in a desperate economic situation without the possibility of betterment.

Measures that cut welfare benefits to those who really need them, that eliminate hot-lunch programs for impoverished school children, and that limit the availability of student loans to those from low-income families—all elements of the "Contract" that many religious conservatives support—have serious, adverse, long-term effects for the less fortunate, indeed, for all of society. Jean Hessburg, California director of People for the American Way, which monitors Religious Right politics, perhaps best sums up the point: "Once people truly understand the [Religious Right] agenda, they reject it."[38]

Toward Unity in the Diversity of Christian Worship: A Final Word on Appreciation

Let us, for the moment, set aside controversies related to liturgical identity crises, women in ministry, and church political activism, and return our focus to the major aim of this work: to enhance ecumenical unity by promoting an appreciation of the strengths of both formal worship and charismatic worship. Critics of formal worship view it as more Eurocentric in style and flavor, and even as mere dead ritualism; critics accuse Afrocentric charismatic worship of excessive emotionalism, and lack of order and orderliness.

We hope that the detailed discussions of ritual performance in each church have created understanding and respect for a worship form that may be different from your own, and also the desire to visit a different church to experience another style of worship—either as an individual or in a group. I encourage liberal mainline and Pentecostal pastors who have a good rapport with one another to sponsor "field trips," as it were, and pulpit exchanges between their congregations so that their respective members can experience the richness of worship in a contrasting tradition.

I leave you now with a brief summary of things to celebrate about worship in each of the two churches, inviting all to pursue further study of liberal mainline Protestantism, Pentecostalism, black worship, worship in general, issues of church growth, the "women's question," and the role of the church in politics. I hope that many of the insights here have served as spiritual dynamite for many—possibly exploding certain myths and misconceptions in a variety of areas.

Summaries of Worship Strengths at the Two Contrasting Churches

We Celebrate the Following in Relation to the Formal Worship of Eurocentric Origin and Style Offered at Grace United Church of Christ

o Prayerful planning that ensures that sermon, songs, prayers, and Scriptures often are tied together around a single theme on any given Sunday.

o Visible inclusiveness of women as worship leaders, deacons, and preachers.

o Sermonizing that relates the gospel to questions of public policy and social concern, particularly as these affect its mostly African American membership.

o Music that is varied (including anthems, spirituals, and gospels), that is expertly performed, and that is often accompanied by string or brass ensemble on special Sundays of the church year.

o A denominational heritage stressing issues of both personal piety and concern for the transformation of society. This tradition can be traced to such historical figures as Jonathan Edwards of the eighteenth-century Great Awakening of New England (on the Congregational-Christian side of the 1957 UCC merger) and reformers Calvin and Zwingli (on the Evangelical and Reformed side).

We Celebrate the Following in Relation to the Afrocentric, Charismatic Worship Offered at Fire Baptized Assembly of God Church

o Spontaneity and sheer joy in response to the dynamic movement of the Holy Spirit, which allows worshipers to participate holistically in the worship and to be the spiritual, emotional, intellectual, and physical beings God created them to be.

o Sermonizing that gives worshipers theological tools for relating the Bible to everyday problems and concerns, and that creates excitement for and a desire to enjoy the spiritual disciplines (prayer, Bible reading, fasting, etc.) at home between public worship services.

o Operation of the Holy Spirit charismata as described in 1 Corinthians 12 and in accordance with the apostle Paul's prescriptions for maintaining orderliness in worship.

o Its corporate evangelistic burden for souls; its faith that human behavior and lives can change for the better as individuals receive Jesus Christ as personal Savior.

o Friendliness and warm attention to individuals through the altar call for the unsaved, prayer line for those with special concerns, hugging, and a most hearty welcome to visitors, among other things.

Epilogue: A Personal Note

Earlier this year, as I was winding down my writing of this book, the film *Waiting to Exhale,* based on Terry McMillan's best-selling novel of the same name, was a tremendous box-office hit and a topic of controversy. After an enormous amount of work on this project over an extended period of time, amid the joys and challenges of family life and professional struggles, I, too, am glad finally to be able to catch my breath and relax. Yet, if even one congregation successfully enhances its worship based on insights gained here, or if one person is freed of hermeneutical bondages that have hindered her from accepting her (or his significant other's) call to ministry, if one person has been given some helpful ways of thinking about the activism of the Religious Right and about the church's sociopolitical involvements in general, if God has used me to shed any spiritual light on any dark subject for anyone, then the "hyperventilation" caused by the work on this book will have been well worth the effort.

APPENDIX: WORSHIP RATING FORM

Please use this form as a guide or basis for dialogue about worship at your church. Rate items on a scale of one to ten. Ten is the highest rating of satisfaction; one is the lowest. If you need more space for comments, please use the reverse side of this sheet or attach additional pages.

1. *Worship at Our Church—General:*
   Is well planned ____
   Is of appropriate length (if too long or too short, comment below) ____
   Nourishes me spiritually ____
   Nourishes me emotionally ____
   Challenges me intellectually ____
   Fully and consistently utilizes women in all aspects of worship leadership and spiritual authority (e.g., preaching, baptisms, celebration of communion, etc.) ____

Comments:

_____
_____
_____
_____
_____

2. *Music in Our Church's Worship:*
   Is of a good variety ____
   Is performed well vocally (if the church has more than one choir, give appropriate separate ratings in the comment section) ____
   Is performed well instrumentally ____
   Has spiritual power or "anointing" ____
   Has spiritual meaningfulness ____
   Is performed at an enjoyable volume (specify in comments if too loud or too soft) ____
   Relates well to the day's sermon topic, scriptures, prayers ____
   Includes a good selection of hymns ____
   Includes a good amount of congregational singing ____

Comments:

_____
_____
_____
_____
_____

3. *Preaching/Sermons in Our Worship:*
    Are well prepared ____
    Relate the scriptures to my everyday life ____
    Equip me to share my faith with others (evangelize) ____
    Equip me to relate the gospel to pressing social, political, and civic
    concerns of my community and the world (e.g., homelessness, discrimi-
    nation, nuclear war, AIDS, etc.) ____
    Have spiritual power ____
    Promote spiritual vitality and a desire to enjoy the spiritual disciplines
    (e.g., prayer, fasting, Bible reading, etc.) on my own ____
    Promote tolerance and appreciation of other forms of worship ____

Comments:

_____
_____
_____
_____
_____

NOTES

1. Praising: Variations on a Theme

1. Robert H. Culpepper, *Evaluating the Charismatic Movement: A Theological and Biblical Appraisal* (Valley Forge, Pa.: Judson Press, 1977), 11.
2. Ibid., 80–81. The work by Michael Harper that Culpepper refers to in this discussion is *Walk in the Spirit* (Plainfield, N.J.: Logos International, 1968), 79–80.
3. Wade Clark Roof and William McKinney, *American Mainline Religion: Its Changing Shape and Future* (New Brunswick, N.J.: Rutgers University Press, 1987).
4. Ibid., 74.
5. Ibid., 85.
6. Ibid., 87.
7. James D. G. Dunn, *Unity and Diversity in the New Testament* (Philadelphia: Westminster Press, 1977).
8. J. Wendell Mapson Jr., *The Ministry of Music in the Black Church* (Valley Forge, Pa.: Judson Press, 1984), 32. Emphasis mine.
9. Ferdinand Hahn, *The Worship of the Early Church* (Philadelphia: Fortress Press, 1973), 2.

2. Definitions of Praising and a Look at Black Worship

1. James F. White, *Introduction to Christian Worship* (Nashville: Abingdon Press, 1982).
2. Ibid., 17–18.
3. Ibid., xvi.
4. Ibid., xvi–xvii.
5. Frank Senn, *Christian Worship and Its Cultural Setting* (Philadelphia: Fortress Press, 1983), 6.
6. White, *Introduction to Worship*, 17.
7. Ibid., 18. White refers here to Evelyn Underhill's classic study, *Worship* (New York: Harper, 1936).
8. Ibid., 16, 38–43.
9. Cyprian Lamar Rowe, "The Case for a Distinctive Black Culture," in *This Far by Faith: American Black Worship and Its African Roots,*

ed. Robert W. Hovda (Washington, D.C.: National Office for Black Catholics and the Liturgical Conference, 1977), 21.

10. Ibid., 24.

11. Ibid., 26. Emphasis mine.

12. Henry L. Mitchell, "The Continuity of African Culture," in *This Far by Faith,* ed. Robert W. Hovda, 9.

13. Ibid., 13.

14. Ibid., 10.

15. John S. Pobee, *Toward an African Theology* (Nashville: Abingdon Press, 1979), 45–46. Emphasis mine.

16. Mitchell, "The Continuity of African Culture," 9.

17. Mercy Amba Oduyoye, "The Value of African Religious Beliefs and Practices for Christian Theology," in *African Theology en Route,* ed. Kofi Appiah-Kubi and Sergio Torres (Maryknoll, N.Y.: Orbis Books, 1979), 110–11. Emphasis mine.

18. Gwinyai H. Muzorewa, *The Origins and Development of African Theology* (Maryknoll, N.Y.: Orbis Books, 1985), 17. Emphasis mine.

19. J. Deotis Roberts, *Black Theology in Dialogue* (Philadelphia: Westminster Press, 1987), 23–24.

20. Mitchell, "The Continuity of African Culture," 12.

21. Roberts, *Black Theology in Dialogue,* 22–23.

22. Ibid., 23.

23. James H. Cone, "Sanctification, Liberation, and Black Worship," *Theology Today,* July 1978, 139–52.

24. Ibid., 143.

25. Ibid.

26. Ibid.

27. Ibid., 139.

28. Ibid., 144.

29. Ibid., 145.

30. Leon Forrest, "Souls in Motion: Spirited Sundays in Black Churches," *Chicago,* July 1985, 128–35, 148.

31. Cone, "Sanctification, Liberation, and Black Worship," 142.

32. Forrest, "Souls in Motion," 134–35.

33. Cone, "Sanctification, Liberation, and Black Worship," 145–46.

34. Ibid., 146.

35. Ibid.

36. Ibid., 146–47.

37. Ibid., 142–43. Emphasis mine.

38. Ibid., 140. Emphasis mine.

39. Nathan Jones, *Sharing the Old, Old Story* (Winona, Minn.: St. Mary's Press, 1982).

40. Ibid., 35.

41. Clarence Joseph Rivers, "The Oral African Tradition versus the Ocular Western Tradition," in *This Far by Faith,* 39–41.

42. Jones, *Sharing the Old, Old Story,* 35.

43. Ibid.

44. Ibid. Emphasis mine.

45. Ibid., 35–36.

46. U.S. Bureau of the Census, *Statistical Abstract of the United States: 1995,* 115th ed. (Washington, D.C.: Bureau of the Census, 1995), Table no. 752, 484.

47. Jones, *Sharing the Old, Old Story,* 36.

48. Ibid.

49. Ibid.

50. Ibid.

51. Cone, "Sanctification, Liberation, and Black Worship," 140. Emphasis mine.

52. Jones, *Sharing the Old, Old Story,* 36.

3. Praising as Majestic, Spiritual Homage

1. *Pilgrim Hymnal* (Boston: The Pilgrim Press, 1967), 491.

2. Senn, *Christian Worship,* 56.

3. White, *Introduction to Worship,* 77–78. Emphasis mine.

4. Ibid., 96.

5. Michael H. Ducey, *Sunday Morning: Aspects of Urban Ritual* (New York: The Free Press, 1977), 123.

6. *United Church of Christ Hymnal* (New York: United Church Press, 1974), 12.

7. Senn, *Christian Worship,* 52.

8. Grayson W. Brown, "Music in the Black Spiritual Tradition," in *This Far by Faith,* 92.

9. Mapson, *The Ministry of Music,* 82.

10. Clarence Rivers, "The Oral African Tradition," 41.

11. Mapson, *The Ministry of Music,* 41–42.

12. *United Church of Christ Constitution and By-Laws* (St. Louis: UCC Church Leadership Resources, 1984), 4. Emphasis mine.

13. *The Hymnal* (St. Louis: Eden Publishing House, 1941).

14. *National Baptist Hymnal* (Nashville: Triad Publications, 1984).

15. White, *Introduction to Christian Worship,* 33.

16. Ibid.

17. André Godin, *The Psychological Dynamics of Religious Experience* (Birmingham, Ala.: Religious Education Press, 1985), 100. Emphasis mine. Godin quotes from Abraham Maslow, *Religions, Values, and Peak-Experiences* (Lafayette, Ind.: Kappa Delta Pi, an international honor society in education).

18. Walter J. Ong, *Orality and Literacy: The Technologizing of the Word* (London and New York: Melthuen & Co., 1982).

19. Ibid., 39–40.

20. Ibid., 42–43.

21. Ibid., 45–46.

22. Ibid., 49–52.

23. Ibid., 74. Emphasis mine.

4. Praising as Spiritual Ecstasy

1. William W. Menzies, *Anointed to Serve* (Springfield, Mo.: Gospel Publishing House, 1971), 375–76.

2. Ducey, *Sunday Morning,* 129.

3. Cheryl Townsend Gilkes, "The Black Church as a Therapeutic Community: Suggested Areas for Research into the Black Religious Experience," *Journal of the Interdenominational Theological Center* 8, no. 1 (fall 1980): 29–44.

4. Ibid., 29. Emphasis mine.

5. Ibid., 33. Gilkes quotes from Thomas J. Scheff, *Labeling Madness* (Englewood Cliffs, N.J.: Prentice-Hall, 1975), 86. Emphasis mine.

6. Gilkes, "The Black Church," 34.

7. Ibid.

8. Ibid., 37.

9. Ibid.

10. Ralph H. Elliott, *Church Growth That Counts* (Valley Forge, Pa.: Judson Press, 1982), 32.

11. *Hymns of Glorious Praise* (Springfield, Mo.: Gospel Publishing House, 1969).

12. Arthur R. Paris, *Black Pentecostalism: Southern Religion in an Urban World* (Amherst: University of Massachusetts Press, 1982), 132.

13. Ibid., 133–34.

14. Ibid., 134.

15. Ibid., 135.

16. Elisabeth Kübler-Ross, *On Death and Dying* (New York: Macmillan, 1969).

5. Praising as Experienced Through the Eyes, Ears, and Hearts of Worshipers

1. Max Weber, *The Sociology of Religion* (Boston: Beacon Press, 1922), 46.

2. *The New Century Hymnal* (Cleveland: The Pilgrim Press, 1995).

3. *Songs of Zion* (Nashville: Abingdon Press, 1981).

4. *Lead Me Guide Me: The African American Catholic Hymnal* (Chicago: G.I.A. Publications, 1987).

5. From the *Book of Worship: United Church of Christ* (New York: UCC Office for Church Life and Leadership, 1986), 512.

6. *American Heritage Dictionary,* 2d college ed., 1985.

6. Key Issues of Praising Revisited

1. *Songs of Zion.*

2. Carlyle Fielding Stewart III, *African American Church Growth* (Nashville: Abingdon Press, 1994), 116.

3. Kenneth B. Bedell, ed., *Yearbook of American and Canadian Churches* (Nashville: Abingdon Press, 1995).

4. Stewart, *African American Church Growth,* 56–57.

5. Ibid., 122.

6. Ibid., 125.

7. From the October 1995 issue of the UCC's communiqué, *Keeping You Posted.*

8. Bruce Buursma, "Protestants Find Mainstream Drying Up," *Chicago Tribune,* 18 May 1986, sec. 1, p. 12.

꽃 ☙❧

9. Ibid.

10. Alan R. Tippitt, *Church Growth and the Word of God* (Grand Rapids, Mich.: Eerdmans, 1970), 39. Quoted by Elliott in *Church Growth That Counts,* 37.

11. Dean Hoge and David Roozen, *Understanding Church Growth and Decline: 1950–1978* (New York: The Pilgrim Press, 1979), 332–33.

12. Ibid., 179–80.

13. Buursma, "Protestants Find Mainstream Drying Up," 12.

14. Louis H. Gunnemann, *The Shaping of the United Church of Christ* (New York: United Church Press, 1977), 148.

15. Ibid., 149.

16. Ibid., 124–26.

17. C. Eric Lincoln and Lawrence H. Mamiya, *The Black Church in the African American Experience* (Durham and London: Duke University Press, 1990), 275.

18. Stewart, *African American Church Growth,* 136–37.

19. E. Margaret Howe, *Women and Church Leadership* (Grand Rapids, Mich.: Zondervan, 1982), 39.

20. Ibid., 38.

21. From Vashti M. McKenzie's *Not Without a Struggle: Leadership Development for African American Women in Ministry* (Cleveland: United Church Press, 1996), 53. She quotes from Gayraud S. Wilmore and James H. Cone, *Black Theology: A Documentary History, 1966–1979* (Maryknoll, N.Y.: Orbis, 1979), 365.

22. Alice L. Hageman, with the Women's Caucus of Harvard Divinity School, *Sexist Religion and Women in the Church: No More Silence!* (New York: Association Press, 1974), 19–20.

23. Elisabeth Schüssler Fiorenza, "Women in the Pre-Pauline and Pauline Churches," *Union Seminary Quarterly Review,* spring and summer 1978.

24. Rosemary Radford Ruether, *Religion and Sexism: Images of Women in the Jewish and Christian Traditions* (New York: Simon & Schuster, 1974).

25. Leonard Swidler, *Biblical Affirmations of Women* (Philadelphia: Westminster Press, 1979).

26. Anne Carr, "Is a Christian Feminist Theology Possible?" *Theological Studies,* June 1982.

27. Letha Scanzoni and Nancy Hardesty, *All We're Meant to Be* (Waco, Tex.: Word Books, 1974).

28. Jacquelyn Grant, "Womanist Theology: Black Women's Experience as a Source for Doing Theology, with Special Reference to Christology," *The Journal of the Interdenominational Theological Center 13, no. 2* (spring 1986).

29. "Win-Lose Situation for SBC Women," *The Christian Century,* 7–14 June 1995, 600.

30. Gail Buckwalter King, "Trends in Seminary Education," in *Yearbook of American and Canadian Churches,* 279.

31. Harvey Cox, "Pentecostalism at Harvard," *Christian Century,* 25 Aug.– 1 Sept. 1993, 807.

32. "The First, and Next, 100 Days," *Christian Century,* 26 April 1995, 448.

33. Randy Frame, "Payback Time?: Conservative Christians Support GOP 'Contract' as Profamily Agenda Takes a Back Seat," *Christianity Today,* 6 March 1995, 44.

34. Ibid.

35. Ibid.

36. "The First, and Next, 100 Days," 448.

37. From a press release on Rev. Jackson's remarks, which I prepared as I worked in the Delta convention press room.

38. Jim Impoco, "Separating Church and School," *U.S. News & World Report,* 24 April 1994, 30.

BIBLIOGRAPHY

Bedell, Kenneth B., ed. *Yearbook of American and Canadian Churches.* Nashville: Abingdon Press, 1995.

Brown, Grayson W. "Music in the Black Spiritual Tradition." In *This Far by Faith: American Black Worship and Its African Roots,* edited by Robert W. Hovda. Washington, D.C.: National Office for Black Catholics and The Liturgical Conference, 1977.

Buursma, Bruce. "Protestants Find Mainstream Drying Up." *Chicago Tribune,* 18 May 1986, sec. 1, p. 12.

Carr, Anne. "Is a Christian Feminist Theology Possible?" *Theological Studies,* June 1982.

Cone, James H. "Sanctification, Liberation, and Black Worship." *Theology Today,* July 1978, 139–52.

Cox, Harvey. "Pentecostalism at Harvard." *Christian Century,* 25 Aug.–1 Sept. 1993, 806–8.

Culpepper, Robert H. *Evaluating the Charismatic Movement: A Theological and Biblical Appraisal.* Valley Forge, Pa.: Judson Press, 1977.

Ducey, Michael H. *Sunday Morning: Aspects of Urban Ritual.* New York: The Free Press, 1977.

Dunn, James D. G. *Unity and Diversity in the New Testament.* Philadelphia: Westminster Press, 1977.

Elliott, Ralph H. *Church Growth That Counts.* Valley Forge, Pa.: Judson Press, 1982.

Fiorenza, Elisabeth Schüssler. "Women in the Pre-Pauline and Pauline Churches." *Union Seminary Quarterly Review,* spring and summer 1978.

"The First, and Next, 100 Days." *Christian Century,* 26 April 1995, 448.

Forrest, Leon. "Souls in Motion: Spirited Sundays in Black Churches." *Chicago,* July 1985, 128–35, 148.

Frame, Randy. "Payback Time?: Conservative Christians Support GOP 'Contract' as Profamily Agenda Takes a Back Seat." *Christianity Today,* 6 March 1995, 42–44.

Gilkes, Cheryl Townsend. "The Black Church as a Therapeutic Community: Suggested Areas for Research into the Black Religious Experience." *Journal of the Interdenominational Theological Center* 8, no. 1 (fall 1980): 29–44.

Godin, André. *The Psychological Dynamics of Religious Experience.* Birmingham, Ala.: Religious Education Press, 1985.

Grant, Jacquelyn. "Womanist Theology: Black Women's Experience as a Source for Doing Theology, with Special Reference to Christology." *The Journal of the Interdenominational Theological Center* 13, no. 2 (spring 1986).

Gunnemann, Louis H. *The Shaping of the United Church of Christ.* New York: United Church Press, 1977.

Hageman, Alice L., with the Women's Caucus of Harvard Divinity School. *Sexist Religion and Women in the Church: No More Silence!* New York: Association Press, 1974.

Hahn, Ferdinand. *The Worship of the Early Church.* Philadelphia: Fortress Press, 1973.

Harper, Michael. *Walk in the Spirit.* Plainfield, N.J.: Logos International, 1968.

Hoge, Dean, and David Roozen. *Understanding Church Growth and Decline: 1950–1978.* New York: The Pilgrim Press, 1979.

Howe, E. Margaret. *Women and Church Leadership.* Grand Rapids, Mich.: Zondervan, 1982.

Hymns of Glorious Praise. Springfield, Mo.: Gospel Publishing House, 1969.

Impoco, Jim. "Separating Church and School." *U.S. News & World Report,* 24 April 1994, 30.

Jones, Nathan. *Sharing the Old, Old Story.* Winona, Minn.: St. Mary's Press, 1982.

King, Gail Buckwalter. "Trends in Seminary Education." In *Yearbook of American and Canadian Churches: 1995,* edited by Kenneth B. Bedell. Nashville: Abingdon Press, 1995.

Kübler-Ross, Elisabeth. *On Death and Dying.* New York: Macmillan, 1969.

Lead Me Guide Me: The African American Catholic Hymnal. Chicago: G.I.A. Publications, 1987.

Lincoln, C. Eric, and Lawrence H. Mamiya. *The Black Church in the African American Experience.* Durham, N.C., and London: Duke University Press, 1990.

Mapson, J. Wendell, Jr. *The Ministry of Music in the Black Church.* Valley Forge, Pa.: Judson Press, 1984.

McKenzie, Vashti M. *Not Without a Struggle: Leadership Development for African American Women in Ministry.* Cleveland: United Church Press, 1996.

Menzies, William W. *Anointed to Serve.* Springfield, Mo.: Gospel Publishing House, 1971.

Mitchell, Henry L. "The Continuity of African Culture." In *This Far by Faith: American Black Worship and Its African Roots,* edited by Robert W. Hovda. Washington, D.C.: National Office for Black Catholics and The Liturgical Conference, 1977.

Muzorewa, Gwinyai H. *The Origins and Development of African Theology.* Maryknoll, N.Y.: Orbis Books, 1985.

The New Century Hymnal. Cleveland: The Pilgrim Press, 1995.

Oduyoye, Mercy Amba. "The Value of African Religious Beliefs and Practices for Christian Theology." In *African Theology en Route,* edited by Kofi Appiah-Kubi and Sergio Torres. Maryknoll, N.Y.: Orbis Books, 1979.

Ong, Walter J. *Orality and Literacy: The Technologizing of the Word.* London and New York: Melthuen, 1982.

Paris, Arthur R. *Black Pentecostalism: Southern Religion in an Urban World.* Amherst: University of Massachusetts Press, 1982.

Pilgrim Hymnal. Boston: The Pilgrim Press, 1967.

Pobee, John S. *Toward an African Theology.* Nashville: Abingdon Press, 1979.

Rivers, Clarence Joseph. "The Oral African Tradition versus the Ocular Western Tradition." In *This Far By Faith: American Black Worship and Its African Roots,* edited by Robert W. Hovda. Washington, D.C.: National Office for Black Catholics and The Liturgical Conference, 1977.

Roberts, J. Deotis. *Black Theology in Dialogue.* Philadelphia: Westminster Press, 1987.

Roof, Wade Clark, and William McKinney. *American Mainline Religion: Its Changing Shape and Future.* New Brunswick, N.J.: Rutgers University Press, 1987.

Rowe, Cyprian Lamar. "The Case for a Distinctive Black Culture." In *This Far by Faith: American Black Worship and Its African Roots,* edited by Robert W. Hovda. Washington, D.C.: National Office for Black Catholics and The Liturgical Conference, 1977.

Ruether, Rosemary Radford. *Religion and Sexism: Images of Women in the Jewish and Christian Traditions.* New York: Simon & Schuster, 1974.

Scanzoni, Letha, and Nancy Hardesty. *All We're Meant to Be.* Waco, Tex.: Word Books, 1974.

Scheff, Thomas J. *Labeling Madness.* Englewood Cliffs, N.J.: Prentice-Hall, 1975.

Senn, Frank C. *Christian Worship and Its Cultural Setting.* Philadelphia: Fortress Press, 1983.

Songs of Zion. Nashville: Abingdon Press, 1981.

Stewart, Carlyle Fielding, III. *African American Church Growth*. Nashville: Abingdon Press, 1994.

Swidler, Leonard. *Biblical Affirmations of Women*. Philadelphia: Westminster Press, 1979.

Tippitt, Alan R. *Church Growth and the Word of God*. Grand Rapids, Mich.: Eerdmans, 1970.

Underhill, Evelyn. *Worship*. New York: Harper, 1936.

United Church of Christ. *Book of Worship: United Church of Christ*. New York: UCC Office for Church Life and Leadership, 1986.

———. *Constitution and By-Laws*. St. Louis, Mo.: UCC Church Leadership Resources, 1984.

———. *Keeping You Posted*, October 1995.

———. *United Church of Christ Hymnal*. New York: United Church Press, 1974.

United States Bureau of the Census. *Statistical Abstract of the United States: 1995*, 115th ed. Washington, D.C.: Bureau of the Census, 1995.

Weber, Max. *The Sociology of Religion*. Boston: Beacon Press, 1922.

White, James F. *Introduction to Christian Worship*. Nashville: Abingdon Press, 1982.

Wilmore, Gayraud S., and James H. Cone. *Black Theology: A Documentary History, 1966–1979*. Maryknoll, N.Y.: Orbis, 1979.

"Win-Lose Situation for SBC Women." *The Christian Century*, 7–14 June 1995, 600.

CREDITS

Grateful acknowledgment is made to the following for permission to use reprinted material in this book:

Chapter 1

From J. Wendell Mapson Jr., *The Ministry of Music in the Black Church* (Valley Forge, Pa.: Judson Press, 1984), 32, 41–42, 82. Reprinted by permission of Judson Press.

Reprinted from *The Worship of the Early Church* by Ferdinand Hahn, copyright © 1973 Fortress Press. Used by permission of Augsburg Fortress.

Chapter 2

Reprinted from *Christian Worship and Its Cultural Setting* by Frank Senn, copyright © 1983 Fortress Press. Used by permission of Augsburg Fortress.

Quotes from Cyprian Rowe, Henry Mitchell, and Clarence Rivers from *This Far by Faith: American Black Worship and Its African Roots,* ed. Robert W. Hovda (Washington, D.C.: National Office for Black Catholics and the Liturgical Conference, 1977). Copyright 1977 The National Office for Black Catholics and The Liturgical Conference, 8750 Georgia Avenue, Suite 123, Silver Spring MD 20910-3621.

All rights reserved. Used with permission.

From John S. Pobee, *Toward an African Theology* (Nashville: Abingdon Press, 1979). Reprinted by permission of the author.

From James H. Cone, "Santification, Liberation, and Black Worship," *Theology Today,* July 1978, 139–52. Quotes reprinted by permission from *Theology Today,* P.O. Box 29, Princeton, N.J. 08542.

From Leon Forrest, "Souls in Motion: Spirited Sundays in Black Churches," *Chicago,* July 1985, 128–35, 148. Reprinted by permission of the author.

Chapter 3

From *Sunday Morning: Aspects of Urban Ritual* by Michael H. Ducey. Copyright © 1977 by The Free Press, an imprint of Simon & Schuster. Reprinted with permission of the publisher.

Quotes from Clarence Rivers and Grayson Brown reprinted from *This Far by Faith*. See credit in chapter 2.

Chapter 4

Chapter 6

INDEX